A. W. (Annesley William) Streane

The Age of the Maccabees

With special Reference to the religious Literature of the Period

A. W. (Annesley William) Streane

The Age of the Maccabees
With special Reference to the religious Literature of the Period

ISBN/EAN: 9783337143756

Printed in Europe, USA, Canada, Australia, Japan

Cover: Foto ©ninafisch / pixelio.de

More available books at **www.hansebooks.com**

THE
AGE OF THE MACCABEES.

The Bible Student's Library.

1.—FOURTH EDITION.
THE FOUNDATIONS OF THE BIBLE: Studies in Old Testament Criticism. By Canon GIRDLESTONE, M.A.

2.—SECOND EDITION.
THE LAW IN THE PROPHETS. By the Rev. STANLEY LEATHES, D.D.

3.
PRINCIPLES OF BIBLICAL CRITICISM. By the Rev. J. J. LIAS, M.A., *Chancellor of Llandaff Cathedral.*

4.—511 pages.
SANCTUARY AND SACRIFICE: A Reply to Wellhausen. By the Rev. W. L. BAXTER, M.A., D.D.

5.
HEZEKIAH AND HIS AGE. By the Rev. R. SINKER, D.D., *Librarian of Trinity College, Cambridge.*

6.
ABRAHAM AND HIS AGE. By the Rev. H. G. TOMKINS. *With Illustrations.*

7.
THE BOOK OF DANIEL. By the Rev. JOHN KENNEDY, M.A., D.D. *With Illustrations.*

8.
THE AGE OF THE MACCABEES. By the Rev. A. W. STREANE, D.D., *Fellow, and formerly Theological Lecturer, of Corpus Christi College, Cambridge.*

For particulars of the above see advertisement at the end of the Volume. Other Volumes in preparation.

THE AGE OF THE MACCABEES.

WITH SPECIAL REFERENCE TO

The Religious Literature of the Period.

BY

A. W. STREANE, D.D.,

Fellow, and formerly Theological Lecturer, of Corpus Christi College, Cambridge.

EYRE AND SPOTTISWOODE,
Her Majesty's Printers,
LONDON—GREAT NEW STREET, FLEET STREET, E.C.
EDINBURGH, GLASGOW, MELBOURNE, SYDNEY, AND NEW YORK.

1898.

All rights reserved.

PREFACE.

THE aim of this volume of the Bible Student's Library is to give the average educated reader as clear a view as is attainable of the main features which are characteristic of Jewish literature during the period dealt with. That period, though it may briefly be called the Age of the Maccabees, embraces, in fact, as will at once be seen, a much larger space.

We have thought it well, therefore, to commence by giving a sketch of the history of the period from the Return of the Jews in accordance with the decree of Cyrus, till the accession of Herod the Great (37 B.C.).

We seek, in the next place, to estimate the social, political, and religious condition of the Jewish people during the period dealt with; and the rest of the book is mainly occupied with an examination of the literature of the time, as closely bound up with the aspirations and various modes of thought which are exhibited in the life of the nation, mainly, though we cannot say exclusively, in Palestine and Egypt.

This period is often neglected, even by the student of religious history, yet it is one which indicates no less clearly than earlier epochs the presence of God with His people, and that in various ways. To say nothing of the stirring events and successful results of the Maccabean contest, we cannot fail to see the action of Divine Providence in the exclusion from the Old Testament Canon of Books which might well have obtained the suffrages of many for their admission, had it been merely a question of the amount of value and interest which they possessed on their literary or historical side. Again, the LXX., viewed merely as a bond of religious unity, and an influence which counteracted the disintegrating tendencies involved in the dispersion of the nation, forms one of the many proofs that the hand of God was still stretched out over His people.

Questions involving the "Higher Criticism" of the Old Testament enter but slightly into the times here treated of. There is, however, one exception, viz., the date and authorship of the Book of Daniel. Inasmuch as eminent theologians in England as well as abroad place the origin of that book—at least in the form in which we now have it—in Maccabean days, it seemed impossible to ignore the question. An attempt has accordingly been made in one of the Appendices to furnish a kind of *précis* of the controversy. For a full discussion of the matter on the conservative side, the reader may be referred to Dr. Kennedy's newly-published work, forming a volume of the present series.

While writing in the main for the non-expert in matters theological, I have sought in my footnotes to point the reader to such further sources of information —ancient as well as modern—as he might desire to consult.

In this, as in earlier literary work, I have had the advantage of unfailing help in the way of suggestion and criticism from my friend, the Rev. R. Sinker, D.D., Librarian of Trinity College, Cambridge.

A. W. S.

CAMBRIDGE,
September, 1898.

CONTENTS.

CHAPTER I.

SKETCH OF JEWISH HISTORY AFTER THE RETURN FROM THE CAPTIVITY 1

CHAPTER II.

THE CONDITION OF PALESTINE FROM THE RETURN TO THE ACCESSION OF ANTIOCHUS THE GREAT 14

CHAPTER III.

THE HISTORY FROM THE ACCESSION OF ANTIOCHUS THE GREAT TO THE TIME OF THE MACCABEAN REVOLT (222–168 B.C.) . . 25

CHAPTER IV.

THE MACCABEAN REVOLT TO THE DEATH OF JUDAS (168–160 B.C.) . 35

CHAPTER V.

FROM THE DEATH OF JUDAS TO THE DEATH OF SIMON III. (160–135 B.C.) 46

CHAPTER VI.

THE REIGN OF JOHN HYRCANUS (135–106 B.C.) . . 54

CHAPTER VII.

From the Accession of Aristobulus to the Death of Jannæus (106–78 B.C.) . . . 64

CHAPTER VIII.

The Reign of Alexandra (78–69 B.C.) . . . 71

CHAPTER IX.

From the Death of Alexandra to Herod's Capture of Jerusalem (69–37 B.C.) 76

CHAPTER X.

General Features of the Religious Literature of the Maccabean Age 89

CHAPTER XI.

The Apocrypha 96

CHAPTER XII.

Historical or Quasi-Historical Books 112

CHAPTER XIII.

Other Pseudepigraphic Additions to the Canonical Literature 167

CHAPTER XIV.

Gnomic and Philosophical Writings 172

CHAPTER XV.

Poetic Literature 197

CHAPTER XVI.

Apocalyptic Literature 213

CHAPTER XVII.

The Septuagint . . 235

CHAPTER XVIII.

Conclusion . . . 246

APPENDICES.

A.—The Assideans and their Relation to the Pharisees . . 249

B.—Traditional Account of the Succession of Jewish Teachers 253

C.—The Date of the Book of Daniel . 257

Index . 271

AGE OF THE MACCABEES.

CHAPTER I.

SKETCH OF JEWISH HISTORY AFTER THE RETURN FROM CAPTIVITY.

BEFORE entering on our main subject, it is desirable that we should take a brief retrospective glance over that part of the earlier history which lies between the return of the Jews from their captivity in Babylon (538 B.C.) and the commencement of that which we may call the Maccabean period.

The decree of Cyrus* (538 B.C.) seems to have been acted upon with all speed by a portion of the Jews resident in Babylon. That portion, however, doubtless consisted of the less well-to-do and those who had formed no very close ties, commercial or otherwise, with the locality in which they had grown up. Many had acted to the full upon the advice given them by Jeremiah (29. 5–7), and, to borrow a Jewish phrase which has been applied to the present case, the bran returned, the fine flour was left behind in Babylon.†

Thus it came to pass that the returned exiles‡ were the more easily reduced to inactivity by the difficulties which speedily came upon them in their attempts at the renovation of their

---

* 2 Chron. 36. 22, 23; Ezra 1. 1–3.
† *See* Deutsch, *Remains*, p. 321, London, 1874.
‡ They numbered (Ezra 2. 64) 42,360. But these figures may indicate only the heads of families.

old home. Mainly through the hostility of the Samaritans on their offer of co-operation being repulsed, but perhaps in some degree owing to the absence of royal favour on the part of Cyrus's two successors, Cambyses and the Pseudo-Smerdis, the work of restoration was for more than nine years (529–520 B.C.) in abeyance. In the year 520 B.C., however, two years after the accession of Darius, the heartening which their prophets, Haggai and Zechariah, sought to give them, and the efforts of Joshua the high priest and Zerubbabel,* evoked renewed energy. Darius's approval was obtained, and four years later the Temple was dedicated to the service of God.

There is little or nothing to record in the way of history until, in 458 B.C., Ezra is sent by Artaxerxes to Jerusalem, and finds it in a ruinous condition. The nature of the rule exercised there had been changed, and the policy of exclusiveness reversed, probably at an early date in the intervening period. The priests, in whose hands lay all the guidance of the community, evidently exercised a sway which, while seeking to conciliate their non-Jewish neighbours, was harsh towards their poorer fellow countrymen. Ezra took a line which certainly did not err on the side of laxity. He had not, indeed, the practical ability of Nehemiah, but he could at any rate, as Graetz says,† "pray and arouse the feelings of others." This he did to some purpose, and it is to his influence that we are to ascribe the establishment of the written Law as henceforward the rule of faith for his people, as well as the rigid exclusiveness which was to be the national safeguard then and subsequently. Nehemiah arrived twelve years later. The wretched condition to which he found the city reduced has

---

* Probably to be identified with Sheshbazzar. So Dr. Ryle, *Ezra and Nehemiah* (Camb. Bible for Sch.), p. xxxi. But see Dr. Sayce, *Higher Criticism and the Monuments*, pp. 530 ff.

† *Hist. of the Jews*, i. 382, Eng. Trans., London, 1892.

been thought to point to a reaction against an amount of strictness for which his countrymen were unprepared.* Whatever may have been the cause or causes of the disastrous state of things found by Nehemiah, there appeared everywhere the need of an energetic administration such as he was well able to supply. On the completion of Nehemiah's task Ezra's name, which has disappeared for a while from the record, returns. He instructs the people in the Law, and takes part in the dedication of the walls.

From the time of Megabyzus may be dated the gradual break-up of the Persian power. In particular, Egypt, about 405 B.C., threw off the foreign yoke, and was not re-subjugated till 344 B.C. The geographical position of Judea must have exposed it to the predatory attacks of armed forces, or to a guerilla warfare no longer repressed by the wide-reaching rule administered hitherto by imperial power. Egyptian kings and satraps of Phœnicia, in a common hostility to the control which Persia still sought to exercise over the remoter provinces of the empire, made the inhabitants of Judea to be unpleasantly familiar with their own troops, as well as with the Greek mercenary soldiers in the pay of both parties.

A fresh trouble also assailed the Jews, this time on the religious side. Artaxerxes II. (Mnemon, 405–358 B.C.) had adopted an idolatrous and licentious worship,† hitherto unknown to the Persians, and insisted on its acceptance by all his subjects. On the Jews resisting the image-worship which the

---

* This prostrate condition of Jewish affairs may, however, have well arisen from the opportunity given to their enemies to cripple their power by the help of Megabyzus, satrap of Syria. In 449 B.C. he had re-established Persian rule in Egypt, driving the Athenian forces from that country, and in consequence of this success had been able to make himself for several years independent of the Persian monarch, Artaxerxes Longimanus. With so powerful an auxiliary as Megabyzus the enemies of the Jews would find it an easy matter to wreck the fortunes of that community, who seem to have possessed no leader capable of rallying them to a successful resistance.

† That of the deity Anahita or Anaitis.

king thus imposed, he is said to have banished many of them to Hyrcania, on the shores of the Caspian.* Bagoas (or Bagoses), who had profited by his opportunities as military commander in Syria and Phœnicia, established himself in power at Jerusalem. The severity of his rule is shewn by the daily exaction of 50 drachmæ for each lamb offered in the Temple precincts.†

Artaxerxes III. (Ochus), who succeeded to the Persian throne in 358 B.C. and reigned for 20 years, was a strong ruler, suppressing revolts in Egypt, which in this reign became again a province of the empire (344 B.C.), as well as in Phœnicia and Cyprus. Much suffering accordingly still fell to the lot of the inhabitants of Palestine. Orophernes, a conspicuous leader in this war, was probably the original of the Holophernes of the Book of Judith.

Artaxerxes III. died by violence in 338 B.C., and after the short reign of his son Arses (338–335), Darius III. (Codomannus) came to the throne (335–331 B.C.). The year following his accession marks the beginning of the end. In that year Alexander entered Asia by the Hellespont, in 333 he won the battle of Issus, and in 331 finally overthrew Darius at Arbela. Most of the time between these two battles was spent by Alexander in establishing his authority in Phœnicia and Egypt. He besieged and captured Tyre and Gaza. The Jews on this occasion refused to furnish him with a contingent of troops or with provisions, pleading their oath of loyalty to Darius. In this connexion his visit to Jerusalem is related, a visit which, if it took place at all, has doubtless been much adorned by legendary detail. "And when he [Jaddua, the high

---

* See *Syncellus*, ed. Dindorf, i. 486. It is, however, possible that this event may have taken place in the time of his successor, Artaxerxes III. (Ochus).

† For his connexion with the murderous strife between the two sons of Joiada, rival candidates for the high priesthood, *see* Josephus, *Antiquities*, xi. 7. 1.

priest] understood that he was not far from the city, he went out in procession with the priests and the multitude of the citizens. . . . Alexander, when he saw the multitude at a distance in white garments, while the priests stood clothed with fine linen, and the high priest in purple and scarlet clothing, with his mitre on his head, with the golden plate whereon the name of God was engraved, approached by himself and adored that name, and first saluted the high priest. The Jews also did altogether with one voice salute Alexander and encompass him about. . . Parmenio . . . went up to him and asked him how it came to pass that when all others adored *him*, he should adore the high priest of the Jews. To whom he replied, I did not adore *him*, but that God who hath honoured him with this high priesthood; for I saw this very person in a dream in this very habit, when I was at Dios in Macedonia, who, when I was considering with myself how I might obtain the dominion of Asia, exhorted me to make no delay, but boldly to pass over the sea thither, for that he would conduct my army, and give me the dominion over the Persians. . . And when he had said this to Parmenio, and had given the priest his right hand, the priests ran along by him and he came into the city; and when he went up into the Temple, he offered sacrifice to God . . . and when the Book of Daniel was shewed him, wherein Daniel declared * that one of the Greeks should destroy the empire of the Persians, he supposed that himself was the person intended; and as he was then glad, he . . . bade them ask what favours they pleased of him; whereupon the high priest desired that they might enjoy the laws of their forefathers, and might pay no tribute in the seventh year. He granted all they desired; and when they entreated him that he would permit the Jews in Babylonia and

---

* *See* Dan. 7. 6; 8. 3-8, 20, 21, 22; 11. 3.

Media to enjoy their own laws also, he willingly promised to do hereafter what they desired." *

The high priest here referred to has been variously identified with Jaddua, as above, or his son, Onias I., or his grandson, Simon the Just.† Be this as it may, Alexander's tolerance as here displayed quite accords with his general policy of cosmopolitanism in matters of faith.

There were, however, special reasons for the favour shewn by Alexander to the Jews. Their "trading connexions over the world, combined with the regular journeys of the 'Dispersion' to Jerusalem, made them invaluable friends to him as guides to his intelligence department. From them too did he learn the passes into Egypt between the marshes and deserts, and they must have announced to the Egyptians his liberality towards their religion, and his graciousness towards those who submitted promptly and unreservedly to his commands." ‡ Many of these Jews were settled by him in Alexandria, and received rights equal to those of the Macedonians and Greeks in tnat city. §

Judea now was made to form part of the satrapy of Cœle-Syria,|| and the head-quarters of the governor, Andromachus, were placed in Samaria. There speedily followed a revolt, probably inspired, in part at least, by jealousy of the favour shewn by Alexander to the Jews. Andromachus was burned alive ; and Alexander hastened back from Egypt to avenge the death of his representative, and continued to mark the difference of his attitude towards the Samaritans and their hereditary enemies at Jerusalem by planting in the city of the former

---

* Josephus, *Ant.* xi. 8. 5.
† This last view is supported by the Talmud of Babylon, *Tamid*, f. 27b.
‡ Mahaffy, *Empire of the Ptolemies*, p. 7 ; comp. p. 85. *See also* his *Greek Life and Thought*, p. 470.
§ Josephus, *c. Apion.* ii. 4.
|| "So called to distinguish it from the Higher Syria, which lay in the neighbourhood of the Euphrates." Graetz, *op. cit.*, i. 427.

people a Macedonian colony. Thenceforward, and till Alexander's death, the affairs of Cœle-Syria seem to have been conducted in peace.

Had Alexander lived to employ the practically unlimited resources which lay to his hand in the empire which he had won, for the purpose of extending his power westward into Europe, the history of the world would in all probability have been changed, and the power of Rome crushed at an early stage of its existence. As things were, upon the great king's death (June 13, 323 B.C.), not one of his generals was of sufficiently conspicuous merit to stand out as an acknowledged successor. Hence there arose a period of varied conflicts which continued for forty-five years.

The kingdom of the Seleucidæ, with which the main portion of this historical sketch will be so closely connected, does not yet come into view. Seleucus its founder was at the time of Alexander's death only about thirty years of age, and thus was unable to assert as yet his claims against those of the older commanders. Perdiccas, the senior officer of the household at the time, became regent and took the central management. The chief of his rivals were appointed to the government of various provinces with full military power. This arrangement is said to owe its origin to Ptolemy I. (Soter), son of Lagus, who himself took Egypt, and worthily carried out his duties as its ruler, founding a dynasty which was destined to have much influence upon the welfare of men of Jewish race.*

The reason probably of his choice of a province, and certainly of his success in maintaining himself against invasion, was the security afforded from an attack by land, and, as regards a great stretch of its coast, from the sea as well.

---

* We may note however that he did not assume the title of king till 306 B.C.

"Even the Romans were exceedingly afraid of this peculiar and isolated position, owing to the power it conferred on its ruler, and so they took special care to let no ambitious or distinguished person assume so unchecked an authority."*
Any Egyptian ruler, having the wisdom to secure the support both of the priesthood, who treasured the traditions of power and wealth, and also of the military caste, who were very jealous of the introduction of foreign mercenaries, might count on holding a position of exceptional strength against the forces of rival sovereigns.†

An early attempt of Ptolemy to extend his dominion was, while occupying Cyprus by the way, to seek the subjugation of the whole of Cœle-Syria, which in the partition of Alexander's Empire had fallen to Laomedon. The Jews declining to submit, Ptolemy approached Jerusalem with an army on the Sabbath,‡ professing that his intentions were peaceable, and that he merely desired to offer sacrifice, as Alexander had done before him. On obtaining permission he seized upon the city and carried many of the inhabitants captive, while others voluntarily accompanied him.§

Egypt appears to have had four immigrations of this sort under his rule. It appears that he, unlike the others of the Diadochi with whom the Jews were brought into contact, was popular with that nation. The causes of this were probably twofold : (1) The Jews' traditional friendliness on the whole

---

* Mahaffy, *Alexander's Empire*, p. 48.
† See Mahaffy, *Emp. of the Ptol.*, pp. 4, 5, and for Ptolemy's conciliatory policy with regard to the Egyptian priesthood see the hieroglyphic inscription given in substance *op. cit.*, pp. 45 f.
‡ It is doubtful whether the following incident took place during this first occupation of Syria (320 B.C.) or later (circ. 312 B.C.) See Mahaffy, *Emp. of the Ptol.* pp. 34, 43.
§ A fragment (found in Jos. *c. Apion.* i. 22) of Hecatæus of Abdera (No. 14 in Müller's *Fragg. Hist. Græc.* ii. 393, quoted in *Emp. of the Ptol.*, p. 43) tells us that Hezekias, the high priest, became Ptolemy's firm friend, and accompanied him to Egypt.

to Egypt, as opposed to the sentiment ever entertained towards their Asiatic conquerors; (2) the fact that Seleucus, contrary to Ptolemy's policy, made a point of establishing a multitude of cities founded on the Hellenic type, repugnant in many respects to genuine Jewish feeling.* Egypt had the further advantages of great fertility, and of the facilities which such a city as Alexandria afforded for carrying on commerce on an immense scale.

Some of those whom he thus transferred to Egypt he employed in his army; for in spite of his readiness to conciliate, so far as was possible, the native military caste, he could not forego the employment of some foreign troops. Others settled as civilians in Alexandria (founded about eleven years previously) with full rights of citizenship. For the next few years Judea was the scene of conflicts of varying issue between the forces of Ptolemy and those of Antigonus, one of Alexander's generals. The latter, however, was slain at the decisive battle of Ipsus (301 B.C.), whereupon the victors divided his possessions among themselves. The fate of Judea and Samaria is somewhat obscure. Palestine and Cœle-Syria may have become at this time an Egyptian province.† On the other hand, the foundation (circ. 300 B.C.) of Antioch by Seleucus as his capital must have rendered Ptolemy's grasp of Cœle-Syria, to say the least of it, uncertain. On the whole, it would seem that Judea was under Egyptian sway for the next eighty years.‡ The deaths of the last three of the Diadochi, Lysimachus, Seleucus, and Ptolemy I., almost synchronized. The last named was succeeded in 285 B.C. by his son Ptolemy II. (Philadelphus), who had however reigned for the two previous

---

* See Mahaffy, *Emp. of the Ptol.*, pp. 87-90.

† See further in Mahaffy, *Emp. of the Ptol.*, pp. 65-67 and 131, and comp. his *Alex. Emp.* p. 69.

‡ But for another view see Poole, *Coins of the Ptolemies*, p. xxix., and Mahaffy, *Alex. Emp.*, p. 69.

years conjointly with his father. His wars with Syria and extension of the Egyptian rule in that direction had an important bearing upon Judea through the encouragement which he gave to the Greek element in the cities bordering upon that country, such as Gaza, Joppa, Ashkelon, Ashdod, Samaria, and Scythopolis. The new king "built Philadelphia on the site of the ancient 'Rabbah of the Ammonites,' Ptolemais on the site of Acco, Philoteria on the Lake of Gennesaret."* We shall see in the next chapter the great influence which these cities soon began to exercise upon Judean ways of thought and living.

On the death of Philadelphus, which took place in 247 B.C., his eldest son Euergetes † (Ptolemy III.) came to the throne. Josephus ‡ relates that on one of the occasions when his Syrian wars § brought him to the neighbourhood of Jerusalem, he "offered many sacrifices to God, and dedicated to Him such things as were suitable." "With the third Ptolemy, all the virtues of that great race, except, perhaps, the taste for patronising learning, seem to take their departure." ||

In the course of his reign (about 230 B.C.) there came into prominence Joseph, a nephew of the high priest Onias II., and grandson of Simon the Just, being son of the Tobiah who had married the daughter of Simon. He attained his position from his exceptional strength of purpose and the acquisition of great wealth. By the skilful carrying out of ambitious aims this man obtained paramount authority from both a military and a

---

* Moss, *From Malachi to Matthew*, p. 35.
† He is said to have obtained this name by bringing back, as part of the immense spoils won in the course of his war with Syria and Babylonia at the beginning of his reign, the statues of Egyptian gods, which had been captured by Cambyses.
‡ *C. Apion.*, ii. 5.
§ These were undertaken by way of avenging the murder of Berenice, daughter of Philadelphus, whom the latter had given in marriage to Antiochus Theos, father of the present Syrian king, viz., Seleucus II. (Callinicus).
|| Mahaffy, *Alex. Emp.*, p. 159.

financial point of view in Cœle-Syria and Phœnicia. He came to the front at a time when his uncle Onias was coquetting with Seleucus II. (Callinicus) of Syria and refusing to pay to Egypt the annual tribute of twenty talents. Joseph addressed the people in the court of the Temple, secured their enthusiastic support, as well as that of Athenion, the Egyptian envoy, and having also raised a loan from the Samaritans, met Euergetes near Memphis, and established himself in his special favour. He held office till his death (208 B.C.), and constituted himself throughout a formidable rival to the high priestly power, both by the riches which he amassed during his twenty-two years of office, and by the almost absolute power which the support of Egypt secured him. That he had "stripped the flesh from all Syria and left only the bones," * was a remark which was made about him in the presence of Philopator.

Philopator (Ptolemy IV.), who succeeded his father in 222 B.C., a year earlier than the commencement of Antiochus the Great's reign, after defeating the Syrian forces at Raphia near Gaza (217 B.C.), and thereby regaining Palestine and Phœnicia, is said † to have visited Jerusalem. While attempting, in spite of the protests of the high priest and people generally, to enter the Holy of Holies, he was seized with a fit and carried away by his attendants. It is impossible to say what substratum of fact lies under the subsequent highly coloured details as related in the same connexion, viz., how the king shewed his spite against the Jews of Alexandria, and how in commemoration of their deliverance by providential interpositions a feast was established. This last must of course have had some historical origin, and probably points to the fact that in spite of the hostility shewn towards them for some

---

* For the full form of the story see Jos. *Ant.* xii. 4. 9.
† 3 Macc. 1. 1—2. 24. But the Jews told pretty much the same story of Ptolemy IX. (Physcon). See Mahaffy, *Empire of the Ptolemies*, p. 381.

reason by Philopator, they succeeded in regaining or obtaining "the privilege of Alexandrian citizenship by payment of a large sum of money, of which the memory rankled in their hearts, and caused them to regard him as a national enemy. We can assert with confidence that Philopator earned the hostility of that people, and that they looked back upon his reign as one of oppression and injustice."* Philopator's death (205 B.C.) was speedily followed by the breaking up of the kingdom of the Nile outside Egypt proper. The next ruler was Philopator's son, Epiphanes, aged but six years, and by no means equal to a contest with Antiochus III. (the Great), who had succeeded Seleucus III. (Soter) as king of Syria in 221 B.C. As part of a scheme for the subjugation of Egypt entered into between Philip V. of Macedon (accession 222 B.C.) and Antiochus, the latter advanced for the purpose of seizing Cœle-Syria. Scopas, an Aetolian, was the leader of the forces sent against him from Alexandria. After some signal successes, that general was defeated by Antiochus at Mount Panium.†

The Jews, still cherishing the hostility to Egypt which had sprung up during the reign of Philopator, favoured the Syrian monarch, and became included in his kingdom; and, although Scopas, returning somewhat later from Egypt, ravaged the country, dismantled the fortresses, and caused much bloodshed, Antiochus (in 198 B.C.), receiving ready aid from Jerusalem in the shape of provisions for his troops, proceeded to reconquer the territory, and finally brought it under the Syrian sway. Ten years previously, Joseph, the powerful satrap of Cœle-Syria, had passed from the scene. His seven sons by his first wife were bitterly opposed to Hyrcanus, his son by a second union. The latter seems to have inherited his father's ambition

---

* Mahaffy, *Emp. of the Ptol.*, pp. 269 f.
† "Juxta fontes Jordanis, ubi nunc Paneas condita est." St. Jer. *Comm. in Dan.* xi. 15 (Migne, *Patrol.* xxv. 563).

as well as his intellectual ability, and early acquired favour at the court of Philopator. On one occasion while returning thence to Jerusalem, Hyrcanus was murderously attacked by his brothers, slew two of them in a skirmish, and being received coldly by his father on his arrival, returned to take up his abode for the time in Alexandria, from which place in the years that followed he exerted, we may be sure, all the force at his disposal, to keep in check the growing power of Antiochus in Palestine. The other Tobiades, as they were called, that is to say, the other sons and the grandsons of the satrap Joseph, were on the side of Syria. Hyrcanus preserved his fealty to Egypt, although his power to render that kingdom any effectual aid in recovering Syria seems to have been practically nil.

CHAPTER II.

THE CONDITION OF PALESTINE FROM THE RETURN TO THE ACCESSION OF ANTIOCHUS THE GREAT.

THE vitality of the Jewish patriotic spirit seems to have been preserved throughout the period of the Exile. There was a continuous faith in the prophecies* that within the space of about two generations the banished would return and take up the broken thread of national existence in their own land. It is true that comparatively few † availed themselves of Cyrus's permission. The descendants of the captives made by Babylonian conquerors preferred, as far as the majority were concerned, not to renounce the ties they had formed within the great city in Mesopotamia. But the enthusiasm of those who accompanied Zerubbabel across the wide plains which lay between them and Judea, is plainly marked in later Biblical literature.‡

It was clearly impossible that such shrunken numbers should attempt to spread themselves over the whole of the land which once was theirs, or even over Judea. Perhaps it was not altogether a misfortune that they were thus compelled to concentrate their strength, and support each other's courage in the difficulties which faced them. They were recruited by many of their nation, who actually within their country or in its immediate neighbourhood had waited patiently the fulfil-

---

* Jer. 25. 11, 12; 29. 10.
† See p. 1.
‡ See Stanley, *Jewish Church*, iii. pp. 78 f., London, 1875-76.

ment of their patriotic hopes. Proselytes also were not wanting in the building-up of the community.

In many points their religious life had undergone a change during the years of exile. The first and most prominent of these changes consisted in the disappearance of idolatry and the abhorrence of its memories. That reformation, which both prophetic denunciations and the efforts of such kings as Hezekiah and Josiah had been able only very partially to effect, had been once and for ever accomplished. After they had come to be familiar during the years of captivity with idol worship as practised at Babylon, this form of sin disappeared from the Jewish nation.

On the other hand, even as early as the time of the prophet Malachi, there are found traces of the sceptical and discontented spirit, whose existence is dealt with in a more developed form in the Book Koheleth (Ecclesiastes). The problem involved in the prosperity of the wicked presented difficulties which, as we can see, both in the Persian and Greek periods, keenly tried men's faith in an over-ruling Providence. The saying of men of Malachi's day "Everyone that doeth evil is good in the sight of the LORD, and He delighteth in them,"* and "Where is the God of judgment?" † finds its echo in the words of the Preacher, "All things have I seen in the days of my vanity : there is a just man that perisheth in his righteousness, and there is a wicked man that prolongeth his life in his wickedness."‡ *Vanitas vanitatum, omnia vanitas*, must have represented the attitude of many minds, which failed to accept the faith expressed in the concluding words of the book last quoted, "Fear God, and keep His commandments ; for this is the whole duty of man.

---

* Mal. 2. 17; comp. 3. 13-18.
† *Ibid.*
‡ Eccles. 7. 15.

For God shall bring every work into judgment, with every secret thing, whether it be good, or whether it be evil."*

To the Exile also we may with some confidence trace the beginnings at any rate of that rule which the individual conscience came to have among the more spiritually minded members of the race. Such narratives as those of Daniel or of Susannah shew that when they were written there was an audience to be appealed to, who would not fail to sympathise with the resolve to risk life itself in faithful adherence to duty.

Again, prayer assumed a new position. This feature is illustrated in the Books of Ezra and Nehemiah † as well as Daniel ‡ and elsewhere. With the enforced suspension of sacrificial offerings during the Captivity, the more spiritual forms of worship acquired a prominence, which they retained after the Return. Synagogue services were established here and there as need arose. In Jerusalem there was now joined with the animal and other offerings in kind, a ritual consisting of psalms and prayers, the latter doubtless for a time at least unrestricted by any hard-and-fast form.

Moreover, almsgiving acquired prominence. He that displayed this form of charity was considered to have thereby so amply acquitted himself of his religious obligations that his gifts became worthy of being described by the word "Righteousness,"§ without further qualification.

Once more, the Jewish outlook upon the world, hitherto so narrow, became somewhat less circumscribed. They were now re-established, not so much upon a national as upon a religious basis. They are henceforward "Judeans,"‖ but the word has

---

* Eccles. 12. 13, 14.   † Ezra 9. 6; Nch. 1. 4; 2. 4; 4. 9; comp. chap. 9.
‡ Dan. 6. 10; 9. 3.
§ צְדָקָה often rendered (e.g., Deut. 6. 25; 24. 13; Ps. 24. [Greek 23] 5) in LXX. by ἐλεημοσύνη: so the Aramaic form צִדְקָה in both LXX. and Theod. of Dan. 4. 24 [Eng. 27].
‖ Jos. Ant. xi. 5. 7.

not a strictly racial significance. It does not exclude a willingness to embrace all who would receive their faith and unite with them in worship of Jehovah. The Exile had so far familiarised them with the thought of the extent of humanity, that they were ready to picture to themselves the acceptance of their religion by the other kingdoms of the earth.*

The impression made upon the Jewish mind through the wealth and luxury affected by the higher classes in Babylon is manifest from the description of the king's palace in the Book of Esther.† The signal honour with which the Jews treated that book may indeed be ascribed to its relation of the overthrow of their would-be oppressors, and the triumph secured them by an overruling Providence working through the good fortune and resolution of a Jewish maiden. But it also shews the pleasure which they felt in dwelling upon the description of the magnificence exhibited in the appointments and surroundings of an Oriental court.

The purity of the Persian mode of worship, the absence of all grossness in the way of sacrificial offering, and the identification of Truth with the Deity in the Zoroastrian creed, had an undoubted effect upon the Judaism of post-captivity days. The elaborate purificatory rites, characteristic of later Judaism, arose in large measure from customs which had become familiar to the nation during its sojourn in Babylon. "The veneration for the holy fire which was kindled from the sacred naphtha fountains of Persia by the Caspian Sea, penetrated into the Jewish traditions in the story that, when Nehemiah rekindled the consecrated fire of the Temple from the stones of the altar, he called it 'naphthar,' giving it a Hebrew meaning, 'a cleansing,' though many call it 'nephi.'" ‡

---

* *See* Stanley, *op. cit.*, iii. 41 ff.
† Esth. 1. 6, 7.
‡ Stanley, *op. cit.*, iii. 184. *See* 2 Macc. 1. 36, and Smith's *Dict. of Bible*, ii. 465.

The development of the Jewish doctrine of angels at this period of their history may also be connected with Persian influences. In that country's faith the hierarchy of celestial intelligences had been set forth with much elaborateness. But although the two religions thus had much in common, the Jewish teaching on the subject possessed a decided advantage in leading the way towards the light to be thrown upon angelic offices by Christian revelation. In the Persian religion there seems little, if any, trace of an interest taken by angels in the affairs or the well-being of men; while such books as Daniel * and Tobit † shew heavenly guardians appointed for the surveillance and protection alike of individuals and of states.

It is, however, specially worthy of note in this connexion that the dualism which was so prominent a feature of the Zoroastrian religion fails to find a counterpart in Jewish teaching. The rival powers of good and evil are never placed by the latter on anything like a footing of equality. Satan is represented as subordinate in position, though having in some sort access to the courts of heaven; and as making his assaults upon the human race only by permission of a higher power. The words of the LORD's message, "I form the light . . . and create evil" ‡ express the attitude of the Jew in this matter in direct antagonism to that of the worshipper of Ormuzd, who gave co-ordinated powers to Ahriman. The "adversary," the opposer of God and man, was the main idea in the mind of the Jew, when he thought of an evil agency as personified; not the one who makes calumnious accusations, not the "slanderer" ($\delta\iota\dot{\alpha}\beta o\lambda o\varsigma$), but the power which, within the limits allowed him by the Most High, makes for *unrighteousness*.

But the characteristic which penetrated most deeply into the national life of the post-exilic people was the reverence

---

* Dan. 8. 15, 16; 10. 5, etc.   † Tobit 3. 17, etc.   ‡ Is. 45. 7.

and study bestowed on the Law, viewed as an absolute rule of conduct, and an inexhaustible storehouse of precepts applicable without exception to every circumstance of life. Ewald,* comparing the working out of this conception in detail with the elaborate literary structures of the schoolmen and with other modern labours of a juristic character, points out that "the difference between the legal movement over which Ezra presided and its modern parallels lies chiefly in this simple fact, that the former found in every ancient law which it worked up the immediate presence of the holy itself, and therefore treated it with the utmost awe and the most scrupulous care, and with admirable patience made the most strenuous efforts possible to secure the legal obedience, and, by that path, the outward sanctity of man."

But this identification, or close conformity, of the things which were required by the Law, and holiness of life, soon worked out in many instances to the natural result of contentment with the careful discharge of duty, ceremonial and other, and failure to recognise the vital power derived from unity with the Divine source of sanctity. Moreover, when the yoke of the Law, thus interpreted, became over burdensome to the individual, recourse was had, especially among the higher ranks, to various devices by which an equivalent in the shape of money or other offerings was held as a release in full from more irksome demands.

It is very significant, as Ewald shews,† that, as ceremonial developed, and ritual holiness became more and more emphasized in the national life, the Divine author of the Law came to be looked upon as further and further removed from direct spiritual contact or converse with His people, so that the highest of His names became completely disused, and for

---

* *History of Israel*, v. 196 (Eng. Trans. 1880). † *Op. cit.*, v. 197 f.

'Jehovah' was invariably substituted in utterance one of the common titles, Adonai, El, Elohim, Heaven, or later, the simple expression, The Name.

The prophetic period of Israel's history had been fraught with deep benefit to their spiritual life. Moral, as contrasted with mere ceremonial, holiness had been powerfully enforced upon the nation before, and even after, the Exile. But when the last of the prophets had protested against the sins of the ecclesiastical leaders of the time, and had pointed once more to the immutable bases of morality, this teaching more and more lost its hold and was practically to a large extent forgotten, while formality in ritual established itself as the all-sufficient substitute.

Comments such as the above on the religious and social condition of the people during the period which followed the Return are necessarily of a somewhat impersonal character. When once the generation which saw the labours of Ezra and Nehemiah had passed away, there is a singular lack of any conspicuous figure.*

We may assume that the Persian power kept up at least a nominal control through its governor, who seems for a while at any rate to have lived within Jerusalem. It is probable, however, that the Jews were left pretty much to themselves as regards administrative functions. Their position between two rival powers like Persia and Egypt must have exposed them to occasional depredations from contending forces. At the same time the condition of the people themselves, as portrayed for us by Malachi, was in many respects lamentable. The enthusiasm which marked the return from the Captivity had evidently died away after a very few generations. The priests

---

* The Prophet Malachi (*See* Driver, *Introd. to Lit. of O. T.*, p. 357, 6th ed.) is to be set down to the generation of Ezra and Nehemiah rather than to a subsequent one.

were chargeable with peculation, adultery, and crimes of violence. They mocked at purity either of ritual or life, and found the observance of the Law a weariness. On the other hand, there were still to be found a few faithful ones, an inner circle whose spirituality of mind caused them to cherish the worship of God, and listen to His prophet. For them the Messianic hope was not extinguished. Yet even they were willing to a large extent to merge that hope in the watching for the messenger who should herald His approach. On the appearance of Elijah the Prophet—for so they named him who was to come in the spirit and power of the Tishbite of old— not only should the Jewish nation be at harmony with itself, and the hearts of parents and children turned towards one another, but the worship of the true God should be diffused through the nations. "From the rising of the sun even unto the going down of the same My name shall be great among the Gentiles; and in every place incense shall be offered unto My name and a pure offering; for My name shall be great among the heathen, saith the LORD of hosts."*

As there was no great scope for political energy at this period, and no leader at once possessed of ability and of patriotic instincts to enter upon any schemes for directing the relationship between the Jews and their neighbours, the best interests of the nation were naturally centred upon religion. Even the Samaritan schism no doubt had its influence in this direction. The enquiry had to be faced, "What is the essential difference between us and other nations or even that community which worships on Mount Gerizim?" And the answer was found in the minute study of the Torah, and the elaboration of endless minutiæ in the form of precepts intended to provide for all conceivable combinations of

---

* Mal. 1. 11.

circumstances. This process of framing elaborate directions and thorny restrictions, this making of 'a fence to the Torah,'* commenced now, and continued for centuries to be the ruling passion of religious spirits. Thus the scribe element in the nation acquired a vast importance. This may be seen in the position (referred to above) which such matters as prayers, fasting, and alms obtained in the life of the people, as shewn, *e.g.*, in Tobit, Judith, and other books of the Apocrypha.†

The high-priestly power had always been an important factor in the life of the Jewish people. In important crises, before and after the establishment of the monarchy, it had discharged a most important function. It was only to be expected that, aided by the hereditary character of the office, its lofty traditions, and the popular enthusiasm for the Law—of which, on its ceremonial side, the priests were the natural guardians—the high priest should acquire during this period, even independently of any claims to distinction from personal excellence, a powerful position as a leader.

The high priests, as we might expect, were not slow to perceive the advantages which their position gave them. We are not without instances ‡ in which they made use of their power for unworthy purposes. On the other hand, about twenty years after the establishment of the Ptolemaic dynasty there arose in Judea a conspicuous high priest, Simon the Just (circ. 300—290). "In an age deficient in great men, he appears like a lofty and luxuriant tree in the midst of a barren country," § "the only high priest who restored the priesthood to honour." ‖ His repairs of the city-walls and

---

* *Pirke Aboth* i. 1. The term means the prohibition of things innocent in themselves, but bordering too closely for safety on things forbidden.
† See abundant illustrations in Smith's *Dict. of Bible* (Art. Apocrypha), i. 192, ed. 1893.
‡ *See* Neh. 13. 4-9 : and for a specially flagrant case, p. 31, *infra*.
§ Graetz, *op. cit.*, p. 435.   ‖ *Ibid*.

of the Temple, his introduction of a much-needed and constant supply of water, and his other merits are set forth in the eulogy bestowed on him in Ecclesiasticus (ch. 50). From him the study and practice of religion received a strong impulse. " The world," he said,* " subsists on three things : the Law, the service in the Temple, and acts of love."

The injunction, " bring up many disciples," † attributed to " the men of the Great Synagogue," reflected the spirit which even now prevailed. Schools for the instruction of the young in the written and unwritten traditions of the Law sprang up in Jerusalem and elsewhere, and there the pupils of the wise (*Talmude Chákhamim*) were instructed by the scribes in the ever-increasing mass of decisions (Halachah) and illustrative tales (Haggadah) which culminated later in the compilation of the Talmuds of Jerusalem and Babylon.

The fervid admirers of the Torah and its developments were only strengthened in their faith with regard to its all-embracing efficacy as a rule of life and morals by the laxity and indifference which they saw around them. As we noticed in the last chapter, it is probably in part to the prevalence of legalism that we are to ascribe the tendency to support the earlier Ptolemies against the Seleucid dynasty. Although a Hellenizing party is scarcely discernible in the political life of Judea till towards the close of the third or beginning of the second century B.C., the policy of the Macedonian conqueror must have at once acted in this direction. That policy was, as we have noticed (*see* p. 9), in accordance with what was the general Hellenic instinct, to plant Greek colonies in the various towns which came under his rule, so as gradually to introduce the language and manners of Greece throughout the empire. It is clear how effectual were the means thus adopted by him, and

---

* *Pirke Aboth*, i. 2. † *Ibid*. i. 1.

carried out by his successors, for the Hellenization of his wide dominions. In particular, the planting of Greeks in such cities as Gaza, Ashkelon, Ashdod, Joppa, and the founding of new cities in attractive localities, such as Anthedon and Apollonia, would have an influence, more or less gradual, on their Jewish neighbours.* That influence was of a twofold character. On the one hand, to those whose training or temperament disposed them firmly to resist all change, and to cling closely to Jewish models in thought and practice, the Greek laxity in belief and habit was simply a thing which called for unqualified censure. On the other hand, the necessary acquisition of the language of the settlers for purposes of commerce and general intercourse had given, as we shall see, by the time of Antiochus, if not earlier, a hold to the Greek element, which implies a considerable antecedent period of growth.† Accordingly in, and even before, Maccabean times we shall find a strong party, in the majority at Jerusalem, in favour of Hellenism, while in stout opposition to them was the party which upheld the Law as the only rule of life, and clung to the ideal as taught by the scribes. The premature violence of Antiochus Epiphanes, forming the occasion of the outbreak of the Jewish wars in the second century B.C., was the cause which enabled the minority, headed by Judas and his brethren, through their vehement appeal to the patriotic and religious sentiment, to gain the day against the force of numbers.

---

* Ewald (op. cit., v. 237) points out that purely Judean districts during these centuries succeeded in excluding such settlements.
† It has been suggested that it was the spread of Hellenic culture which led to the introduction of the public reading of the "prophets" in the synagogue. See Ryle, Canon of the O.T. (2nd ed.), p. 118, London, 1895.

CHAPTER III.

THE HISTORY FROM THE ACCESSION OF ANTIOCHUS THE GREAT TO THE TIME OF THE MACCABEAN REVOLT (222–168 B.C.).

"POLYBIUS chose the year 221 B.C. for the opening of his great history of the civilized world, because in his opinion it marked a curious turning-point in the affairs of men. Several of the greatest monarchs of the world died at that time— Antigonus Doson, Ptolemy Euergetes, Cleomenes. Antiochus III. of Syria was only just come to the throne, a mere youth, and other inexperienced youths, Ptolemy Philopator and Philip V., ascended the vacant thrones. To those who expected a Roman invasion it must now have seemed inevitable, and at this time the Romans could have conquered the empire of Alexander with no difficulty. But suddenly there arose for them too the cloud in the west; Hannibal was before Saguntum, and crossed the Ebro, and for the next twenty years they were struggling for bare existence against the mighty Carthaginian. So then the interference of Rome was stayed, and Hellenistic life was allowed another generation of development."* We have already (ch. I.) touched upon the position of affairs in Egypt and Judea during the earlier years of the long reign of Antiochus the Great (221–175 B.C.). As we have seen (p. 12), he did not establish his power in Jerusalem till twenty-four years later. Although the Hellenizing party in the city was strong enough to assure him of support, things were different elsewhere. The Jews in the country parts were much harassed by the exactions

---

* Mahaffy, *Alex. Emp.*, p. 213.

and depredations practised by the troops of the rival claimants. Owing to the wise administration of Aristomenes, an Acarnanian, virtually governor of Egypt during the infancy of Ptolemy Epiphanes, Antiochus III., after his decisive victory over the Egyptians at Panion, on the upper Jordan, made peace with the king, and undertook to give him his daughter Cleopatra in marriage, and with her Cœle-Syria and Palestine as her dowry. In the meanwhile, however, it was arranged that the taxes should be divided between the two kings, thus practically subjecting the people to a double amount of oppression.

Antiochus at first treated the Jews with much consideration, causing their religious scruples to be respected, and even directing that the city walls and the Temple should be repaired. On the whole, Jewish feeling at this time was decidedly against Egypt;* and, in general, it may be said that association with a kingdom like that of the Seleucidæ, who ruled over such very various nationalities, would naturally present a certain amount of attraction, as against Egypt, the character of whose government would be likely to permit much less of elasticity. Ptolemy Philopator (*ob.* 204 B.C.) by the severe imposts which he enforced had alienated the nation, and they sided consequently with the Syrian power. There appear to have been more Jews in Antioch and its neighbourhood than were to be found in Alexandria itself. From Babylon two thousand families had been transferred to Phrygia and Lydia; in fact, the Jews were nearly the most numerous nationality within the Syrian kingdom. We are told in the Second Book of Maccabees (**8.** 20)—and probably the story is true, with some amount of exaggeration in detail—that eight thousand Babylonian Jews had gained a victory for Antiochus over an army of Galatians of fifteen times their own size.

---

* For the reason, *see* Mahaffy, *Alex. Emp.*, p. 232.

The seven sons of Joseph, the leader of the Egyptian party (*see* p. 12), by his first wife, who were named after their paternal grandfather the sons of Tobiah, formed the champions of Hellenism during the time of Antiochus III. Their half-brother, Hyrcanus, on the other hand, inherited his father's policy, and by his ability and social qualities became, as we have already seen (p. 13), a *persona grata* at the Egyptian court. There he acquired much wealth, which, on the death of his patron Philopator, he transferred in part to the Temple treasury for security, while with another portion he erected for himself on the eastern side of Jordan, not far from Heshbon, a costly castle,* in which he took up his abode as representative of the Egyptian interest in those quarters. Domestic broils between him and his brethren constantly led on to civil disorder, and the state of the country was deplorable enough during the earlier part of Antiochus the Great's reign, while desultory attacks from their old enemies the Idumeans, Philistines, and Samaritans, added to the troubles of the nation.

Antiochus suffered a severe defeat at the hands of the Roman general Lucius Scipio near Magnesia in 190 B.C., a blow which involved the loss of much territory and money, as well as of his fleet. We now for the first time hear of his son, Antiochus Epiphanes, whom he was compelled to send to Rome as a hostage, to remain (as it turned out) thus confined for thirteen years.

In order to pay the excessively heavy impost which the Roman power inflicted, Antiochus betook himself to robbing temples,† and the resentment and tumult which was brought about by his attack upon the temple of Bel at Elymais was

---

* The ruins of it perhaps still exist at *Arak-el-Emir*.
† Which were not only full of rich offerings, like the Temple at Jerusalem, but served as banks of deposit.

the cause of his being slain there, 187 B.C. His son, Seleucus Philopator, succeeded him and reigned in an uneventful manner for about eleven years. He devoted himself to finding the money which Rome continued to demand, while the Jews remained, in a manner, subjected to both the Egyptian and Syrian kingdoms.

The chief incident connected with Jerusalem during Seleucus's reign was the attempt of Heliodorus to seize upon the Temple treasures. An official, described as "steward of the Temple," named Simon the Benjamite, in order to curry favour with Seleucus, informed Apollonius, governor of Cœle-Syria, that there was much wealth to be had for the capture. He reported the matter to Seleucus, who, hard pressed for means wherewith to pay the heavy demands of the Romans, sent his chief minister, Heliodorus, to Jerusalem. The Second Book of Maccabees (ch. **3**) relates the terror that took possession of the city on the arrival of the Syrian envoy, and the subsequent incidents, at least in the form which the memory of them assumed several generations later. "The priests, prostrating themselves before the altar in their priestly garments, and looking toward heaven, called upon him that gave the law concerning deposits that he should preserve these treasures safe for those that had deposited them." "And they that were in the houses rushed flocking out to make a universal supplication, because the place was like to come into contempt. And the women, girt with sackcloth under their breasts, thronged the streets, and the virgins that were kept in ward ran together, some to the gates, others to the walls, and some looked out through the windows."* Thereupon appeared a horse "with a terrible rider" clothed in armour of gold, and two young men who scourged the impious intruder, at length laid prostrate,

---

* 2 Macc. 3. 15, 18, 19.

"speechless and bereft of all hope and deliverance."* The high priest offers a sacrifice of propitiation. Heliodorus too makes vows, offers sacrifice, and returns to the king. "And when the king asked Heliodorus what manner of man was fit to be sent once again to Jerusalem, he said : If thou hast any enemy or conspirator against the state, send him thither, and thou shalt receive him back well scourged, if he even escape with his life ; because of a truth there is about the place a power of God." †

The high priest above-mentioned was Onias III., who succeeded his father Simon II. in 198 or 195 B.C. He was a prominent member of the Assidean sect, and remarkable for his holiness of life and close observance of the Law. As a ruler, he aimed at strict impartiality between rival factions. He supported Hyrcanus in his use of the Temple as a place of security for the treasures which he had obtained through siding with Egypt, while, although he was viewed with hostility by the Hellenistic party led by his own brother Jason,‡ he seems to have been regarded, for a while at least, with much favour by Seleucus. At length, however, owing to the continual slanders of Simon the Benjamite, who remained at the Syrian court, Onias, in the interests of his people, proceeded to Antioch, where he abode for some years. Soon after his arrival there Antiochus Epiphanes obtained permission to terminate his thirteen years' detention at Rome. On his arrival at Antioch he found that his brother was dead, probably

---

* Raphael's celebrated representation of this scene in the Stanze of the Vatican (in allusion to Pope Julius II.'s overthrow and expulsion of the usurpers of Church property. See Bellori, *Descrizioni*, etc., Rome, 1821, pp. 57 ff.) is a reproduction (as is pointed out by Symonds, *Sketches in Italy and Greece*, London, 1879, p. 74) of the expulsion of foes from the market-place at Perugia by Simonetto and Astorre (Baglioni), as seen by Raphael when painting at the studio there in his youth.
† 2 Macc. 3. 37, 38.
‡ Jason was originally called Jesus, according to Jos. *Ant.* xii. 5, 1.

murdered by Heliodorus, who had assumed the throne. Epiphanes banished the murderer, and thus unexpectedly obtained the kingdom (175 B.C.),* Demetrius, son of the late king, and thus the rightful heir, being now a hostage at Rome. This arrangement met with the favour of the Roman power, which, on the principle '*Divide et impera*,' had for its interest to sow dissensions among members of a royal family, and thus gain over kingdoms which still retained more or less of independence.

Antiochus IV. (Epiphanes) reigned 175–164 B.C. "He was by nature a genuine despot, eccentric and undependable, sometimes extravagantly liberal and fraternizing with the common people in an affected manner; at other times cruel and tyrannical."† The latter side of his character is made abundantly evident by his treatment of the Jews. The former qualities are brought out in detail by Polybius in his history,‡ who there speaks of him as 'Επιμανής (Epimanes, madman) rather than 'Επιφανής (Epiphanes, magnificent). He was thoroughly imbued with the spirit of Hellenism, and his great purpose was to introduce Greek worship and practices throughout his dominions, not sparing any amount of violence or religious persecution, should they be needful to attain his ends. The feuds which prevailed in Judea of themselves would have attracted his attention. He received, however, a direct appeal from the Hellenizing party there, who pointed out that Hyrcanus was still collecting taxes in the neighbourhood of his castle in the interests of Egypt.

Hyrcanus committed suicide, and Antiochus seized his property. In his need of money he proceeded to plunder the Temple, a proceeding which would fall in well with his natural dislike of the stricter party among the Jews. Jason, brother

---

* *See* Dan. 11. 21 ff. † Schürer, *op. cit.*, 1. i. 199.
‡ Polyb. xxvi. 10, translated at length by Schürer, *l.c.*

of Onias, who had been acting as high priest since the latter had taken up his abode at Antioch, undertook, on condition of his being confirmed in the possession of that office, to provide amply for the king's pecuniary needs, and to encourage Hellenism in every way in Jerusalem. In pursuance of this arrangement, " seeking to overthrow the lawful modes of life, he brought in new customs forbidden by the Law,"* the very priests hurrying from their sacrifices to the contests conducted in the Greek manner in a gymnasium below the citadel. Many sought to efface the marks of circumcision. "The Greek cap," a broad-brimmed hat, such as appeared on the figure of Hermes (Mercury), was ordered to be worn by the noblest of the young men.† A festival in honour of Hercules was celebrated every fourth year at Tyre, and to this Jason sent a money contribution. But the courage of his messengers failed them, and when it came to the point, they asked that the money should be applied to the fitting out of additional vessels for Antiochus's fleet.

Jason held office for three years (174—171 B.C.), and his influential position is shewn by the fact that when Antiochus in 172 B.C. paid a short visit to Jerusalem, he was received with acclamations and a torchlight procession.

Jason's tenure of power however was, after all, far from secure. Menelaus, brother of Simon the Benjamite,‡ was sent to Antioch with some of the promised money. He took the opportunity of outbidding Jason and thus obtained his office ; but his attempts at fulfilling the pecuniary obligations which he had thus incurred, by rifling the Temple-stores and carrying off its sacred vessels, procured him not only the rebuke of the aged Onias, soon afterwards slain (171 B.C.), but arraignment

---

* 2 Macc. 4. 11.   † *Ibid.*, *v.* 12.
‡ Sc 2 Macc. 4. 23 ; but Josephus (*Ant.* xii. 5. 1), with less probability, says that he was Jason's own brother.

before the king as being the cause of riots in Jerusalem brought about by his sacrilegious conduct. But the attack upon him proved abortive. "Menelaus, through the covetous dealings of them that were in power, remained still in his office." *

Antiochus now (170 B.C.) relying, though without adequate grounds, on immunity from the side of Rome, which was becoming involved in a war with Perseus, king of Macedonia, attacked and defeated Ptolemy Philometor near Pelusium. A report that the king of Syria had been slain brought such encouragement to the enemies of Menelaus, that Jason, who had fled to the Ammonites, returned to the city, and compelled Menelaus to take refuge in the citadel. The report soon proved to be erroneous; Jason's career was at an end; he fled to Sparta and died there unmourned.

The ferocious side of the king of Syria's nature was now fully revealed. He held a three days' massacre in Jerusalem, sparing neither age nor sex. Menelaus himself brought the king into the Holy of Holies, where the latter declared afterwards that he had seen the statue of a long-bearded man (Moses), riding an ass, and with a roll in his hand.† He carried off everything of value to Antioch, leaving, as rulers in Jerusalem, Menelaus as high priest and Philip, a Phrygian, as governor. Of the latter it is said that he was "in character more barbarous than him that set him there." ‡

On Antiochus's conduct at this time Prof. Mahaffy comments as follows : " I think his savage outbreak at Jerusalem, where he sacrificed swine upon the altar, defiled the Holy of Holies, and forced all the priests to pollute themselves, must have been caused by some more special personal injuries on

---

* 2 Macc. 4. 50.
† Hence perhaps the later assertion that a golden ass was an object worshipped by the Jews. For various conjectures as to the reasons for such a belief, see Dr. Hatch's Article *Asinarii* in Smith's *Dict. of Christian Antiquities*.
‡ 2 Macc. 5. 22.

their part than the mere resistance to his innovations. Our information is so scanty that we can only guess. In some way the nationalist party in Judæa, and their relations in Egypt, must have thwarted his advance and marred his campaign. We hear that his third advance was slow; had he reached Alexandria but a few days sooner, he might have seized the capital, murdered the royal princes, and then made his peace with the Romans when the game was won. It seems likely that the opposition of the patriotic party in Judæa hindered his march, and so caused his signal failure at the moment of victory."*

On the occasion of another expedition against Egypt two years later (168 B.C.), Antiochus was met by a Roman envoy,† Caius Popilius Lænas, who handed him the Senate's written order to discontinue the war, and on his hesitation to promise acquiescence, drew a circle around him with his stick on the sand, and required his decision before he stepped across that boundary.‡ At the moment that Antiochus yielded to this peremptory demand, the empire of Alexander may be said to have visibly passed over to the Romans. But to a man of the king's ferocity of temper the occasion proved one on which he had to wreak his vengeance in some direction, and now, as before, the Jews were the victims. Sending Apollonius,§ his collector of tribute, with 20,000 men to Jerusalem, he gave command that it should be thoroughly Hellenized.‖ On the first Sabbath after his arrival Apollonius proceeded to carry

---

* Mahaffy, *Emp. of the Ptol.*, p. 341. For further particulars as to Antiochus's acts of severity see Farrar's *Daniel*, p. 244. London, 1895.
† Ptolemy Philometor and his brother Euergetes II., who were reigning conjointly at this time, had already requested help from Rome and Achaia against the Syrian power.
‡ Polyb. xxix. 27.
§ So 2 Macc. 5. 24. In 1 Macc. 1. 29 his name is not given.
‖ This is expressed in Daniel (11. 30) by the words, he had regard "unto them that forsake the holy covenant."

out his orders. Those who opposed were killed or sold into slavery, and colonists brought in to fill their places.* The city walls were demolished, but the citadel was fortified, and the Syrian garrison held it securely through Maccabean times till 142 B.C. All distinctively Jewish practices were forbidden, circumcision, the sacrificial system, abstinence from unclean food, even the possession of the sacred Books. On the 15th of Chisleu, *i.e.* late in December, 168 B.C.,† an altar to the Olympian Zeus was placed on the altar of burnt-offering, and ten days later it was hanselled by the sacrifice of a sow. The Jews were compelled to keep the festival of Dionysus (Bacchus), crowned with ivy. Violence, including death, was the penalty for detection in the infringement of any of these commands, which were rigidly enforced by officers appointed to see to their observance in all parts of the country. To this time belong the well-known stories of the martyrdom of the aged scribe Eleazar, and of the mother and her seven sons.‡ It was emphatically a time of sifting. "Judah was searched, and that which was unworthy cast out. Waverers turned with rekindled fervour to the God of their fathers. In their hiding-places on the outskirts of the land, the faces of the Chasidim (Assideans) grew stern. The soldiers of Jehovah were ready for battle, waiting in prayer for a God-sent man to lead them."§

---

* The policy of expelling the inhabitants of a city and re-peopling it with persons who would carry out the desire of the conquerors was practised by the Jews themselves later at Joppa and Gazara (1 Macc. 13. 11 and 43-48).
† So Schürer, *op. cit.*, 1. i. 208; but some make this to take place a year later.
‡ 2 Macc. 6. 9—7. 42.
§ Moss, *From Malachi to Matthew*, p. 66.

CHAPTER IV.

THE MACCABEAN REVOLT TO THE DEATH OF JUDAS (168—160 B.C.).

IN order to understand the importance of the Maccabean revolt as a specially important epoch in the history of Judaism, we must contemplate it on the one hand in its relation to the establishment of the Law under Ezra and Nehemiah, and on the other hand in its reference to the completion of the literary work which goes by the name of the Mishnah (circ. 200 A.D.).

When the Temple-worship at Jerusalem was re-established, there was placed before the pious Jew in detail the ceremonial, as well as other, duties which that Law entailed. The festival celebrations, the sacrifices and other offerings on stated occasions, the tribute to be paid to the priests, and in general the rites necessary to be performed regularly or on special occasions, on the penalty of forfeiting the favour of the Almighty—all these were set forth with particularity, to be carried out with the utmost punctilio. Further, the study of the Law was given in charge to a body of men, the scribes, whose duty should be to enforce its regulations, explain its meaning, and draw such inferences as might be needed in the complicated circumstances of religious duty. Absolute precision was essential in carrying out the requirements of the Law. How should that precision be attained, except by an authorised interpretation? In the course of centuries these guardians of the Law had heaped up a vast number of traditions, more or less directly based on the groundwork of the text which was in their keeping, and intended to provide answers for the variety of questions actually arising, or which might well be expected to arise, touching its requirements. This gradually growing body of decisions, which by the end of the second century A.D. was formed into the Mishnah (the common basis of the Talmuds of Jerusalem and Babylon), had not of course acquired in Maccabean times the fulness which it afterwards exhibits. Nevertheless, it is clear that the Assideans, and all those who with them placed a high value upon the distinctive religious rites of the nation, were even at this date strong supporters of the sanctity of the ceremonial enjoined, or suggested by inference from that which was enjoined, in the five "Books of Moses" (the Torah). A considerable measure of enthusiasm for the Law already doubtless existed among those who were wholly opposed to the encroachments of the Hellenistic spirit, to which we have referred in previous chapters.

On the other hand, we gather from the general tenor of the history that those who favoured Hellenism were in the majority in Judea during the times immediately preceding the Maccabean outbreak. Not only were the Jews compelled from the needs of commerce to acquaint themselves with the Greek language, but it is also evident that the attempts to introduce Greek customs into Judea met with considerable success. If then there had been no violent means used to this end, and things had been permitted to go smoothly on in Judea, as had been the case in Syria and in Egypt, it seems humanly speaking probable that as in the latter cases, so in the former, the Judaism of Palestine would have taken a more or less Hellenistic form. "For it belonged to the very essence of Hellenism that it should dominate and colour the modes of religious worship, and at least clothe them in Grecian garments. We find it so in Syria as well as in Egypt."*

---

* Schürer, *op. cit.*, 1. i. 198.

THE MACCABEAN REVOLT TO DEATH OF JUDAS. 37

But although, as far as numbers go, those who favoured Greek ways seem to have been in the ascendant in Judea, the check was sudden and effective. The violent attempt of Antiochus Epiphanes to "rush" (in modern phrase) his policy and abolish Judaism at one blow, aroused the spirit which found expression in the Maccabean revolt. "It was just the extreme and radical character of the attempt that saved Judaism. For now not only the strict party of *Chasidim*, but the whole mass of the people, was roused to do battle for the old faith. And the further development of events led to the complete expulsion of Hellenism from Jewish soil, at least in matters of religion. So far as our information reaches, this is the only example of an Oriental religion completely emancipating itself from the influence of Hellenism." * It is true that the need in pre-Maccabean days of resisting the seduction of Greek manners had already done something in this direction. None the less did the savagery of Epiphanes bring about the saving crisis of Judaism.

The contemplation, however, of the Maccabean revolt from this point of view must not cause us to forget that its leaders were in constant intercourse with Greeks. Although in one sense those leaders were fiercely Semitic and national in their aims, they were willing to deal in the way of treaties with the Seleucid kings or the Roman Senate, and, as Prof. Mahaffy observes,† in a case of the latter kind (circ. 129 B.C.) "the very names of the ambassadors—Simon, son of Dositheus; Apollonius, son of Alexander; and Diodorus, son of Jason, cultivated men ($ἄνδρες$ $καλοὶ$ $καὶ$ $ἀγαθοί$),who doubtless spoke Greek perfectly at Rome—shew the worldly side of John Hyrcanus."

We have spoken (pp. 33, 34) of the barbarities practised upon the Jews by order of Antiochus Epiphanes, and the

---

* Schürer, *op. cit.*, 1. i. 198.   † *Greek World under Roman Sway*, p. 43.

martyrdoms which were the outcome of Jewish heroism. The Assideans and those whom by preaching and example they encouraged to resistance, took refuge, as their forefathers had done, in caves and other hiding-places. At first the Assideans would not permit their followers to defend their positions if assailed on the Sabbath, and we are told that on one such occasion Philip, the Phrygian commander of the Syrian forces, was able to destroy vast numbers of the fugitives by applying fire to the caves in which they had sought refuge.

Hope at last appeared, and the heroism of Mattathias and his family supplied the leadership which was needed by the afflicted nation. He belonged to the priestly family of the Hasmoneans, so called from *Chasmon*,* his great-grandfather. He was an old man, and his sons were all in their prime. He had withdrawn from Jerusalem, when the state of affairs rendered it impossible for him to discharge his priestly functions there, to Modin,† his home. The emissaries of the king, in the course of their expeditions for the purpose of extirpating Jewish rites, arrived at Modin, and urged Mattathias to sacrifice to Jupiter, promising advancement, if he would comply. When he stoutly refused, on behalf of himself and his family, to forsake the law of his fathers, even should he stand alone in resistance, he saw a Jew step forward to comply with the commissioners' demand. This spark kindled the flame. With his own hand he slew his recreant fellow-countryman, while his sons killed Apelles, the leader, and his soldiers, and destroyed the altar of sacrifice. Thereupon Mattathias summoned all to follow him to the mountains, where he carried on for a year a successful warfare,

---

* *Prince*, or *magnate*. See plural of the word in Ps. 68. 32 [Eng. 31].
† The Modiim of the Talmud (Tal. Bab. *Chagigah*, 25b), now known as *El-Mediyeh*, 16 miles N. of Jerusalem. Mattathias's son Simon adorned his father's tomb with pillars and carvings of ships, placed so as to be visible from the sea (1 Macc. 13. 29). *See* Neubauer's *Geog. du Thalmud*, p. 99. The monument still existed in the time of Eusebius.

harassing the enemy, and careful not to meet them in the open, as long as his forces were still untrained to cope with anything like disciplined troops. He persuaded even the more rigid of his followers to give up their scruples as to self-defence on the Sabbath. His adherents constantly increased, and although, as in the times of the Judges and early in the reign of Saul, they had to live for the most part in hiding-places, they gradually gained experience in warfare, as well as courage from the successes gained in unlooked-for descents upon towns occupied by the enemy, where he slew foes and apostates alike, circumcised the children, and destroyed symbols of idolatry.

In 167 B.C., feeling death approaching, he committed the cause to his five sons, exhorting them to be faithful to the charge thus laid on them. Each of them had a distinguishing epithet. John was Gaddis, "the Holy"; Simon, Thassi, "Guide"; Judas, Maccabeus, "the Hammer";* Eleazar, Avaran, "the Beastslayer"; Jonathan, Apphus, "the Cunning." John, as the eldest, was head of the family, but their father, knowing their natural aptitudes, named Simon as the adviser, and Judas the leader in war. The selection was justified by events. Judas shewed himself possessed of ability, patriotism, modesty, tactical skill, unfailing courage, and military ardour, and won undying fame among heroes. "He was renowned unto the utmost part of the earth, and he gathered together

---

* Heb. מַקֶּבֶת. Compare the application of this simile to the grandfather of Charles the Great, Charles *Martel*, who conquered the Saracens at Tours in 732 A.D., as well as to Edward I. of England, on whose tomb in Westminster Abbey are inscribed the words "Scotorum *Malleus*." This explanation of the word, however, though highly probable, is not absolutely certain. The view indeed that it is formed from the initial letters of the Hebrew *Mi kamoka baelim J'hovah*, "Who is like Thee among the gods, O LORD?" (Ex. 15. 11), may safely be rejected. But we may possibly, with Curtiss (*The Name Machabee*. Leipzic, 1876), explain it in connexion with Is. 43. 17, as "the extinguisher," that is, the exterminator of his enemies. Both these views, however, involve the unlikely assumption that the Greek κ (Μακκαβαῖος) can be used to represent the Heb. *Caph* as well as *Koph*. See further in Schürer, *op. cit.*, I. i. 213.

such as were ready to perish," * is the enthusiastic summing up of his merits by the native historian of his times.

After a while spent in completing the training and organisation of his men by the same tactics as had been adopted by his father, he soon succeeded in defeating and slaying Apollonius, the commander of the Syrian detachment, and set an example of turning the enemy's arms upon himself, by ever after using the sword which he had thus captured. Not long subsequently, in the pass of Beth-horon, encouraged no doubt by the memory of Joshua's overthrow of the five kings of the Amorites,† he completely routed the army of Cœle-Syria under Seron.

Antiochus, roused to indignation by these unexpected defeats, and prevented from avenging them in person by the need of suppressing insurrections against his authority in Parthia and Armenia, entrusted an army of mercenaries to Lysias, his son's guardian. His policy towards the Jews was now changed. Hitherto he had sought to Hellenize them by planting colonists, who should induce them to give up all their distinctive features as a nation, and become absorbed into the Greek world. But now his end was to be obtained, not by absorption, but by annihilation, and his orders were that the Jews should be exterminated, and the land colonised by external troops.

Lysias for this service chose three generals, Ptolemy, Nicanor, and Gorgias, with a force variously estimated at twenty thousand and at forty thousand soldiers. His troops were so confident of success that they were accompanied by Phœnician slave-traders, with chains and money ready for the acquisition of the captives on whom they reckoned, and whose price they had already fixed. They proceeded by the coast

---

* 1 Macc. 3. 9.   † Josh. 10, 11.

route to Emmaus (now Amwas),* twenty-two Roman miles
N.W. of Jerusalem, near the Jaffa road. Judas took up his
quarters in the first instance at Mizpah,† where in old time,
when the nation was in sore need, Samuel had procured for
them a victory decisive and with lasting results.‡ Having
inspired his followers with enthusiasm by the display of a
scroll of the Law, for the maintenance of whose precepts they
were about to fight, he led his forces, 6,000 in number, to a
position on the south of Emmaus, and thence into the hills.
Gorgias, leaving part of the Syrian army in charge of Nicanor,
who was commander-in-chief, proceeded by night to the hills
to attack Judas's camp. Forewarned of this plan, Judas had
withdrawn his men, and, descending under cover of darkness to
the plain, appeared at Emmaus, and attacked and destroyed
his enemy's position with great slaughter. Gorgias, when day
dawned, perceived the camp in flames, and, not venturing to
hazard a conflict with the foe thus flushed with success, withdrew
to the Philistine country. The booty, including much
gold and silver, proved of considerable value in facilitating the
continuance of the struggle. "And they returned home, and
sang a song of thanksgiving, and gave praise unto heaven;
because His mercy is good, because His mercy endureth for
ever."§

This took place in 166 B.C. In the following year Lysias
resumed hostilities, this time leading in person a large army of

---

* Emmaus was a place of note also in the campaigns of Vespasian and Titus. It was destroyed by an earthquake in 131 A.D., and was rebuilt under the name Nicopolis in the latter part of the third century. It sent a bishop to the Council of Nicæa (325 A.D.) and to that held at Constantinople, 553 A.D. From the times of Eusebius and St. Jerome till the fourteenth century it was confused with the village of Luke 24. 13.

† It was "over against Jerusalem" according to 1 Macc. 3. 46. Its position is otherwise uncertain; but it would seem from this expression that Jerusalem was visible from it, a fact which then, as now, would probably attach an additional sanctity to the spot.

‡ 1 Sam. 7. 5-13.

§ 1 Macc. 4. 24.

horse and foot along a circuitous route by way of Idumea. He met with no better success, being completely overthrown at Beth-zur,* a town which commands the main road from Beersheba and Hebron to Jerusalem, and which played an important part in the Maccabean struggle.

These signal successes put a completely new face upon the Jewish resistance, and a lull in the contest with their oppressors having now set in, Judas proceeded to Jerusalem, where the citadel was still held by Menelaus under the protection of Syrian forces. The deserted sanctuary, idolatrous altars, and images of Zeus and of Antiochus would remind the Jewish leader that much yet remained to be done. The Temple was now thoroughly cleansed of its pollutions. A new altar and new vessels were provided, while a wall with two towers was erected as a defence against attacks from the citadel. We gather that Hellenizing priests were rigidly excluded from taking part in the restoration of the national religion, and doubtless Menelaus, though still titular high priest, had no share in the proceedings. On the removal of the polluted altar, a council of elders determined to place its stones in one of the porches of the entrance court, "until there should come a prophet to shew † what should be done with them" (1 Macc. 5. 46). In order that the fire for the new sacrifice might come from a source of unquestioned purity, it was obtained by striking stones together. Just three years to the day from the defilement of the altar of burnt-offering by idolatrous sacrifice, the consecration was effected. It was ordained that each year

---

* *Beit-zur*, about 15 miles S. of Jerusalem.

† This refers to the expectation, current also in N.T. times, that one of the old prophets would re-appear. Sometimes Jeremiah (Matt. 16. 14), sometimes Elijah (*ib.* and 17. 10), was named in this connexion. In the Talmud we have frequent references to the supposed re-appearances of the latter. I may be permitted to refer to the general Index (*s.v. Elijah*) of my translation of the treatise *Chagigah*, Tal. Bab. For Passover usages connected with this expectation *see* Smith's *Dict. of Bible* (Art. *Passover*), ii. 715, note *r*.

the festival commemorative of this re-dedication should be held (the ἐγκαίνια of John 10. 22) for eight days * "with gladness and joy" (1 Macc. 4. 59). Its name to this day is Chānukah (Consecration) or the Feast of Lights, the latter symbolizing the re-establishment of the Divine illumination of the Law.

The freedom from active service in the field was, as might be expected, but temporary. The Jews' inveterate enemies, Idumeans and the rest, were as hostile as ever. Judas fortified Beth-zur, and rescued and brought to Judea many of his countrymen who were suffering ill treatment at the hands of their heathen neighbours in Galilee and Gilead or among the Ammonites and Edomites.

Lysias meanwhile, probably from lack of money wherewith to pay mercenaries, left Judea to itself. Antiochus failed in his Parthian expedition, and on his return died in Taba, a Persian city, appointing his relative Philip guardian of his son Antiochus v. (Eupator). This appointment of a rival to Lysias (who already held the same office) had the natural result of giving the final blow to the strength of the Seleucid kingdom. Judas ventured under these circumstances to lay vigorous siege to the citadel. Probably through the collusion of Hellenistic priests, whom he had excluded from participation in his restoration of worship, those who held the fortress, Menelaus included, made their escape to Antioch, and urged that strong measures should be taken by the king. Lysias, with his youthful charge, accordingly laid siege to Beth-zur, which was the key of that part of the country. The Sabbatical year (163 B.C.), in which there could be neither sowing nor reaping, increased their difficulties, and the garrison was reduced to surrender. Thereupon Judas went out to meet the Syrian troops at Beth-zachariah (between Jerusalem and Beth-zur),

---

* It commenced on the 25th of Chisleu, a month which corresponded roughly with our December.

but his force, a mere handful by comparison, in spite of prodigies of valour was driven back to Jerusalem, and took refuge in the Temple precincts. Even these would have been carried by assault, had not the advance of Lysias's rival Philip upon Antioch compelled the former to make terms with the Jews and withdraw. In the treaty thus obtained they secured a promise of complete religious freedom, and although, in spite of the terms of peace, the fortifications of the city were razed to the ground, the people had at least gained through their leader the main object for which they had for years been contending.

Henceforward accordingly we may observe that the character of the contest was altered. None of the successors of Epiphanes attempted to overturn the Jewish religion by force. The struggle was henceforward primarily within the nation, between the stricter and the Hellenizing parties, the one or the other of them calling in the Syrian power to their aid. At present the national party were in possession. But presently Demetrius (Soter), son of Seleucus IV. (Philopator), and thus nephew of Epiphanes, made his escape * from Rome, slew his cousin Antiochus Eupator and Lysias, and with the support of the Romans assumed the kingdom of Syria (162 B.C.). Menelaus had been put to death by Lysias, and Alcimus (or Jakim) named by Demetrius as his successor. The new high priest, with other leaders of the Hellenist party at Jerusalem, urged upon Demetrius that he should relieve them from what they represented as the oppression of Judas Maccabeus. In reply to their request, Bacchides was sent as general to carry out their demands. Alcimus, as a lineal descendant of Aaron, as well as by the assurances which he gave, had secured the support of the Assidean party, who, however, were taught by his treacherous murder of sixty of their number that their allegiance was misplaced. This and a further outrage on the

---

* See Polyb. xxxi. 19 for picturesque circumstances which attended it.

part of the Syrian general Bacchides had the effect of strengthening anew the party of Judas. Alcimus sought additional help from Demetrius, who, in reply, sent Nicanor with a commission to take strong measures against the rebels. After a conference with Judas, and complimentary speeches on the part of Nicanor, there followed a battle at Caphar-salama,* and another at Adasa,† in both of which the Syrian forces were utterly routed. On the latter occasion Nicanor himself fell.

Judas now, fearing the vengeance of Demetrius, sent an embassy to the Roman Senate, who readily tendered their support, in pursuance of their general policy to extend their influence by taking up the cause of one of the parties to a dispute, and so acquiring a footing from which to advance their own interests. In this case their policy was doubtless influenced by their desire to adopt measures at once easy and effective to keep up control over the power to which, in the days of Epiphanes, they had administered so peremptory a check by the hand of Popilius Laenas (p. 33). Their order to Demetrius in pursuance of this treaty, that he should no longer trouble the Jews, came too late. Only about two months after the death of Nicanor, Bacchides, despatched to Judea, inflicted a crushing defeat at Elasa ‡ upon Judas, who himself fell in the engagement, and was buried by permission of the victors with his father at Modin.

After all, it is not to be wondered at that even such a hero was unable to maintain his ground permanently against a foe so overwhelmingly superior in numbers. His earlier victories, surprising as they were, may be accounted for in part at least by his powers in strategy. Never afterwards were the Jews successful against their foes, except when the Syrians were themselves weakened by internal dissension.

---

* Its position is unknown.   † N.E. of Beth-horon.
‡ Its position is unknown; perhaps *Khurbet Il'asa*.

CHAPTER V.

FROM THE DEATH OF JUDAS TO THE DEATH OF SIMON III.

(160—135 B.C.)

GREAT as was the blank left by the death of the chief leader among the Maccabean brothers, yet the condition in which he left his countrymen was at any rate to be preferred to that from which he had rescued them. Now, as we have said, there was no longer a question of their being compelled to conform to idolatrous customs. Further, they had gained a knowledge of what they could do in the way of resistance to a foreign foe. Self-respect and self-reliance had been to some extent impressed upon them by the victories which Judas had gained by a rare combination of skill, courage, and enthusiastic confidence in his cause as being that of God.

Internal dissensions were however rife, and there was no longer a sufficiently commanding personality to overcome any of the evils of faction. The Assideans, the Hellenists, and the adherents of the three surviving brothers of the Hasmonean family, divided the nation. The first-named, narrow in their sympathies, had no very definite views of policy, except to give a general support to the high priest Alcimus; holding that his Aaronic descent sufficiently counterbalanced his treachery towards them and his undoubtedly Syrian sympathies. The Hasmoneans looked to the treaty which Rome, on the principle of obtaining a hold on the weaker of the two contending powers, had made with Judas Maccabeus.

The Hellenists continued their former aims; they still held the citadel at Jerusalem, where they proved a thorn in the side of their fellow-countrymen.

The sufferings of famine were now added to intestine troubles, and it was evident that only by the efforts of the Hasmonean party could any brighter future be looked for. Jonathan, the present leader, was more of a politician than a general. His brother Jochanan was slain in an attack by a hostile tribe, and Bacchides in the course of a year practically reduced the country to submission to the Syrian yoke. Alcimus, who, apparently with the object of giving the heathen access to the Temple, had ordered the destruction of a line of demarcation * which stood between the inner and outer courts, was seized with paralysis and died, owing, as the stricter Jews believed, to the wrath of heaven at his sacrilegious purpose.

For some years (160—153 B.C.) the Jews were without a high priest, and Bacchides for the first two of them left the country to itself, a circumstance of which Jonathan made good use by seeking to improve his position for taking the offensive. This endeavour of his so far succeeded, that, after a certain amount of strife with both Hellenists and Syrian forces, the land had rest for five years.

But more striking success was now in store, of a character that shews the powerful position which the Maccabean leader had succeeded in acquiring. The Hellenizers evidently failed to command the sympathies of any large number of the people. The Assideans doubtless were in general accord with the party of Jonathan, and the people over whom he presided at the end of those years of respite had a real claim to be regarded as a united nation. The war of faction had been put down.

---

* See its exact nature discussed in Schürer, *op. cit.*, l. i. 237.

Jonathan's supremacy was conceded, and so apparent to Syria that the rivals for power were eager to secure his support.

Balas, son of Epiphanes, bore an extraordinary likeness to Antiochus Eupator, the late king of Syria. He took the name of Alexander, and with the countenance of Attalus of Pergamum and Ptolemy Philometor of Egypt in his pretensions, as well as of the Roman Senate,* he claimed the Syrian throne. Demetrius, whose cruelties had alienated his subjects, was alarmed, and wrote to secure Jonathan's aid, "with words of peace, so as to magnify him." † Balas, on the other hand, successfully capped this attempt by a present of a purple robe and a golden crown; so that he at once became prince in Judea and officiated as high priest at the Feast of Tabernacles, 152 B.C., the first of his family ‡ who had held that office. Demetrius still endeavoured to outbid his rival for Jewish support, and the letter which he now wrote, preserved by Josephus,§ illustrates the extremely severe character of the taxation which had been imposed by Syria. He says: "I will remit you most of the taxes and contributions which ye paid to my predecessors and myself. . . . I give you as a favour the value of the salt-tax and the (golden) crowns which ye did bring to me, and my share, even one-third of ground crops, and one-half of the fruit trees, I surrender from to-day. Also the poll-tax paid by every inhabitant of Judæa, viz., Samaria, Galilee, Peræa, I grant you in perpetuity." Among further concessions he promises honourable posts in military service, a larger contribution to the Temple expenses, the

---

* Although they had recognised Demetrius as king, yet they would be able to justify themselves by the fact that he had escaped, a bad precedent, which could be conveniently condemned, if needful.
† 1 Macc. 10. 3.
‡ For there is no real ground for supposing that Judas was ever high priest.
§ Ant. xiii. 4. 9. See Mahaffy, Emp. of the Ptol., p. 183.

remission of the annual tax of 10,000 drachmæ paid by those who came to sacrifice at Jerusalem, and that even Jews settled in Syrian provinces should be exempt on all Sabbaths and festivals, and for three days before and after the festivals, from being called before any court of justice.

Jonathan was prudently deaf to these appeals. Alexander overthrew his rival, who was slain in the battle, and Philometor offering to give the victor his daughter Cleopatra, the marriage was celebrated at Ptolemais, Jonathan being present as a specially honoured guest.* Jonathan's position henceforward was such that he was able to aim at the extension of Jewish dominion by taking advantage of the political condition of Syria, and obtaining, partly by demand, partly by conquest, such concessions of power or territory as he desired. In the exercise of this general policy he continued to support Alexander Balas when Demetrius II., son of Demetrius I., set himself up (147 B.C.) as rival claimant for the throne, and he more than once defeated Demetrius's forces, and brought home rich booty. As an acknowledgment of this service he acquired from Balas Ekron and its territory.

In 145 B.C., however, Demetrius obtained the throne with the help of Ptolemy, who transferred his daughter Cleopatra from Balas to his rival. Jonathan at this time, trusting that the Syrian forces were sufficiently employed, sought to obtain possession of the citadel at Jerusalem, which still contained a Syrian garrison. Demetrius hearing of this, summoned Jonathan to Ptolemais. The latter, however, was able as a result of that interview to obtain his own confirmation in his dignities, the promise for Judea of freedom from tribute, and the addition of the three Samaritan provinces of Ephraim,

---

* It is remarkable that, although upon this occasion, among other honours, Jonathan was named "general" ($\sigma\tau\rho\alpha\tau\eta\gamma\acute{o}\varsigma$), the citadel at Jerusalem continued to be held by a Syrian commander.

Lydda, and Ramathaim—all this apparently on condition that Jonathan should raise the siege of the citadel.

Antiochus VI., son of Alexander Balas, was now brought forward by Trypho (the leader of some troops whom Demetrius had disbanded) as rival king to Demetrius, and thereupon an opportunity was furnished Jonathan to make still further demands as the price of aid. Before, however, effect could be given to these, Demetrius was driven from power, and Jonathan passed over to the side of the new ruler, taking the field on his behalf, while at the same time he sent ambassadors to open up friendly relations with Sparta, as well as to Rome to renew the treaty made in the time of Judas. At this time also the city was re-fortified and a wall erected so as to cut off the citadel effectually from the rest of Jerusalem. At length, Trypho suspecting, and not without cause, that Jonathan was advancing rapidly towards the step of casting off completely the Syrian suzerainty, treacherously secured the person of the Jewish leader, and after a further exhibition of successful craft in his dealings with Simon Maccabeus, who had taken the command, caused Jonathan to be murdered at Bascama,* and returned home.

Simon, on his succession to power (142 B.C.), reaped the benefit of his predecessor's skilful policy and generalship. All that was needed was to obtain from Syria the confirmation of the concessions made to Jonathan. These were readily granted by Demetrius, who indeed had no power to refuse them, and Simon's position as an independent prince was virtually conceded, though not perhaps in language wholly free from ambiguity. He now proceeded to secure the fortress of Beth-zur and Gazara. The latter was of special importance to obtain, as being on the route between Jerusalem and Joppa,

---

* E. of the Jordan, but otherwise unknown.

a town which was one of the most valuable acquisitions made at this time, as its trading dues were a source of large income to the Jewish commonwealth. Above all, he at last obtained possession of the citadel itself, and demolished its forts, the Hellenists who occupied it either withdrawing to Egypt, or accepting the new conditions of life in their own country, or lastly, in some few cases where they were unwilling to yield, being put to death for their idolatrous leanings. Public documents were dated from the commencement of Simon's reign (142 B.C.), as a new era, thus following the example of neighbouring independent states. Embassies sent by him to Sparta and to Rome procured promises of friendship and support from both. Prosperity prevailed throughout the land. According to the description of the Maccabean historian, "Then they tilled their ground in peace, and the land gave her increase, and the trees of the plains their fruit. The ancient men sat in the streets, they communed all of them together of good things, and the young men put on glorious and warlike apparel. He provided victuals for the cities, and furnished them with all manner of munition, until the name of his glory was named unto the end of the earth. He made peace in the land, and Israel rejoiced with great joy: and they sat each man under his vine and his fig-tree, and there was none to make them afraid: and there ceased in the land any that fought against them: and the kings were discomfited in those days. And he strengthened all those of his people that were brought low: the law he searched out, and every lawless and wicked person he took away. He glorified the sanctuary, and the vessels of the Temple he multiplied."* One more step was needed to crown the position. The office of high priesthood had been held by Jonathan with the permission of the

---

* 1 Macc. 14. 8-15.

Syrian power. Simon must assume it at the call of his own nation, and this was done with all due pomp and ceremony in September 141 B.C., when it was resolved that Simon should be ecclesiastically, as well as in civil and military affairs, supreme " for ever, until there should arise a faithful prophet."* Brazen tablets recording the decree were set up in the Temple court. The announcement of this solemn confirmation of the high priesthood in the house of Joarib was made to the Jews resident in Egypt in a carefully worded communication, having regard to the susceptibilities of men who had not only set up a novel temple in their adopted country, but also had among them a representative of the ancient high-priestly family of Jaddua.

Now that the culmination had been reached, Simon, or rather, probably, the council of chief men over whom he presided, proceeded to issue shekels and half-shekels with the words (in old Hebrew characters) "Jerusalem the Holy" on one side, and on the other, " shekel (or half-shekel) of Israel," with the number of the year, dating apparently from his consecration to the high priesthood. Emblems of his office were added in the shape of a budding rod, and a cup suggesting incense. Simon's name does not occur on those extant, of which we have specimens of the years (142—138 B.C.)† 1, 2, 3, 4, 5.

After several years of peace, during which Simon obtained the renewed expression of Roman goodwill—of value less than doubtful, could men have foreseen the future—he was called upon by Antiochus Sidetes (138 B.C.) to recognise his authority as successor to Demetrius, who had been defeated and captured

---

* 1 Macc. 14. 41. For this expression *see* above, p. 21.

† See the discussion in Schürer (*op. cit.*, 1. i. pp. 258 ff.), who, against the opinion of the majority of numismatists, sees reason to doubt whether the specimens in question were coined under Simon.

in the course of his Parthian expedition. Sidetes, while the contest between himself and Demetrius's general Trypho was still doubtful, readily confirmed Simon in his independence and immunities. As soon as that leader had been captured and put to death, Sidetes claimed the restoration to Syria of the citadel in Jerusalem and other fortresses on payment of suitable compensation, and followed up his claim by an appeal to arms. Simon, now an old man, sent his sons, Judas and John, to meet the invader between Modin and Ekron. The Syrians were vanquished, and Simon was left in peace by Sidetes during the few remaining months of the Jewish prince's life. He and his sons, Mattathias and Judas, were treacherously slain at Jericho by his son-in-law Ptolemy, son of Abubus, who had been appointed by Simon civil and military governor of that district. Ptolemy's ambitious designs, which had prompted him to this deed of violence, were unsuccessful. John, the sole remaining son, was forewarned that Ptolemy's agents were approaching in order to complete the murderous designs of their master. He hastened to Jerusalem, where he received the support of the people, and succeeded to his father's position (135 B.C.).

CHAPTER VI.

THE REIGN OF JOHN HYRCANUS (135—106 B.C.).

THE reign of John Hyrcanus,* who now succeeded to the priestly and princely dignities of his father, has been compared to that of Solomon. They both began under troublous circumstances. Both extended the bounds of their country's dominion and its influence over neighbouring states, and both, after a period of much prosperity, declined in glory and at length ended with gloom and party strife.

Hyrcanus's first duty he considered to be to avenge the deaths of his father and brothers. Ptolemy took refuge in Dok, near Jericho, where his main defence against capture by siege seems to have been his possession of the person of the mother of Hyrcanus, whom he threatened to hurl from the walls, if extreme measures were resorted to by the besiegers. After a considerable time the approach of the Sabbatical year compelled Hyrcanus to withdraw his forces, whereupon Ptolemy slew his mother-in-law, and fled to the wilderness east of Jordan. We hear of him no more. That Hyrcanus took no further measures against him is sufficiently explained by the need which befell that he should himself sustain a siege from Antiochus III. (Sidetes), who approached Jerusalem, laying

---

* So named, not from having conquered the Hyrcanians (Euseb. *Chron.*, i. 548, ed. Syncellus) when he was associated with Sidetes in his Parthian war; for the name had been in use among the Jews long previously (Jos. *Ant.* xii. 4. 6-11; 2 Macc. 3. 11); but perhaps from his belonging to a family which had settled in Hyrcania, and had subsequently returned to Palestine. *See* Schürer's note (*op. cit.*, 1. i. 274) for parallels.

waste the neighbouring country.* After carefully investing the city for more than a year, without much progress being made, and both sides apparently suffering from lack of food while the besieged were still sufficiently supplied with water, Hyrcanus turned out all who were incapable of bearing arms, and as they were refused succour from the outside forces many of them perished. At length Hyrcanus asked for seven days' cessation of hostilities in order to keep the feast of Tabernacles. Antiochus's favourable response was accompanied by a present, including offerings of animals prepared for sacrifice. Negotiations for peace commenced, and it was concluded, the Jews agreeing "to deliver up their arms, to demolish the fortifications of Jerusalem, to pay tribute for the towns they had seized outside the narrower limits of Judea, and to give hostages for their good behaviour."†

That the towns here referred to (Joppa, Gazara, and others) were not taken from the Jews at this time, when Syria was able to re-assert her supremacy, is doubtless to be ascribed to the interference of the Romans, with whom Hyrcanus was in communication, and who, from motives of self-interest, sided, as heretofore, and as usual, with the weaker state.

Hyrcanus soon rebuilt the walls, and we are told that he proceeded also to hire mercenary troops, a novel step which, however little approved by the straiter sect of his countrymen, would at least afford a welcome relief from military service to many of the nation. The money needed for their pay or for the tribute to Antiochus, is said to have been obtained from the tomb of David.‡

Hyrcanus now accompanied his late foe in the expedition of the latter to Parthia to rescue his brother Demetrius

---

* Circ. 134 B.C., but *see* Schürer's note (*op. cit.*, 1. i. 275) for the uncertainty whic hangs over the precise date.
† Moss, *op. cit.*, p. 108.   ‡ Jos. *Ant.* vii. 15. 3; but comp. xiii. 8. 4.

Nicator, who had been forcibly detained there for the last ten years. The Parthian general was defeated, and the king set Nicator free, that Sidetes might be drawn homewards by the need of protecting himself against his rival. Antiochus was soon afterwards slain in an attack of the enemy on his camp. Hyrcanus, who had been treated with much consideration by Antiochus, now escaped, and on reaching Jerusalem proceeded to take advantage of the strife which followed among claimants for the crown of the Seleucidæ, to render his country once more independent and to extend its limits.

Nicator, who had designs upon Egypt, was soon defeated, captured, and put to death (circ. 125 B.C.) by Alexander, nicknamed by the Syrians Zabinas, "the purchased," who was said by some to be the son of Alexander Balas, by others an adopted son of Sidetes. Antiochus VIII. (Gryphus), son of Demetrius Nicator, soon asserted his supremacy over Zabinas (122 B.C.), and for eight years reigned in peace over a kingdom reduced in size. At the end of this period there followed three years (114—111 B.C.) of civil war between him and his halfbrother, Antiochus IX. (Cyzicenus), remarkable mainly for his love of pleasure and sensuality, and apparent desire to pose as a second Antiochus Epiphanes in point of character. Cyzicenus, unlike his two immediate predecessors, ventured to meddle with Hyrcanus, who, however, on the one occasion on which their forces met, inflicted on him a decisive defeat.

Hyrcanus, taking advantage of the helplessness of Syria to check his schemes of extension, obtained forcible possession of considerable districts east of Jordan, as well as of Idumean and Samaritan territory. The Idumeans, who seem to have reaped much advantage from the destruction of Jerusalem by Nebuchadnezzar (586 B.C.) in the way of extension of territory northward,* now weakened in all probability by the rising power of the Nabateans, who had spread from the south in their wake, were unable to resist the Jewish attack. To them he gave the alternative of exile or the embracing of Judaism. Many of them accepted the latter, and thenceforward such were considered as Jews, but, as we see from Josephus,† they were liable to be looked on with some contempt by the Jewish aristocracy, who considered Herod, for example, as only a "half Jew." "For the first time the Judæans under their leader, John Hyrcanus, practised intolerance against other faiths; but they soon found out, to their painful cost, how dangerous it is to allow religious zeal to degenerate into the spirit of arbitrary conversion. The enforced union of the sons of Edom with the sons of Jacob was fraught with disaster to the latter. It was through the Idumæans and the Romans that the Hasmonæan dynasty was overthrown and the Judæan nation destroyed."‡

In the Samaritan territory, Shechem and the temple on Mount Gerizim had been already destroyed by Hyrcanus. He now proceeded to plant Idumean settlers in the neighbourhood of Samaria. The colonists there received sorry handling. Hyrcanus besieged Samaria, Cyzicenus, with some support from Egypt,§ vainly endeavouring to divert his attention by ravaging the country around. After a year's siege Samaria fell (108 B.C.) and was completely demolished, the ground on which it stood being cut up into ditches and canals. "When the sons of Hyrcanus [Aristobulus and Antigonus] returned to Jerusalem,

---

* See Ewald, *op. cit.*, v. 81. † *Ant.* xiv. 15. 2.
‡ Graetz, *op. cit.*, ii. pp. 8, 9.
§ An ineffective support only. It came from Ptolemy Soter II. (Lathyrus), who contributed a force of 6,000 men, but did so in opposition to the policy of the powerful queen-mother, Cleopatra, "who had two distinguished Jews, Chelkias and Ananias, the sons of Onias of Heliopolis, for her generals in Palestine, and these were doubtless acting in the interest of the Jews against the Samaritans."—Mahaffy, *Emp. of the Ptol.*, p. 109.

the boundary between their father's kingdom and that of the Syrians was substantially a line running from Mount Carmel on the west to Scythopolis on the Jordan. The authority of the holy city extended over a larger area than in any previous period since the Exile; and the country was so administered that the people prospered, and the nations outside were either jealous or respectful." *

A stage of advance in the way of personal claims on the part of Hyrcanus was marked by the occurrence of his own name on coins of this time: "Jochanan, high priest, and the commonwealth of the Judeans;" in some even "Jochanan, high priest, and head of the commonwealth of the Judeans." Thus, while still claiming the priestly character of the government of which he appeared as ecclesiastical head, a distinct step forward was taken in the prominence given to his civil prerogatives.

We now come face to face with two parties destined to take an important position in Judaism. Neither the Pharisees † nor the Sadducees ‡ are wholly out of relationship to views which we have already noticed as held by important factors of the community. But while they may thus remind us respectively of the Assideans and the Hellenists of the earlier period, the distinctions are also obvious. Those who from their natural bent of mind or from training took the narrowest

---

* Moss, *op. cit.*, p. 116.

† פְּרוּשִׁים *separated, set apart*, in contrast to עַם הָאָרֶץ, *a common person*. Comp. ὄχλος (as against λαὸς) in John 7. 49. For an interesting parallel between the Pharisees, both as regards name and religious, political, and social characteristics, and Puritans or Nonconformists among ourselves, further illustrated by the relations between the Roman Catholic clergy and their flock in Ireland, *see* J. E. H. Thomson, *Books which Influenced our Lord and His Apostles*, pp. 61 ff. Edinburgh, 1891.

‡ The etymology of the name is obscure, some deriving it from Tsaddik, *righteous*; others from Zadok, who with another disciple of Antigonus of Socho (who fl. in the first half of the 3rd c-nt. B.C.) is said to have founded the school; others again from the Zadok of 2 Sam. 8. 17.

view as to the duty of exclusiveness, were henceforward known as Essenes. Practising strict asceticism, and in some cases at least forbidding marriage, these exercised a comparatively slight influence upon the community, with which they generally renounced all connexion. The Pharisees, on the other hand, although their rise is not clearly marked, had evidently in Hyrcanus's day acquired the position of the popular party. They were, however, a religious rather than a political body. To the close study of the Law they added that of the superimposed and elaborated traditions as to its meaning and extent of application. Thus while inheriting the essential ideas of the Assideans, they gave a much more unqualified support to the policy of exclusiveness and national self-assertion which arose naturally out of the success of the Maccabean movement, and they had a real interest in their country's welfare and prestige. Although closely connected with the scribes, the two were not, at least in later times,* coincident. The relation between the scribes and Pharisees " was practically the same as that which exists between teachers and taught. The Pharisees were the men who endeavoured to reduce the teachings and theories of the scribes to practice, and all those scribes, who in addition to the written Law also believed in the binding authority of tradition, were Pharisees as well as scribes."†

The Sadducees, on the other hand, may be considered as akin to, or even a branch of the Hellenistic party. They were distinguished, however, by accepting with the utmost loyalty the Pentateuch, although declining to be bound by the traditions which had grown up around it. It may well be, as Ewald says,‡ that the disappearance of the early literature of this school is to be attributed to the disrepute into which it fell

---

* Mark 2. 16; Luke 5. 30.; Acts 23. 9.
† Morrison, *Jews under Roman Rule* (*Story of the Nations Series*), p. 305. London, 1890.   ‡ *Op. cit.*, v. 276.

politically in Maccabean times. For as the Pharisees were *primarily* a religious, so the Sadducees were rather a political, party. They included the aristocratic families, the generals and others who were disposed to take a laxer view on the subject of exclusiveness, as having mixed more with the outer world, and acquired a knowledge of, and respect for, customs outside those proper to the Jewish race. "The main principle of the Sadducees was that . . . good and evil, human weal or woe, depended solely on man's own choice, and on his knowledge or ignorance. This almost Stoic-sounding principle, which they could easily set themselves to prove by detached passages of the Pentateuch, involved the sharpest contrast with the rigid system which had prevailed from the time of Ezra ; but not less so with all true religion. At the same time, it quickens the impulse of human freedom and activity, places the whole world of sense within its reach, and, while it flatters able minds, seems free from danger so long as the conception of God derived from ancient faith remains unimpaired, and the hereditary morality of the mass of the people is but little shaken. From this point it was but one step further to the denial of the immortality of the soul and eternal retribution, and therefore of the actual existence of angels and spirits ; * so that in this the Sadducees consciously repudiated what was by no means disclaimed in the Book of the Law, even if it was not sufficiently clearly asserted ; and fell into the very doubts from which Koheleth had with difficulty escaped. Moreover, though they accepted the authority of the Law, yet they would only maintain a very independent position with respect to it, and they rejected all the further extensions and statutes of which the dominant school was so fond. This was the natural result of placing

---

* Comp. Acts 23. 8, which, however, as has been pointed out (J. E. H. Thomson, *op. cit.*, p. 56), taken strictly, only shews that they disbelieved all such alleged appearances *in their own day.*

their fundamental principle in the merely human resolve to allow no power to determine or hinder their conduct save the civil laws." *

Their repudiation of the doctrine of the resurrection of the body may be closely connected with the Hellenic influence, to which they so readily lent themselves. We are reminded of the Greek view of the matter by St. Paul's experience at Athens. † "Associating continually with those who thus regarded the very notion of the resurrection as incredible, it was but natural that the Sadducees should not believe in it themselves." ‡

It would be an error to suppose that in all matters where religion or administration was concerned the Sadducees leaned to milder measures than their rivals. "The Sadducees thought that the punishment ordered by the Pentateuch for the infliction of any bodily injury—'an eye for an eye, a tooth for a tooth'—should be literally interpreted and followed out, and obtained in consequence the reputation of being cruel administrators of justice; whilst the Pharisees, appealing to traditional interpretations of the Scriptures, allowed mercy to preponderate, and only required a pecuniary compensation from the offender. The Sadducees, on the other hand, were more lenient in their judgment of those false witnesses whose evidence might have occasioned a judicial murder, as they only inflicted punishment if the execution of the defendant actually took place." §

So long as the struggle was for religious freedom, as it was in the days of the first generation of Maccabean brothers, the Pharisees were heartily on the side of the rulers. When this contest had been brought to a successful issue, and Hyrcanus shewed that his aim was for the aggrandisement and

---

* Ewald, *op. cit.*, v. 278 f.   † Acts 17. 32.
‡ Thomson, *op. cit.*, p. 56.
§ Graetz, *op. cit.*, ii. 22. *See also* infra, p. 73.

extension of the Jewish state, and even for his personal glorification as the civil prince, and not merely the chief ecclesiastical personage, their support began to be exchanged to some extent for suspicion and coldness. For all the earlier portion of his rule, however, he contrived to prevent a formal difference from manifesting itself. At length the crisis came.

On the occasion of a banquet to the chief Pharisees, Hyrcanus, perhaps in order to test the sincerity of their friendship, and lead them to make the attack, for which he may have had good reason to think that they were preparing, asked them to mention anything in his conduct which they considered blameworthy. A certain Eleazar ben Povia replied that he should content himself with princely authority and transfer the high priest's diadem to a worthier head, inasmuch as his mother had been made a captive during an attack on Modin by the Syrians.* The charge which this implied was inquired into and found false. Hyrcanus called upon the Pharisees to inflict punishment for the slander. They condemned their colleague to the penalty assigned to ordinary slander, viz., stripes and imprisonment. The Sadducees suggested that a punishment so trivial in proportion to the offence of making this charge against the chief civil and ecclesiastical ruler shewed disaffection on the part of the Pharisees to his rule. He thenceforward withdrew his favour from them, shewing his estrangement by various changes in the details of administration, civil offices, as well as those connected with the Temple, being now given to the Sadducees.

This clouded the short remainder of Hyrcanus's days, and proved the commencement of discord and disaster to the nation. His house, indeed, appeared thoroughly prosperous.

---

* The reference is apparently to Lev. 21. 13, from which passage were in time deduced the requirements that a priest's wife should be found blameless, with respect to her pedigree, for four generations backwards.

" It was because they had devoted such intense labour, and had been proved in the severest crisis, that the Asmoneans, like David of old, had attained supreme power, which came to them unsought and yet, by the inevitable necessity of circumstances, backed by the acclamation and most earnest co-operation of the people. . . . Their position as rulers, therefore, was if possible more prosperous, and full of brighter promise for a long future, than David's had ever been." * In John Hyrcanus and his five sons, it seemed that the perpetuity of their house was secured. But collapse was near. Hyrcanus died at the age of sixty, after thirty-one years' rule, in the year 106 B.C. Josephus says that " he was esteemed by God worthy of the three privileges—the government of his nation, the dignity of the high-priesthood, and prophecy." † Whatever we think of this last claim, we may at any rate accept it as a sign of the high estimation in which he was held by his countrymen during the greater part of his reign.

---

* Ewald, op. cit., v. 383.   † Ant. xiii. 10. 7.

CHAPTER VII.

FROM THE ACCESSION OF ARISTOBULUS TO THE DEATH OF JANNÆUS (106—78 B.C.).

HYRCANUS, before his death (of which no particulars have come down to us), named his wife as his successor, and his son Judah—better known by his Greek name Aristobulus—as high priest. The latter soon transferred his mother from the throne to a prison, and getting rid of his four brothers in a similar manner, he assumed the title of king, although he did not venture to place it upon the coins struck in his reign. His successors till the time of Pompey continued the regal title. It is doubtful whether he actually was called "Friend of the Greeks." This, at any rate, expressed his line of action.* His Greek leanings, however, did not prevent him from extending the Jewish territory in a northerly direction and Judaizing the inhabitants. The chief event of his reign was this expedition against the Itureans, a large section of whom he compelled to submit to circumcision and conform to the other requirements of the Law. Probably it was mainly Galilee that he thus annexed, extending in this way his country's dominions northwards, as his father had done into the opposite region. "Continued invasions in the same direction would have given the caravan roads leading from the land of the Euphrates to Egypt into the hands of the Judæans, which possessions, combined with the warlike courage of the inhabitants and the defensive

---

* Josephus's words (*Ant.* xiii. 11. 3) are χρηματίσας μὲν φιλελλήν. *See* Schürer *op. cit.*, 1. i. 292, note.

condition of the fortresses, might have permitted Judæa to attain an important position among the nations." *

The accounts which we possess of Aristobulus are in the main drawn from hostile sources. The Greeks, indeed, whose friendship he cultivated, seem naturally to have taken a favourable view of his character. The Pharisees, with whose party he completely broke, did not admit that he was possessed of any virtue. They attribute to him the deaths of his mother and brother, Antigonus. The latter, with, or more probably without, the sanction of Aristobulus, was slain in the palace, and the tragic circumstances of his end are said to have had such an effect on the already weak health of the ruler that his own death quickly ensued (105 B.C.).

He was succeeded by his brother Alexander Jannæus. The latter was a Græcised form of the Hebrew Jonathan, with Jannai as an intermediate stage. He and his brothers were released from the prison to which Aristobulus had consigned them, by the widow of the late ruler, Salome or Alexandra. It is almost certain † that she gave him her hand in wedlock as well. If so, we see that he did not hesitate to violate the law that the high priest should not marry a widow. This falls in with the general character of his reign, in which the kingly side is much more prominent than the priestly. Simon ben Shatach,‡ however, brother of the queen, soon assumed a prominent position, and thus the Pharisees' influence was powerful throughout the reign.

Jannæus inherited the vehemence and warlike inclinations of many of his forbears, without possessing, to an equal extent, the prudence which had characterized the more distinguished of the Maccabees. He succeeded, however, in extending his

---

* Graetz, *op. cit.*, ii. p. 37.
† *See* Schürer, *op. cit.*, 1. i. 295.
‡ For notices of him *see* (besides what follows here) Dr. C. Taylor's *Sayings of the Jewish Fathers* (*Pirke Aboth*), p. 17, note 19. Cambridge, 1897 (2nd ed.).

dominion, with the help of his Pisidian and Cilician mercenaries, and without any very grievous disaster. At this time the rivals for the Syrian throne, Grypus and Cyzicenus, were too busily engaged with each other to cause him much disquietude in his attempt to acquire a firmer hold upon the coast towns. His troops overran the district of Gaza, while he himself proceeded to carry on a vigorous siege of Ptolemais, a city the possession of which was highly important for trading purposes. A further inducement no doubt consisted in the fact that it contained a large body of Jewish colonists.

At this time (circ. 105 B.C.) Ptolemy Lathyrus had been driven from Egypt by his mother Cleopatra, the revolution being probably, in part at least, effected by the help of Egyptian Jews, with whose interests Cleopatra had identified herself. Lathyrus, who had taken up his abode in Cyprus, viewing the intestine troubles of Syria, bethought himself of retrieving his own fortunes by the attempt to bring Palestine again under the Egyptian dominion. Ptolemais refused to receive him. Jannæus sought to keep him in play with friendly expressions, while he sent to Egypt to warn Cleopatra and request aid. Lathyrus, discovering Jannæus's real policy, attacked and routed him at Asophon * near the Jordan, a success which was followed, according to Jewish (probably exaggerated) tradition, by great cruelties practised upon the neighbouring inhabitants. Soon the combined army and fleet of Egypt, led respectively by Cleopatra and her son Alexander, brought Ptolemy's hopes to a close, and he was obliged to return to Cyprus. The opposition of the Jews in Egypt was the only thing which saved Judea from becoming thereupon subject to Cleopatra's rule. Her army had been despatched under the command of two Jews, Helkias and Ananias. The

---

* Unknown.

former had died during the expedition. The latter strongly protested against the annexation, pointing out that his countrymen in Egypt would not be slow to visit upon the queen what they were certain to consider a gross breach of faith.

Jannæus soon renewed his attempts upon various outlying cities, and with success. He captured Gadara on the Lake of Galilee and other towns, and after nearly a year's siege obtained possession of Gaza (96 B.C.) through an act of treachery. The resistance was fierce to the end, and the overthrow complete. "Before the siege the town was one of the busiest and most prosperous in Palestine; afterwards it was little better than a huge ruin, in which fire and spoliation had done their worst."*

On the ecclesiastical side Jannæus was far from popular. The Pharisees, who had the warm support of the people, were offended at the indifference with which the high priest regarded the details of ritual, to which they attached the utmost importance. Simon ben Shatach doubtless fomented these quarrels, and the stories which have come down to us concerning him, while many of them are childish, and doubtless not without considerable accretions of tradition, yet shew at any rate a man who had the skill to secure a powerful share in the conduct of affairs. At length a crisis came. "It could only be with deep-seated resentment that pious Jews could look on and see a wild warrior like Alexander Jannæus discharging the duties of high priest in the holy place, certainly not with the conscientious and painstaking observance of the ordinances regarded by the Pharisees as Divine. Even while he was discharging his priestly office it is said that for the first time they broke out in open rebellion. During the feast of Tabernacles, when every one taking part in it was required to carry

† Moss, *op. cit.*, p. 136.

a palm branch and a citron fruit as a festal emblem, Alexander was once, as he stood beside the altar about to offer sacrifice,* pelted by the assembled people with the citrons. At the same time they insulted him by calling out that he was the son of a prisoner of war, and was unworthy of the office of sacrificing priest. Alexander was not the man to bear this quietly. He called in the aid of his mercenaries, and 600 Jews were massacred."†

Thus unpopular at home, Jannæus proceeded to gratify his military instincts by leading his hired troops to attack Obedas, king of the Arabians. His enemy out-manœuvred him, shut up his forces in a narrow valley, and defeated them with great slaughter. Escaping to Jerusalem with difficulty, he found his people in revolt, and for the next six years (94–89 B.C.) he was engaged in civil war, dismissed by Josephus ‡ in scarcely more than the statement that "in the several battles that were fought on both sides, Jannæus slew not fewer than fifty thousand of the Jews." The disfavour with which he was regarded by the majority of his people was counterbalanced in several ways. His Sadducean leaning induced that party to assist him, and they formed by far the wealthiest portion of the community, and could avail themselves besides of the Temple treasury. The provinces on the east of Jordan, which had been taken from Obedas, were restored to him, and this probably secured him from feeling sufficient interest in the contest to intervene. Egypt, as we have seen, owing to the strong Jewish element there, was unable to make use of the divisions in Palestine for any purpose of aggrandisement, while Syria was still distracted by domestic strife.

---

* The story related in the Babylonian Talmud (*Sukka*, 48*b*) that on one occasion a Sadducee was pelted with lemons because he poured water not on the altar, but on the earth, *may* refer to Jannæus. *See* Schürer, *op. cit.*, I. i. 301.
† Schürer, *ibid.*
‡ *Wars*, i. 4. 4.

At length, however, the side opposed to Jannæus obtained some help from the last-named quarter. Demetrius III. (Eucærus), the ruler of part of Syria, accepted the invitation proffered by the Pharisees, and armies composed, on both sides alike, of Jewish and foreign elements met near Shechem (88 B.C.). Demetrius was on the whole successful after an engagement in which the loss on each side was severe. Jannæus withdrew to the mountain country, and was joined by a number, said to have been 6,000, of deserters from Demetrius. They divined the latter's intentions of annexation, and apparently did not desire, whatever might be Jannæus's faults, that their country should again have experience of the Syrian yoke. Under these circumstances Demetrius hastened homewards, and Jannæus proceeded to seize and punish with great cruelty those who had maintained so prolonged a resistance to his rule. For the rest of his reign the Pharisees were crushed.

Judea now became for a short time the seat of war between the most powerful of the claimants to the Syrian throne, Antiochus XII. (Dionysus) and the Nabatean king, Aretas. The latter, after a victory over Antiochus, vanquished Jannæus, but was persuaded by concessions of territory to withdraw. For the next three years Jannæus's success in arms, and in the consequent acquisition of fresh territory for his country, was such, that when in 81 B.C. he returned to his capital, he was received with enthusiasm by the people who had so long opposed his rule. His health was undermined by a long course of excesses, and while seeking to repress outbreaks of disaffected subjects in 78 B.C. he died at the age of 49 years.

"It was one of the results of the peculiar warfare of the Asmonean princes that Palestine gradually became studded with fortresses or castles apart from the main seats of their ancient history or civilisation, and commanding the passes in which they entrenched themselves against their enemies. Such had been Modin under Mattathias and Judas, and Masada under Jonathan; such was Hyrcaneum under John Hyrcanus; such, under Alexander Jannæus, was Machærus beyond the Dead Sea, and Alexandreum in the mountains between Samaria and the Jordan valley, which subsequently became the recognised burial-place of the later princes of the Asmonean family, as Modin earlier had been of the first. But Hyrcanus and Alexander were interred, in regal or pontifical state, in tombs which long bore their names close to the walls of Jerusalem."*

If extent of dominion be a test of prosperity, Jannæus may certainly claim credit for winning a considerable number of cities with their neighbouring territories. Also, in spite of his carelessness in regard to Pharisaic ritual or traditions, he insisted that those whom he conquered should accept Judaism, on the penalty of devastation of territory and large destruction of life. Accordingly he left the kingdom larger than it had been at any time since the Exile.

"This work of conquest however proved at the same time a work of destruction. It did not lead, as once the conquests of Alexander the Great had done, to the furtherance, but to the extinction, of Greek culture. For in this respect Alexander Jannæus was still always a Jew, who subjected the conquered territories, as far as they went, to Jewish modes of thought and manners. If the cities in question would not consent to this, they were laid waste. Such was the fate which befell the great and hitherto prosperous coast towns and the Hellenistic cities on the east of the Jordan. The Romans, Pompey and Gabinius, were the first to rebuild again those ruins, and re-awaken in them a new prosperity."†

---

* Stanley, *Jewish Church*, iii. 369. † Schürer, *op. cit.*, 1. i. 307.

CHAPTER VIII.

THE REIGN OF ALEXANDRA (78—69 B.C.).

WHEN Alexander was dying, he is said to have advised his wife Alexandra, on whom the sovereignty now devolved, to cultivate the favour of the Pharisees. According to one account,* his words were, "Fear neither the Pharisees nor their opponents, but fear the hypocrites who pretend to be Pharisees, whose deeds are those of Zimri, and who claim a reward like that of Phinehas." Strongly supported by the Pharisees, she succeeded in keeping her kingdom free throughout her reign not only from internal feuds, but to a large extent also from foreign attack. Josephus † speaks of her as "a sagacious woman in the conduct of great affairs, intent always on the gathering of soldiers together, so that she increased the army by one-half, and procured a great body of foreign troops, till her own nation became powerful at home and terrible to foreign potentates."

She had two sons, Hyrcanus the elder, an indolent person, who succeeded to the high priesthood, and Aristobulus, energetic and ambitious. The latter she sent upon an expedition against Damascus, which, however, was not fruitful in results of any kind. Danger also threatened on the part of Tigranes, king of Armenia. Alexandra promptly sent him presents, thereby to procure freedom from attack. These might easily have failed to be effectual, had it not been for the fact of the

---

* Talmud of Bab., *Sota*, 22b.   † *Wars*, i. 5. 2.

gradual advance of the Romans in Tigranes' direction, and his knowledge that the insatiable legions were watching in the rear. "The time was now almost come when the eagles would find their way across the frontiers of Judea itself, and the period of its independence would finally close."*

As regards home administration, Simon ben Shatach, who during the reign of Aristobulus had headed the opposition to that king's Sadducean policy and tastes, was now in full favour with royalty. Hyrcanus, the high priest, was a nonentity, and thus the natural supporter of the Sadducean party was helpless. Josephus† remarks of the queen, that "while she governed other people, the Pharisees governed her." "She had indeed the name of regent, but the Pharisees had the authority; for it was they who restored such as were banished, and set such as were prisoners at liberty, and, to say all at once, they differed nothing from lords."‡ Writers of later times on the Pharisean side record the traditions of the glories of this period from the point of view of their party. "Under Simon ben Shatach and Queen Salome rain fell on the eve of the Sabbath, so that the corns of wheat were large as kidneys, the barley corns as large as olives, and the lentils like golden denarii; the scribes gathered such corns and preserved specimens of them in order to shew future generations what sin entails." §

Simon ben Shatach now sought to obtain further support by associating with himself an ecclesiastical officer who, under the title of Nasi (prince), or president of the council, should have the duty of expounding the intricacies of the legal ritual, and deciding knotty points as they might arise. The most fitting person in respect of attainments appeared to be Jehudah

---

* Moss, *op. cit.*, p. 153.
† *Wars*, i. 5. 2.
‡ *Ant.* xiii. 16. 2.
§ Tal. Bab., *Ta'anith*, 23a in Derenbourg, *Essai sur l'histoire, etc., de la Palestine*, p. 111. Paris, 1867.

ben Tabbai, then resident at Alexandria. Accordingly in a message couched in high-flown language he was invited to accept the post, and in conjunction with Simon completed the enforcement of strictness in Jewish observances. There was a dispute in later times as to which held the higher office. " Wise men say Jehudah ben Tabbai was vice-president (Ab-beth-din) and Simon ben Shatach was prince-president (Nasi). Who is the author of that teaching ? For the converse would appear to be the case ; because our Rabbis have taught thus, viz., that Rabbi Jehudah ben Tabbai said, May I see * the consolation of Israel, if I have not slain a false witness so as to oppose the Sadducees, when they say, False witnesses are not put to death, unless the condemned person shall have been put to death.† Simon ben Shatach said to him, May I see the consolation of Israel, if thou hast not shed innocent blood ; for behold, wise men have said, False witnesses are not to be put to death, until they are both proved to be false, and they are not beaten, until they are both proved to be false, and they do not refund money, until they are both proved to be false. Forthwith Jehudah ben Tabbai undertook that he would not teach doctrine (Halachah) except in the presence of Simon ben Shatach." ‡ This, with the further discussion which thereupon ensues as to the exact meaning of Jehudah ben Tabbai's "undertaking" gives us a glimpse at once of the nature of the discussion, in which he was called on to take a prominent part, and of the style of a

---

* Meaning the reverse, May I *not* see, etc. For the euphemism comp. 1 Sam. 20. 16 and 25. 22. See also Rashi's interpretation of Exod. 1. 10, viz., "drive us out of the land."

† *See* p. 61. The Pharisees and Sadducees were agreed that both witnesses must be proved guilty of perjury, before either of them could be visited with the punishment due to the person whom they accused, had he been guilty. On the other hand, the Pharisees asserted, and the Sadducees denied, that this punishment ought to be inflicted on them, in case it had not yet been inflicted on the person wrongfully sentenced by their means.

‡ Talmud of Bab., *Chagigah*, 16b.

large portion of the Talmud, from which the above passage is an extract. Whatever may have been the exact relative position of the two men, their influence upon religious and intellectual life was unmistakeable. The ceremonial observances which had been neglected were restored. In particular we are told that the ceremony observed at the Feast of Tabernacles, when water drawn in a golden basin from the well of Siloam was poured as a libation upon the altar, was carried out, accompanied by the most impressive ritual. So at the feast held on the 15th of Ab (August) in honour of the wood offered for the use of the altar, the young men chose white-robed maidens in marriage, as they performed the sacred dance and song. Careful attention was given to education. Schools were established for youths above sixteen, while systematic arrangements were for the first time made for teaching boys below that age. "The schools of Judah may be regarded as the first general attempt on the part of the nation to encourage rabbinical scholarship, and to draw youths of promise to professional careers." * "No less than eleven different names for schools now came into vogue . . . 'Our principal care,' such was the boast of Josephus,† dating it from this time, 'is to educate our children.' 'The world,' such became the Talmudical maxim,‡ 'is preserved by the breath of the children in the schools.'" §

The teaching was doubtless narrow; but viewed in connexion with the times, the essay was praiseworthy and patriotic. Improvements in the practice of the law courts and in checking the facilities for obtaining a divorce are also to be ascribed to the same source, as well as the imposition of the half-shekel

---

* Moss, *op. cit.*, p. 160.
† *C. Apion.* i. 12.
‡ For other quotations from the Talmud to the same effect see article " Education " (Ginsburg) in Kitto's *Cyclop. of Bib. Lit.*, i. 728b. Edinb., 1862 (3rd ed.).
§ Stanley, *Jewish Church*, iii. 391.

or temple-tax, in imitation of that which is ordered in Exod. 30. 11–16.* By this last change the religious administration was rendered more independent of the instability necessarily attaching to individual generosity. "As long as the voluntary system prevailed, it was suicidal to alienate those who alone were competent to contribute largely; but when a kind of poll-tax had been welcomed by the nation, every Sadducee could be excluded from the Sanhedrin with financial impunity, and the whole ecclesiastical organisation of Judaism was rendered independent of their grace or generosity." †

Judah ben Tabbai at length resigned his office, owing to his being convicted, according to the tradition, of an error in procedure. Simon succeeded him, and the honour in which he was held is shewn by the story that he accepted with Brutus-like sternness and fidelity the paramount claims of law. His son had been found guilty on the evidence of witnesses, who, ere the place of execution was reached, confessed to perjury. He pleaded nevertheless, with the father's acquiescence, that in the interests of justice the sentence should be executed, lest the general belief in witnesses' testimony should in future cases be shaken.

The position of the Sadducean leaders was indeed a changed one. Aristobulus, however, stood their friend, and induced his mother to appoint them to command the chief fortresses throughout the country, thus getting rid of their presence in Jerusalem. They in return enabled him, when his mother's end drew near, to hire mercenaries, and secure the fortresses on his side. Thereby on her death (69 B.C.) he easily procured his own succession to the vacant throne.

---

* In Nehemiah's time one-third of a shekel was imposed, in our Lord's day, a half-shekel (Matt. 17. 24, Rev. Vers.). For these varying amounts, see Dr. Ryle's note (*Camb. Bible for Schools*) on Neh. 10. 32.

† Moss, *op. cit.*, p. 163.

CHAPTER IX.

FROM THE DEATH OF ALEXANDRA TO HEROD'S CAPTURE OF JERUSALEM (69—37 B.C.).

ON the death of Alexandra, Hyrcanus, as eldest son, claimed to succeed to the vacant throne. But he was soon defeated by his warlike brother in a battle near Jericho, and yielding his ecclesiastical position as well,* retired into private life after a reign of three months, solaced by the wealth that he had accumulated.

The end of the Maccabean power now approached. Evidently there was no great friction between parties within the state, nor did the Pharisees anticipate any serious change in their position through the accession of Aristobulus II. It was from an Idumean that the attack arose which immediately preceded the establishment of Roman rule in Palestine. The governor of Idumea was a certain Antipater, almost to a certainty a descendant of one of those families whom John Hyrcanus had compelled to accept Judaism.† He had a son of the same name, who, being of an ambitious turn, bethought him that he could advance his interests much more successfully with Hyrcanus as nominal ruler, than with Aristobulus as actually at the head of the State. Taking up the cause of the former accordingly, and gaining some influential adherents, he

---

* This point is clear (against Graetz, *op. cit.*, ii. 58, and others) from Jos. *Ant.* xiv. 1. 2; xv. 3. 1; and specially xx. 10. *See* Schürer, *op. cit.*, 1. i. 314.

† For discussion of conflicting statements as to his family antecedents, see Schürer, *op. cit.*, 1. i. 314.

persuaded Hyrcanus, as though in danger from his brother, to flee for protection to Aretas, king of the Nabateans, and obtain his aid in return for large cessions of territory. Aristobulus was vanquished in battle, deserted by many of his soldiers, and obliged to take refuge in the temple-mount. After a blockade of several months, and much privation on the part of the besieged, alike from lack of food and the absence of suitable sacrifices at the Passover feast, which occurred at that time, the siege was raised by the intervention of the Roman Scaurus, whom Pompey had detached for this purpose in the course of the latter's Asiatic conquests. Both brothers appealed to him with presents. Scaurus decided to support Aristobulus and ordered Aretas to withdraw. He was pursued and defeated by Aristobulus, who looked forward to a reign undisputed indeed by his brother, but one from which all independence had been for ever eliminated. Three embassies met Pompey himself at Damascus; viz., from each of the rivals for the sovereignty, and from the Pharisees, the last deprecating the re-establishment of the kingly power in any shape. Pompey, who was on the way to attack Aretas, postponed a decision for the moment, but soon considering that he had cause to doubt the good faith of Aristobulus, he gave up for the time his Nabatean campaign, and turned against him, compelling him to surrender the fortress of Alexandrium, and withdraw to Jerusalem. Thither Pompey followed, learning on his way, to his great satisfaction, that Mithridates, the most dangerous enemy that he had had to encounter, had fallen by his own hand. When Pompey reached Jerusalem, the party of Hyrcanus yielding without resistance, he found that he had only Aristobulus and his followers to deal with. They had secured themselves as they best could in the temple-mount. After a three months' siege the Romans, partly through the rigid observance of the Sabbath-rest by the enemy, forced an entrance. The priests were massacred as they proceeded with their duties at the altars. Twelve thousand Jews are said to have perished.*

Although Pompey on this occasion violated Jewish feeling by forcibly entering the Holy of Holies, yet his mode of dealing with the conquered people was far from severe. He left them nominally under the hierarchical government which they desired, nominating Hyrcanus as high priest. A heavy sum of money was exacted and the country was placed under Scaurus, now made Roman governor of Syria. Aristobulus with his sons and daughters, and a large body of other Jewish captives, helped to swell Pompey's triumphal entry to the Capitol.

Pompey had left Hyrcanus, though without the kingly title, as the recognised high priest and still in at least nominal control of the civil administration. The subjection to Scaurus deprived Hyrcanus of all real power, and Gabinius becoming governor a few years later, and taking advantage of a revolt under Alexander, son of Aristobulus, cancelled (57 B.C.) all the remains of self-government, retaining Hyrcanus in the high priesthood only, and dividing Judea into five provinces, each with its independent assembly or Sanhedrin. "Politically Jerusalem ceased to be a centre of rule and influence, and was degraded into the head of a commune; and whatever prerogatives of local government remained, were exercised by an aristocracy, and not even by a titular king, and were recognised or disregarded by the Romans at their will." † "The work of conquest was made light to their Western assailants by the fact that the country was torn with internal strifes, and that the contending parties were so blind to their own interests as to seek protection and help from the strangers. There was no longer any trace left of that spirit which had led the people on to victory a hundred years before."‡

---

* This took place towards the end of autumn, B.C. 63.
† Moss, *op. cit.*, p. 181.   ‡ Schürer, *op. cit.*, 1. i. 325.

The capture of Jerusalem by Pompey, and the political results, were noteworthy in more ways than one. Through his "triumph" as a victorious general, the Jewish nation came under the personal cognisance of his countrymen at home, and thus was formed at the metropolis of the world the nucleus of the Jewish colony, which in later years proved so important an element in connexion with the beginnings of Christianity in that city. Henceforward the Jew became a well-known person at Rome, and a familiar figure in its literature.

To revert, however, to Palestine itself, we may readily grant that the dispositions made by Pompey and his lieutenant Gabinius, as related in the last chapter, although displeasing doubtless to the national pride of the Jews, were on the whole a blessing to their neighbours. The Jewish dominion was restricted to the limits of the country, as re-occupied after the return from Babylon. The districts over which they had in later times acquired authority must on this change of masters have found the Roman rule much less exacting and severe. "Samaria, the commercial cities along the Mediterranean coast, the Decapolis in the north east of Palestine, and many Hellenic communities on the eastern banks of the Jordan, were liberated from a yoke which they detested, and which at times forced Judaism upon them at the point of the sword."*

Gabinius caused many towns, which had been destroyed by the Jews, to be rebuilt. Among the most important of these were Samaria and Scythopolis. His general policy was, by multiplying such flourishing centres of life, to produce a wholesome rivalry among themselves, and thus diminish the danger of political combination against the Roman power.

The above-mentioned policy had of course the result of depriving Jerusalem of its position as the main centre of

---

* Morrison, *op. cit.*, p. 40.

influence, and thereby of exasperating those whose interests or sentiment were keenly affected by the degradation. Accordingly on the re-appearance of Aristobulus and his son Antigonus in Judea (after effecting their escape from Rome), many flocked eagerly to their standard. It was, however, only an ill-armed and untrained force that they would command, little adapted to cope with the troops which Gabinius could bring into the field. Aristobulus took refuge in Machaerus, and after a two years' siege was captured and sent back to his Roman prison. The senate, however, which thus confined him, set his children at liberty.

Gabinius, returning (B.C. 55) from a campaign in support of Ptolemy Auletes, found that Alexander, son of Aristobulus, had made his escape from his Roman guard in Pompey's train, and attempted revolt, which did not long survive the return of the Roman governor.

Meanwhile, political events in Italy had their influence in provinces as remote as Syria. The combination known as the first Triumvirate, consisting of Cæsar, Pompey, and Crassus, was formed in the year B.C. 56. Of these three Crassus was by far the most wealthy, and decided that by directing his attention to the eastern provinces, he was using the means likely to be most successful in enabling him to outstrip his competitors in the race for pre-eminence. In an expedition against the Parthians he was defeated and slain. Before proceeding thither, he had, unlike his colleague Pompey, plundered the Temple, and thereby incurred the enmity of the Jews. They once again rebelled, and the moment seemed an encouraging one. Cassius, whom the death of Crassus placed in command, although he had but 10,000 men under him in the whole of Syria, crushed the revolt, sold 30,000 Jews as slaves, and put the leader of the insurrection to death (B.C. 52). Antipater, who advised this measure, was a farsighted and prudent statesman. He perceived that, in the interests both of his own ambition and of the people over whom he was placed, he was bound to cultivate the friendship of Rome, and therefore of that candidate for the supreme power whose fortunes were for the time uppermost.

In B.C. 49 began the civil wars through which was effected the change from republican to imperial Rome. "During these twenty years, from Cæsar's crossing the Rubicon down to the death of Antony, B.C. 49–30, the whole Roman history was reflected in the history of Syria and also in that of Palestine. . . . During this short period Syria and Palestine changed sides and owned new masters no less than four times." * Like the other portions of the Empire, Judea had to submit to the severest exactions, in order that the strife might be maintained among the would-be autocrats of the world.

The death of Julia, Pompey's wife and daughter of Cæsar, ended the alliance between the two. They promptly sought to secure respectively the eastern and the western provinces. Pompey landed in Egypt, and was immediately murdered. Cæsar, who arrived soon afterwards at Alexandria, was hemmed in, compelled to burn his ships, and blockaded in one quarter of the town both by land and sea. Antipater with his accustomed prudence adopted Cæsar's side, and shewed himself a valuable ally, going to the rescue with 3,000 soldiers, and inducing the Alexandrian Jews to support the Roman cause.†

After rendering the most efficient service in many respects, he received a becoming reward, a large portion of which, to do him justice, consisted in the acquisition of valuable privileges

---

* Schürer, *op. cit.*, 1. i. 376.
† So Jos., *Ant.* xiv. 8. 1–3, *Wars*, i. 9. 3–5. But, as is pointed out by Prof. Mahaffy (*Emp. of the Ptol.*, p. 458, note), Cæsar's letter to the Sidonians (Jos. *Ant.* xiv. 10) gives all the credit to Hyrcanus, and says not a word about Antipater.

for his people. It was doubtless through his advice that Cæsar rejected the claims of Antigonus, the younger son of Aristobulus, to the Jewish sovereignty. Antipater continued, as always, to support Hyrcanus, feeling no doubt that he was too incapable to be at all dangerous to his schemes. Cæsar accordingly confirmed the latter in his high priesthood, and made the office of 'ethnarch' to be hereditary in his family. He secured the Jews in the possession of their temple-tax, and freed them from any such demands for military service as might interfere with the requirements of the Law. They were made autonomous as regards their own affairs. Joppa and some other coast towns were restored to them. The Roman garrisons were withdrawn. Permission was given that the walls of Jerusalem, destroyed by Pompey, should be rebuilt. Antipater was given the charge of the kingdom,* received immunity from all taxation, and was made a Roman citizen.

The benefits conferred by Cæsar on the Jewish people were by no means confined to Palestine. In accordance with his general policy to encourage contentment among provincials, and to humour such customs as did not in his opinion go beyond harmless prejudices, he allowed the 'Dispersion' in Asia Minor freedom to practise their religion, while to those in Egypt, for whom the possession of such a privilege was no novelty, he granted Roman citizenship. Of all peoples under the sway of Rome at this time the Jews, we are told, were the most vehement in lamenting his death.

In Jerusalem, Hyrcanus was of course, as before, nominal ruler, and a mere puppet in the hands of Antipater. The latter, through the advantages procured by his means for the people, of which not the least apparent consisted in the rebuilding of the walls now in course of completion, had

---

* Under the title of ἐπίτροπος. He had, however, it would seem, held the position earlier, perhaps through Gabinius. *See* Schürer, *op. cit.*, p. 376, note 13.

obtained the utmost popularity with the multitude. They realised that to him the material prosperity of the country and the immunities which they enjoyed were mainly due. But to the upper classes he was an object of hatred. Party strife continued, and the combatants failed to see the obvious truth that independence as against such a power as Rome was impossible, even were the nation agreed among themselves, and that the benefits which Antipater had procured to them were the utmost which could be looked for.

"Judæa, during this troubled time, had to suffer much, but it was due to the wisdom of Antipater that she did not suffer more. To his honour it must be said that he made the utmost of the difficult and perilous circumstances in which the Jews were then placed, and by abandoning a hopeless struggle with Rome obtained the most favourable conditions possible for the people whose interests he had in charge. Personal ambition, no doubt, entered into his calculations—it is an element in the character of almost everyone who aspires to rule —but the important fact remains that he possessed a clearer view of the times in which he lived, and utilized his knowledge in the performance of far greater services to the Jewish nation than the Jewish aristocracy who reviled and opposed him. By futile insurrections and by fostering discontent the aristocracy added vastly to the miseries of the population. By their opposition to the Romans they were in reality throwing themselves across the path of the Divine purpose, which was working itself out in history by binding the Mediterranean peoples under one form of civil rule, as a preliminary to the advent and propagation of the Christian faith." *

The Sadducees never ceased to contrast Antipater as an outsider with the Maccabean family, and the glories won for the

---

* Morrison, *op. cit.*, pp. 56 f.

nation by its earlier members. The Pharisees resented his slighting treatment of the Sanhedrin, and of their tenets generally. They sought to attack him through his sons Herod and Phasael, whom he had made governors respectively of Galilee and Jerusalem. The former (the future "Herod the Great"), a clever and ambitious youth, aged probably twenty-five * at this time, had already done good service in his northern province by exterminating the bandits who had invested that region. His enemies at Jerusalem took advantage of his executing one of these miscreants to induce the weak Hyrcanus to summon him before the Sanhedrin, to whom at that time was reserved the power of life and death. Herod came, but overawed the assembly by his showy appearance and armed retinue. Hyrcanus *ex officio* presided. The names of two others of the judges are preserved, Shemaiah † and Abtalion, famous among Rabbis. The following utterances of theirs are preserved in *The Sayings of the Jewish Fathers:* ‡ "Shema'iah said, Love work; and hate lordship; and make not thyself known to the government. Abtalion said, Ye wise, be guarded in your words; perchance ye may incur the debt of exile, and be exiled to the place of evil waters; and the disciples that come after you may drink and die, and the Name of Heaven be profaned."

Although among the most renowned Jewish scholars of their day, their wisdom was scarcely of so practical a character as to add strength to the tribunal, which seems to have been in considerable awe of the accused. When there appeared an imminent danger that the authority of the court would be

---

* *See* Schürer, *op. cit.*, 383, note 29, for the probable misreading "fifteen" in the traditional text of Jos. *Ant.* xiv. 9. 2.

† Ewald, however (*op. cit.*, v. 407, note 2), considers it to have been Shammai, Hillel's rival.

‡ (*Pirke Aboth*), i. 10. *See* Dr. Taylor's ed., p. 18, note 2, for further references to them.

openly defied, Hyrcanus adjourned the trial, the accused withdrew, and in place of holding himself in readiness to obey any further summons, marched with hostile intent against Hyrcanus. He was with difficulty persuaded by his brother Phasael and by Antipater to relinquish his warlike purpose, and return to Galilee.

After a short-lived recovery of power in Syria by the party of Pompey, Cæsar's assassination (March 15, 44 B.C.) gave Antony the leadership. Cassius, whom Cæsar had appointed proconsul of Syria, proceeded to that province, after assisting in the murder of his chief. He levied seven hundred talents upon Palestine, by way of contribution to war expenses, and in default of prompt payment of this heavy exaction, seized and sold as slaves the inhabitants of several Jewish towns. Herod, who fortunately for himself was able to pay the 100 talents which were his share of the impost, was made procurator of Cœle-Syria.

Antipater's position had at this time become insecure through the rising power of one named Malichus, as to whose origin little or nothing is known. Through bribery he procured Antipater's death by poison at a feast given by Hyrcanus (43 B.C.). Herod obtained permission from Cassius to avenge his father's murder, and availed himself of it by means of hired assassins.

After the defeat at Philippi (42 B.C.), Cassius committed suicide. Turbulent times followed in Palestine. Roman troops had been withdrawn to supply the needs of those contending for the rule of the Empire. It is clear that the Jews as a whole had by no means even now accepted the Idumean sway. Phasael had to put down an insurrection in Jerusalem, while Antigonus made an abortive effort to recover the kingdom for the Maccabean family, and though worsted by Herod in an encounter on the borders of Judea, and driven from the country, yet he managed for a while to retain some hold upon the northern part of Palestine.

The same spirit was shewn, though in more peaceable fashion, by the repeated complaints made against the sons of Antipater by representatives of the upper classes before Antony, who was for the time master of the eastern part of the Roman world. He refused to act upon their wishes, confirmed Phasael and Herod in their position, and proceeded to lay a severe impost upon Palestine as upon other provinces, in order to defray the expenses alike of his warlike operations and his luxury.

A Parthian invasion of Syria was made use of by Antigonus as affording him another opportunity of recovering his hereditary rights. He was already established within Jerusalem, and his followers engaged in street encounters with those of his opponents, when the Parthians, appearing before the walls, invited Phasael and Hyrcanus to go out to the camp of Barzaphanes, the satrap in command, for the purpose of arranging terms. They fell into the snare, and were at once thrown into prison. Phasael there committed suicide. Hyrcanus's ears had been cut off by the direction or the act of Antigonus, in order that on account of this mutilation there might under no circumstances be a resumption of his position as high priest; * and he was thereupon led by the Parthians into exile. Herod meanwhile had succeeded in making his escape from Jerusalem, and after various wanderings reached Rome.

This probably was the most critical period of his eventful life. But fortune speedily smiled on his ambition. The triumvirs, Antony and Octavian, who had just been forced by the legions, weary of fighting, to patch up a reconciliation, united to do honour to the fugitive. At their motion the

---

* Lev. 21. 17.

Senate (40 B.C.) nominated him king of Judea. He did not hesitate to offer sacrifice after the manner of the pagan ritual on entering upon office. "Thus within a week of his arrival the exile found himself with a crown upon his head, and the power of Rome at his back." * So far his task was an easy one. He now had to seek to add to the name the reality of power.

The Parthians (40 B.C.) had allowed Antigonus to call himself both king and high priest. His position, however, was a precarious one. He bought off for the moment the hostility of the representative of Rome in Syria, P. Ventidius, but failed to create any enthusiastic following for himself in his kingdom. Herod, on the other hand, though received with some support, found that the general attitude both towards him and his rival was one of indifference. This was the case even on the part of the Roman troops, who were in the pay of Antigonus for the purpose. Herod at first devoted himself to the difficult task of subduing the bandits who still infested Galilee; but it was not till he had had an interview with Antony, at Samosata, and thereby had obtained more active support from this all-powerful source, that he was able to prosecute with effect his purposes against Antigonus, in whose favour Galilee had declared. Now, however, after a rapid and successful progress through the country parts, he laid siege to Jerusalem (37 B.C.). During the time while engines of attack were in course of erection, he celebrated his marriage with Mariamne. She was his second wife, a grand-daughter of Aristobulus II., and thus a descendant in the fourth generation of John Hyrcanus. It is probable that he intended by this union of the rival families—his own and that of the Maccabees—to render the position which he now claimed more acceptable to the people at large.

---

* Moss, *op. cit.*, p. 203.

After a little more than eight weeks Herod, with the help of the Roman general, Sosius, captured the city. Pillage and slaughter followed. It was only by lavish gifts that Herod succeeded in dismissing the Romans from Jerusalem, and persuading them to leave the country. Antigonus pleaded for mercy at the feet of Sosius, who spurned him, calling him Antigone. He took him to Antioch, where Antony soon after caused him to be beheaded. Herod could now contemplate the final ruins of the Maccabean dynasty. After a three years' struggle he had entered upon his kingdom with the full support of the arbiters of the world.

CHAPTER X.

GENERAL FEATURES OF THE RELIGIOUS LITERATURE OF THE MACCABEAN AGE.

STRICTLY speaking, the Maccabean age is comprised within a period of fifty or sixty years. For the purposes of this volume, however, we take it in a more extended sense and consider it as dating, to speak roughly, from the commencement of the Greek period * to the accession of Herod the Great (37 B.C.).

The class of literature with which we have here to deal may be referred to two geographical centres—Palestine and Egypt. That among Palestinian Jews should be found literary energy in various forms need excite no surprise. Their heritage of Sacred Books would stimulate some of their number to leave the impress of the thoughts of their own times on the minds of their countrymen of that and succeeding generations. In Egypt it would have been still stranger if an abundant literature had not sprung up. Alexandria, succeeding to the position which Tyre had once held, had long been a town of great commercial importance, furnishing Rome with its main supply of corn. It was also foremost as an intellectual centre; and no inconsiderable portion of the leading citizens had already for a long time been Jews. These, while still retaining their allegiance to the faith of their nation, could not but be much influenced by the character of their

---

* Alexander the Great died 323 B.C.

environment. Greek forms of philosophy, and in general Greek habits of thought, were familiar to them; and they were thus well qualified to realise the attitude which their neighbours would be inclined to assume towards the tenets of Judaism, and to make use of literary as well as other means of recommending their faith to men who were many of them doubtless keenly acquisitive of information on all such topics.*

It is well to note thus at the outset that we are to be prepared to find a certain amount of difference as regards development in the Palestinian and the Alexandrian literature of this time. Postponing to a later stage any more detailed inquiry into the nature of either of them, we may ask ourselves, without dwelling especially on the above-mentioned distinction, What features do we find to be characteristic of the literature in one or another of the various forms which it presents in the Maccabean age? By a brief enumeration of the chief of those features, we shall be in a better position to notice more particularly the character of the works in which they severally appear.

(*a*) Reverence for the past. A considerable amount of the literature of the time is influenced either in subject or form by earlier writings. Some took Old Testament narratives, and modified or enlarged them, with a view, we must suppose, to attract Gentile readers.† Others ‡ framed their compositions on the form of the older sapiential writings (Job, Proverbs, Ecclesiastes). All, we may say, preserved a conscious continuity of feeling with their nation as it had existed in the past; and all realised (more strongly, probably, in proportion to the degree of heathenism with which they came in contact) the

---

* The endeavour to attain this end by the special means of translations of their Sacred Books into Greek will be dealt with later.

† See instances given by Dr. Salmon in the *Speaker's Commentary*, "Apocrypha," vol i., General Introduction, p. xix.

‡ Such as the writer of Ecclesiasticus (in Palestine) or Wisdom (in Egypt).

unique character of their own history, and of God's dealings with them as a chosen race.

(*b*) Monotheism was firmly maintained by all. The sentence which the stricter Jews bear in their phylacteries: "Hear, O Israel; the LORD our God is one LORD," had lost, we may believe, none of its force in the presence of heathen laxity. "The Creator,"* "The Highest,"† "The Lord of all,"‡ "The Eternal,"§ and other expressions, all testify to the stress which the Jews of this period laid upon their primary dogma, the great differentiating feature of their Creed, as compared with the religious beliefs, or with the unbelief, of Hellenism. With this is connected the abhorrence of idolatry, which we may see alike in the contempt which the story of Bel and the Dragon pours upon such worship, and in the words of the Book of Wisdom (chaps. 12–15): "The worship of those nameless idols is a beginning, and cause, and end of every evil" (*ibid.* 14. 27).

(*c*) The tendency to narrate, or refer to, matters in the nation's history in such a way as unduly to glorify the actors in them, or to give an exaggerated notion either of the importance of the part which Jews took in the events recorded, or of the influence of those events upon others. Examples meet us in the 1st [3rd] Book of Esdras; also in the 2nd and 3rd Books of Maccabees, while even the First Book, although on the whole very trustworthy, is not entirely free from the same influence.∥

(*d*) In many of the books of the period we are considering, there is a conspicuous lack of freshness and originality. We may note this specially in Books of the Apocrypha, as

---

* Judith 9. 12; Ecclus. 24. 8; 2 Macc. 1. 24; 7. 23.
† (ὁ) ὕψιστος, *altissimus*, specially frequent in Ecclesiasticus and Second [Fourth] Esdras.
‡ δεσπότα, ὁ θεὸς πάντων, *O Lord, the God of all*, Ecclus. 33. (Eng. 36.) 1.
§ ὁ αἰώνιος, specially frequent in the Book of Baruch.
∥ *e.g.* the numbers in 6. 30, 37.

compared with the Canonical Books of the Old Testament. A reader who has any feeling for literary style will perceive, on comparing the one with the other, a marked difference of tone, an artificiality, and often a rhetorical style, in contrast with the straightforward simplicity of writings which are not consciously framing themselves on any model, but form the natural expression of the thoughts or circumstances which the writers were moved to record.

(e) Philosophy has left its mark on the literature of that age. This is true not only, as we have already noticed, for the writings which were produced under the intellectual influences prevailing at Alexandria, but also among Palestinian authors as well. Hellenism, as we have seen earlier in this work, was a potent element in national life both around and within Judea, and even those who were most desirous to exclude what they considered to be its disintegrating effects from Jewish soil, were not indisposed to cultivate at any rate "wisdom" in the shape of sententious sayings, proverbs, similitudes, to discuss the dealings of God with man, and seek to solve the problems which have presented themselves, whenever the attempt was made to study the inter-relations of Providence and human affairs.

(f) The avoiding of anthropomorphic expressions was the object of a decided endeavour, although not carried out in its entirety. A few such phrases as "the *eye* of God,"[*] "the *hand* of God"[†] remain, but on the whole the tendency "to keep the Creator and the created more distinctly asunder, belongs to the whole period during which the Books of the Apocrypha were written, and we can trace its influence (i) sometimes in the avoidance of the Sacred Name, (ii) sometimes in the substitution of an abstract expression denoting quality, principle,

---
[*] Chiefly in Ecclesiasticus, but also Bar. 2. 17; 2 Macc. 3. 39.
[†] Often in Ecclesiasticus and Wisdom; so Bar. 2. 11; 3 Macc. 2. 8.

or force, (iii) sometimes in the personification of a Divine attribute."*

(g) A religious element now appeared, either altogether new, or with an added emphasis or distinctness, which we fail to notice in the earlier writings.

(i.) The doctrine of angelic mediation comes under this head, and may well be connected with the tendency just noticed to avoid anthropomorphism. The interposition of angelic beings to bridge over the gulf, now realised as so vast, between God and man, was the object of a belief which is strongly marked not only within the limits of the Apocrypha, as in Tobit, the Song of the Three Children, the History of Susanna, and elsewhere, but beyond it, as in the Book of Enoch, to whom the angels shew a vision, making him thus aware of the fate for good or evil of the future generations of mankind.

(ii.) The doctrine of *the last things* received elaborate treatment in some of the writings of this period. There is but little trace indeed in the Books of the Apocrypha, with one important exception, of the expectation of a personal Messiah.† That exception is found in 2 Esdras, where the advent of such a one, who will confer blessings on the Chosen Nation, and take vengeance on the enemies of Israel, is the subject of a main part of the book. But on the whole, prophecies as to the future seem to have been directed in Palestine by the desire for national deliverance from the yoke of a foreign usurpation, while in Alexandria philosophical speculation, when it dealt with the future of Israel at all, followed a more abstract trend of thought. We may notice accordingly that the Last Judgment and the punishment of the wicked are

---

* Dr. Ryle in Smith's *Dict. of Bible*, ed. 1893, *s.v.* "Apocrypha," p. 187a. See the numerous examples which there follow under the above-mentioned heads.

† For further notice of this point *see* remarks on 1 Maccabees in a later chapter of this work.

elaborately dealt with in the Books of Judith, 4 Maccabees, and 2 [4] Esdras.

(iii.) The doctrine of a future state may with some confidence be said to be wholly absent from those books of the Apocrypha which are of Palestinian origin.* On the other hand, in the Book of Wisdom the doctrine of the immortality of the soul is insisted on with frequency. The thought of the release of the soul from the body, regarded as a prison, was in harmony with current philosophical speculation. The resurrection of the body to life, however, is plainly accepted in 2 Maccabees (7. 9 and elsewhere), and hence prayers and offerings are presented for those who have departed from life, "a reconciliation for the dead, that they might be delivered from sin" (12. 45).

(*h*) Stories told with a moral purpose, and to illustrate religious or moral duties (in Jewish phraseology, Haggadah). As time went on, the imagination allowed itself unfettered licence on the subject of the unseen world, angels, demons, and the future glories of Israel, and doubtless the Jewish mind in the period we are now considering, as well as in later days, amid the suffering which belonged to their actual surroundings, found pleasure and relief in weaving speculations of this sort.†

(*i*) Lastly, in the Palestinian portion of the literature, legalism, the emphasizing of such duties as would be insisted on by the scribe,‡ is a prominent feature. It would appear from many passages that the careful observance of the code of external duties laid down by the religious teachers of the day was all that was requisite. As strict conformity in all respects to the requirements of the Law with regard to worship and

---

* *See* Ryle, *op. cit.*, p. 194*b*.
† *See* Morrison, *op. cit.*, pp. 263 ff., for illustrations of the nature of Haggadah.
‡ *See* p. 22.

sacrifice was difficult or impossible for many Jews, owing to their geographical remoteness from the central Sanctuary at Jerusalem, the more stress was laid on the fact that prayer, fasting, and almsgiving, as duties which could be carried out irrespective of dwelling-place, were acceptable to and demanded by the Creator. This is illustrated by the stories of Tobit and of Judith, while at the same time these narratives teach the duty of presenting one's self at Jerusalem at festivals, as well as that of avoiding ceremonial defilement. Again, the restoration of the Temple is the main subject of the 1st [3rd] Book of Esdras. Both the 1st and 2nd Books of the Maccabees deal with the importance of the services of the Sanctuary, as well as with the obligatory character of the Levitical worship. We have already noticed, moreover, the stringency of the views held by the followers of Judas Maccabeus as to circumcision and the observance of the Sabbath.

The Books of Wisdom and Ecclesiasticus, on the other hand, deal with the matter in a less distinctively Jewish spirit. The fear of God and general uprightness of life are the points on which they dwell. Passing for a moment beyond the Apocrypha, the Psalms of Solomon occupy in this respect somewhat of an intermediate position. "They are pervaded by an earnest moral tone and a sincere piety. But the righteousness which they preach, and the dearth of which they deplore, is, all through, the righteousness that consists in complying with all the Pharisaic prescriptions." *

In general, it may safely be said that the literature of the period shews us that "legalism had invaded every relation of life." †

---

* Schürer, *op. cit.*, II. iii. 21.
† Ryle, in Smith's *Dict. of Bible*, as above cited, p. 192a. *See* the same Article for further illustrations of the points here dealt with.

CHAPTER XI.

THE APOCRYPHA.

WHILE commenting in the last chapter upon the main features to be observed in the religious literature of the age which we are considering, the books commonly called the Apocrypha were mainly, though, as the references there given will have shewn, not exclusively in our thoughts. Their importance is clear indeed, when we remember that they form, substantially, the oldest portion of the literature which followed the close of the Canon of the Old Testament. We now come to deal with these books more particularly, to examine the position to be assigned to them, the value which they can justly claim, and at the same time the broad line of distinction which is fitly drawn between them and the Canonical Books of the Old Testament Scriptures.

There is, after all, in spite of Juliet's frequently-quoted remark,* much in a name, and doubtless the neglect with which these books have often been treated may be in part due to the dubious reputation which adheres to the adjective *apocryphal*, and so to some extent affects the kindred substantive.

The Greek adjective, of which our word represents the neuter plural, has for its earliest meaning *hidden*,† and then *obscure*, *recondite*. In Dan. 2. 22 (Theodotion's version), as well as in

---

* *Romeo and Juliet*, Act II. Sc. 2.
† So in classical Greek, as well as in the LXX., *e.g.* Isa. 45. 3 ; 1 Macc. 1. 23. Compare Col. 2. 3.

various passages in Ecclesiasticus,* the word is applied to things which are hidden from man's understanding ; and hence arose the sense in which it came to be used by certain heretics to indicate those writings, real or pretended, which were to be kept from the knowledge of all outside their own body, as containing secret or esoteric teaching.† Gnostics in this way brought the word into disrepute among the orthodox, inasmuch as it expressed views opposed to the plain teaching of our Lord ‡ (Luke 8. 17). Clement of Alexandria (circ. 200 A.D.), says that the followers of Prodicus claimed the possession of the apocryphal books of Zoroaster.§ 2nd[4th] Esdras (14. 44–47) ‖ contrasts the first 24 books (by which he evidently means our Canonical Old Testament) which are to be published " openly, and let the worthy and unworthy read it," with " the seventy last, that thou mayest deliver them to such as be wise among thy people ; for in them is the spring of understanding, the fountain of wisdom, and the stream of knowledge."

The tinge of heresy, which in this manner had attached itself to those books, passed away with the teaching which had thus induced it. The name now began to have reference not so much to the heterodoxy of the contents of the books, as to the dubious character of their claim from the point of view of authorship or origin. "Apocrypha" thus came to signify books excluded from the Canon.¶ Thereupon, so long as there was no distinct agreement among leaders in the early Church

---

* 14. 21 ; 39. 3, 7 ; 42. 19 ; 48. 25.

† *e.g.*, the secret books of Basilides.

‡ It is noteworthy that Athanasius, on the other hand (*Epist. Pasch.* 39, Migne, Patrol. xxvi. 1438), speaks of certain books of the Apocrypha as used for the instruction of Catechumens.

§ *Strom.* i. 15 (Migne, *ibid.* viii. 775). In *Strom.* iii. 4 (*ibid.* 1154) he calls a Gnostic book which he quotes apocryphal.

‖ Read in *v.* 44 with R.V., " fourscore and fourteen."

¶ *i.e.* writings which, as claiming an authorship which does not belong to them, have never been considered to be in any sense Canonical by the Eastern or Western Church.

as to the exact limits of the Canon of the Old Testament, there necessarily existed a difference as to the comprehensiveness of the word "Apocrypha." While Athanasius * calls such works the "arbitrary inventions of heretics," Cyril of Jerusalem (ob. 386 A.D.) describes them as books that are questioned, as contrasted with "the two and twenty books of the Old Testament." † The Jews, as we shall see below, had always rigidly excluded these books from the Canon. But few of the Fathers were acquainted with Hebrew, and the Greek Bible, for reasons which will presently appear, had always included such books. Thus it came to pass that even Origen, with his great learning, which included a knowledge of Hebrew, shewed a strange inconsistency in this respect, conforming in spite of his acquaintance with what constituted the Hebrew Canon, to the popular use of Alexandria, and appealing, in a certain controversy of the day, to the History of Susanna as part of the Book of Daniel.‡

"Both Jerome and Augustine—the one accepting the shorter Palestinian, the other the longer Alexandrine Canon of the Old Testament—assigned to ἀπόκρυφα the same meaning of 'non-canonical writings.' Unfortunately, their difference of starting-point contributed to great confusion of thought among Western divines, who were accustomed to base opinion and phraseology upon the utterances of the two great doctors."§

We may the more clearly realise the differences of position assigned in early times to the Apocrypha, if we review briefly the attitude assumed towards these books by (a) the Palestinian Jews, (b) the Alexandrian Jews, (c) the Greek and Latin Churches.

---

* *Ep. ad. Amun. Mon.*, Migne, xxvi. 1179.
† In his 4th *Catechesis* (Migne, xxxiii. 496).
‡ *See* Salmon, *op. cit.* p. xxiii. f., for account of Origen's correspondence with Africanus in this connexion (edited by Wetstein, Basle, 1674).
§ Ryle, Smith's *Dict. of Bible*, as above cited, p. 164a.

(a) The Palestinian Jews. Their testimony is decisive, whether we take that of New Testament writers themselves (of whom it may be said with almost absolute confidence that they do not quote any of these books), or of those who naturally derived their information from Jews, such as Justin Martyr (ob. circ. 148 A.D.), or Josephus,* or Melito, bishop of Sardis (circ. 170 A.D.),† or Origen (ob. 253 A.D.)‡

It may be added that, while the Canonical Books were each provided with a Targum, or paraphrase of the original Hebrew, written in Aramaic as the common tongue, such a paraphrase is altogether wanting in the case of the books of the Apocrypha, with the possible exception of Tobit.

(b) The Alexandrian Jews. We have no knowledge of a difference of opinion as existing at any time between these and their brethren in Palestine on the subject of the Canon. In this connexion we naturally turn to Philo,§ in whose writings quotations from the Jewish Scriptures abound. His habit, we may notice, is to exalt the Pentateuch, as being of Mosaic authorship, above the rest of the Old Testament. The holy men and sacred writers that followed, including one who came so many centuries later as Zechariah, he calls the companions ‖ of Moses, as though implying that they, and therefore their writings, derived their authority from the great leader and legislator. Accordingly, Philo quotes the Pentateuch with special frequency, but is far from omitting to cite the later

---

* *C. Apion.* i. 8. Yet it should be observed that in his narrative he often follows the historical books of the Apocrypha. See Salmon, *op. cit.*, p. xvi. for instances.

† In Euseb. *Hist. Eccles.* iv. 26.

‡ His list of O.T. books is given by Euseb. *op. cit.*, vi. 25. But *see* remarks above on Origen's inconsistency in practice.

§ The exact dates of his birth and death are unknown. But we may consider him as "an older contemporary of St. Paul." See Edersheim. *s.v.* "Philo" in Smith's *Dict. of Christian Biography.*

‖ "I have also heard of one of the companions of Moses having uttered such a speech as this: 'Behold a man whose name is the East'" [Zech. 6. 12]. (*De Confusione linguarum,* § 14. Yonge's transl., ii. 14, Bohn's Library, London, 1854.)

books as well. On the other hand, he is so little disposed to place the Apocrypha in any sense on a level with the Canon that he never once cites those books, a fact the more noteworthy in that he frequently introduces into his works extracts from profane authors.

Philo's position, in this respect, is the more remarkable because we should naturally look for a certain amount of laxity among Alexandrian Jews as to the limits of the Canon. The influences of Hellenic culture, as we have already noticed, would themselves lead to a wider interpretation of the idea of inspiration. Philo's own teaching was to the effect that "every good man is a prophet," * and that thus there are practically no limits to be assigned to the Canon. Men inspired by God appear and will appear without restriction of age or country. The "prophetic" gift is not to be tied down to time or place.

(*c*) The Greek and Latin Churches. The lack of contact with Jewish tradition, and almost total ignorance of Hebrew, as soon as the very earliest generations of Christians had passed away, left open a door to laxity in the matter of the Old Testament Canon. Books of the Apocrypha were freely quoted by ante-Nicene fathers, some with, and others without, an accompanying indication that the writer considered them as on a level with other "Scripture." Clement of Alexandria quotes Ecclesiasticus,† Wisdom, Tobit, as Scripture, just as, in the case of the New Testament, he does by the Epistle of Clement of Rome and of Barnabas, and the Shepherd of Hermas. Irenæus, Tertullian, and Cyprian shew from time to time similar laxity.‡

---

* *Quis rer. div. haer.* § 52.
† Often. *See* index in Dindorf's ed. (iii. 618), Oxford, 1869, for references in this and the following cases.
‡ *See index scriptorum* in the same edition, and Smith's *Dict. of Bible*, as above, p. 169.

The Council of Laodicea, it is true (circ. 360 A.D.), in a list of doubtful authenticity, however,* gives the Jewish Canon with the one addition of the Book of Baruch. But the third Council of Carthage (397 A.D.) accepts five Books of Solomon, as well as Tobit, Judith, and the Books of Maccabees.

Even St. Jerome himself was not wholly consistent. We find him,† from time to time, speaking with a certain degree of hesitation on the point, especially with respect to Ecclesiasticus. This, however, in no respect alters his general position, which clearly was that of the Church of England, as defined in Article VI., where his authority is quoted. As we have already seen, his knowledge of Hebrew enabled him to re-establish the Canonical books in their place of superiority to all rivals.‡ His position is clearly shewn in one of his letters § advising his correspondent on the subject of her daughter's education.

After enumerating the books of the Old and New Testament as we now receive them, and placing them in the order in which she shall study them with most edification, he adds, "Let her beware of all Apocrypha," ‖ adding that if at any time she should wish to read them, she is to be warned that they differ essentially from the former writings.

St. Jerome's powerful defence of the limits of the Old Testament Canon, and his insisting on the term Apocrypha as applied to the books which had sought, and to some extent found, admission, still bear fruit in the position adopted by the Church of England, and all other Churches included in her communion.

The Western Church as a whole however refused to be bound even by so high an authority as St. Jerome. Before his

---

* *See* Westcott, *Canon, etc.*, pp. 400 ff.
† *See Dict. of Bible* as before, p. 171, for instances.
‡ *e.g.*, in *Prologus Galeatus in libr. Reg.*
§ Ep. 107 (*ad Laetam*) (Migne, *Patrol. Lat.* xxii. 877).
‖ " *Caveat omnia apocrypha.*"

time Latin versions of various books external to the Hebrew Canon had been made, and he himself, though reluctantly, had consented to translate Tobit and Judith. The force of custom was powerful enough to retain these in the Latin Bibles, while at the same time St. Jerome's prefaces emphasized the distinction between the Canonical Books and the rest.

The Council of Trent (in 1546 A.D.) declared (by a small majority) that all the Books contained in the Latin Vulgate were Canonical. This excluded the Prayer of Manasses and 1st [3rd] and 2nd [4th] Esdras.

In the Reformed Church the tendency, specially of late years, has been to reduce the amount of the Apocrypha publicly read. For this restrained use two reasons may be assigned.*

(*a*) The fear of confusion of these books with Canonical Scripture. We may find a parallel in early times. The Shepherd of Hermas and other such works were then publicly read in the assemblies of Christians. It may well be believed that one cause of the discontinuance of such reading is to be found in the fact that as the times passed away in which the uninspired source of those writings was a matter of common knowledge, there began to be a risk of confusion with the actual writings of the New Testament; while the letters of living bishops were still read, inasmuch as no such mistake could in their case be made.

(*b*) The reading of such books, owing to the change of manners and modes of thought, began to prove less edifying than other ways of teaching, *e.g.* sermons, which could be adopted to modern needs and modes of expression.

Having thus touched upon the regard in which the Books of the Apocrypha were held at various epochs, it may be well to

---

* *See* Salmon, *op. cit.*, p. xxxviii.

attempt to give ourselves an account, as clear as circumstances will permit, of the reasons why the Jewish Church so decidedly excluded them from the Sacred Canon. From what has been already said, it is manifest that their acceptance or rejection did not depend simply upon the language in which they were composed. Ecclesiasticus, 1 Maccabees, and probably others of these books were written in Hebrew; yet this did not secure them a position as Canonical. We may however go so far as to say that no book not originally Hebrew or Aramaic would have had any chance of admission to the Jewish Canon, however strong might be its appeal on other grounds.

Again, it has been said that the "Great Synagogue," a body of learned men formed under the presidency of Ezra, and continuing to exist till about 300 B.C., had weighed carefully the individual merits of all books which might have any claim to be considered as Canonical, and that the result of their labours in the way of acceptance and rejection is that which we now possess in the Jewish Canon of the Old Testament.

We are saved from any discussion of the probabilities of this view by the fact that the evidence for the very existence of such a body as the "Great Synagogue" is of the most shadowy nature.* So long as this is the case, it seems waste of time to consider any share which they may be thought to have had in the formation of the Canon.

Can we then discern any of the reasons which guided the Church of the Old Dispensation in so solemn and important a decision? The often quoted statement of Josephus that after Malachi the succession of prophets was not preserved † probably

---

* See Ryle, *Canon, etc.*, pp. 261 ff.
† *C. Apion*, i. 8. The records of the later history of the nation, he there says, have for this reason not been deemed worthy of the same credit as the earlier (διὰ τὸ μὴ γενέσθαι τὴν τῶν προφητῶν ἀκριβῆ διαδοχήν).

expresses the view generally held by his countrymen in his own time. It is true that he is speaking in that context of Ahasuerus * (whom he calls Artaxerxes), and that his belief that neither Esther or any other of the books contained in the Canon were of later date than the times of Malachi may be the origin and not the result of his view as to the time of the cessation of the prophetic element. It is true also that he himself elsewhere † speaks of John Hyrcanus (ob. 105 B.C.) as a prophet. Nevertheless the statement seems to give us the clearest clue that we are likely to attain for the solution of the problem. It represents, although coming to us from a writer of so much later date, what we may well assume to have been the instinctive feeling of the Jews of Maccabean and pre-Maccabean times. The more intense the reverence which from the days of Ezra downwards grew up for the Law and the Prophets, the greater would be the hesitation in adding to the Sacred Collection any writings which did not thoroughly harmonize with the religious thought of the people, and commend themselves alike by the circumstances of their origin or supposed origin, and by addressing themselves to the best instincts of the nation through appeals to patriotism or through their methods of dealing with its history or its faith. If we are to assume (and it is difficult to conceive that it can have been otherwise) that there was in some way a more or less formal recognition of the K'thubim as having a right of incorporation with the earlier collections, then, whatever shape that act of inclusion took, it represented and officially sanctioned a use by which many of those books had already for generations been recognised and honoured as the work of inspired men. That there was a certain amount of hesitation as to the acceptance of one or more of the books is of course possible. Some see

---

* This is shewn by Ryle, *op. cit.*, p. 252, note.   † *Wars*, i. 2. 8.

a reflection of it in the subsequent differences of opinion, *e.g.* as to the Canonicity of Esther * or Ezekiel.†

Accordingly, by the time that the Seleucid persecutions had given an intensity of practical interest to the question, what were the precise limits of the Sacred Books of which their oppressors sought by violence to deprive them, many of the later books of the K'thubim had already received a place in the Canon. The reasons in each several case must doubtless in their entirety remain unknown to us, although in individual instances we may form very probable conjectures as to their nature. They "all enjoyed some exceptional cause of recommendation. In each case some distinctively religious element connected with either the faith, the worship, the patriotism, or the antiquities of the people, prepared the way for their public recognition."‡

It is true that we should not be justified in asserting that pre-Maccabean or Maccabean times witnessed no additions to books already accepted as Canonical. To these times may well belong explanatory notes, additional Psalms, appendices, or even other insertions. But it seems plain that the admission of anything like a whole book to the Canon in times at all approaching Maccabean days would have been impossible unless either from its known age, or from its subject-matter, or its mode of treatment, it had carried with it the strongest conviction of its prophetic origin.§

Although so many centuries have passed away, we can see plainly a difference in the strength of claim, even as between, say, Proverbs on the one hand, and Ecclesiasticus on the other; or, to take works of an historical character, the Books of Chronicles as compared with the First Book of Maccabees.

---

* Omitted apparently from a Jewish list as late as 178 A.D. *See* Ryle, *op. cit.*, pp. 149 ff., 214 ff.
† *Chagigah, Talmud of Babylon, Trans. of*, p. 71, note 1.
‡ Ryle, in Smith's *Dict. of Bible* as above, p. 1689*a*.
§ For the case of Daniel *see* Appendix C.

In the case of the former pair there is doubtless a similarity of style and of aim. Ecclesiasticus is "perhaps the earliest in date and the most Jewish in tone of all the Apocryphal Books."* But even if we were to grant that it was composed before the final close of the Canon, yet it could not claim from the Jew to be considered anything but modern, while the Book of Proverbs was ascribed to Solomon and his successsor in a similar form of wisdom. Moreover, the teaching contained in Proverbs was of a value never called in question. The Book of Ecclesiasticus on the other hand, if it were to claim recognition on any such level of excellence, would, we may be sure, have met with sharp criticism from the side of the Pharisees, on the ground that it seemed to dispute the doctrine of man's immortality (ch. 17. 30).

When we compare the Chronicles with 1 Maccabees, we may note that in both the language, as in the case of the former pair, was Hebrew,† and if it had been enough to be a history of stirring times, when the Lord wrought deliverance for Israel from their oppressors, the Maccabean story might well be considered as having claims of the strongest nature. But in spite of its merits and of its subject, there was the fact that the glories of the Hasmonean family did not find any special favour with those of the nation who objected to their liberation so far as that liberation meant the encroachment of Greek influence upon the strictness of Jewish observances. There was not, so far as we know, the faintest indication of a desire that even the admission to the Canon of individual Psalms in Maccabean days (if, as most commentators now admit to be *possible*, a few such be deemed to have found a place there) should be held to justify the introduction of a whole book, whose recent date was unquestion-

---

* Ryle, *ibid*.
† The extant 1 Maccabees in Greek is a translation from a lost original.

able, and which laid no claim in any sense to "prophetic" authorship.*

In general it may be said, as we have already indicated, that the subsequent introduction of books would become more than ever impossible owing to the rivalry of Jewish factions. We seem now in a position to arrange *seriatim* our reasons for declining to accept the estimate which many of the Fathers placed upon these books, as set forth on earlier pages in this chapter.

A.—Historical Reasons.

(i.) For the reasons which we have just examined, they were not acknowledged by the Jewish Church as Canonical. The Christian Church, as the successor and development of the Older Dispensation (Matt. 5. 17) has received from it the Divine Deposit of the Old Testament Scriptures.

(ii.) They are not quoted by the writers of the New Testament.† It is true that neither are certain Canonical Books (viz. Judges, Song of Solomon, Ecclesiastes, Esther, Ezra, Nehemiah) quoted in the New Testament. But then we have clear independent testimony to the fact that those books formed an undoubted part of the Jewish Canon.

(iii.) The strong presumption, drawn from expressions of our Lord and the Apostles, that the Canon had long been closed. He appealed to the Scriptures as to a well-defined collection of writings, held in absolute reverence.‡ The veneration paid to them, of which we have ample proof, shews that there could have been nothing fluctuating about their

---

* For the belief that Divine Revelation was at an end, or at least indefinitely suspended, *see* 1 Macc. 4. 46; 9. 27; 14. 41.

† On the other hand for some suggestions of *familiarity* with them on the part of N. T. writers, see Ryle, in Smith's *Dict. of Bible*, i. p. 183a.

‡ John 5. 39; comp. Rom. 3. 2.

limits. His allusion (Matt. 23. 35) to Old Testament history from Genesis to 2 Chron. (24. 21) indicates the probable limits, then as now, of the Hebrew Volume,* and therefore plainly supports the belief that the K'thubim, the last of the three divisions of the Scriptures, was complete.†

B.—Internal Evidence.

(i.) Feebleness of style is a frequent characteristic as compared with the books that preceded. They shew a stiffness, a lack of originality, and an artificiality of expression, which contrast unfavourably with the Canonical Books. The vigour and simplicity of these latter have passed away, and have been replaced, sometimes by a rhetorical style of language, sometimes by the attempt to imitate older modes of writing, when the spirit which gave freshness to these has evidently departed. The writers themselves more than once express the sense of their inferiority to the older literature (1 Macc. 4. 46; 9. 27; 14. 41; Ecclus. 36. 15).

(ii.) Improbable or impossible statements. Much of the narrative in the Second Book of Maccabees comes under this head, while in the case of the didactic romances, as we may call the Books of Tobit and Judith, many of the circumstances in the story are not only obvious inventions, but destitute of historic verisimilitude. We may instance the magical element which comes into the former of these books. The stories of Bel and the Dragon and of Susanna are also fully open to similar criticism.

---

* See Ryle, Canon, etc., p. 151, although it has been held that the arrangement of the Palestinian, as opposed to the Babylonian, Jews, placed the Books of Chronicles at the beginning, not the end of the K'thubim.

† Luke 24. 44 certainly appears to indicate the same, but this obvious inference has been challenged by some.

(iii.) Distortions of Old Testament narratives. Examples of this are the exaggerated account of the Egyptian plagues and the miracles wrought in the Desert-wanderings (*see* Wisd. 11. 2–20). Compare also the additions to the Books of Esther and Daniel with the Canonical portions of these books.

(iv.) The introduction of fictitious letters and other documents, and the attempt to gain glory for the Jewish nation or its conspicuous men by the invention or exaggeration of incidents tending to their credit. Examples are to be found in 1st [3rd] Esdras and 2 and 3 Maccabees.

So much we may say as to the less favourable characteristics of the books of the Apocrypha, and the reasons, whether connected with these characteristics or not, which draw a broad line of demarcation between them and the books which we receive as Canonical.

On the other hand, they form an extremely valuable branch of religious literature:—

(i.) They supply a connecting link between the Old and New Testaments. When we compare the religious condition of the Jews in the earlier period after the Return, with that of the same nation as disclosed to us in the time of our Lord's earthly ministry, we become aware of a considerable advance. Between the days of Nehemiah and of John the Baptist much had happened. Not only is there no mention of any inclination to idolatry, but monotheism is securely established. There is in the air a strong Messianic hope. The doctrine of the resurrection of the body and of a future life now holds a place in the most cherished convictions of the most religious portion of the nation. The Scriptures are the objects of deep reverence and of earnest study, even if that study be not always of the most enlightened kind.

Now the books of the Apocrypha give us by far the fullest and the most trustworthy accounts obtainable as to the process of change which produced these results. When inspired authority is silent, we have recourse to such information as we can obtain, and we here find a portion of the unconscious "Praeparatio Evangelica," paving the way for the central event in the world's history. Dr. Salmon * supplies us with illustrations of the historical value of the Apocrypha from this point of view, in relation to the doctrine of a future life. He points out that "the third part of the Homily on the Fear of Death offers proof of the belief in a future life held by 'the holy fathers of the old Law,' but these proofs are taken exclusively from the Book of Wisdom. And it would not be possible to replace the two passages from that book selected as the lesson for All Saints' Day, by two other Old Testament chapters expressing the same belief with equal distinctness."†

(ii.) The same writer points out the value of a knowledge of these books as supplying a key to the interpretation of current allusions in modern literature, otherwise incomprehensible, e.g. "A Daniel come to judgment," ‡ "The affable archangel " § ; or,

"the sociable spirit, that deign'd
To travel with Tobias, and secured
His marriage with the seven-times-wedded maid." ||

or "magna est veritas et praevalet."¶

(iii.) Again, they preserve to us the peculiar features which were the result of the contact of Jewish religious thought and

---

* *Op. cit.*, p. xl*b*.
† P. xxxvi.
‡ *Merchant of Venice*, Act. iv., Sc. 1.
§ *Paradise Lost*, vii. 41.
|| *Ibid.*, v. 221 ff.
¶ Dr. Salmon, however, in common with nearly everyone else, has *praevalebit*, and thus fails to give the saying quite in accordance with the Greek, in which the tense is *present*, not future. (Μεγάλη ἡ ἀλήθεια καὶ ὑπερισχύει, 1 Esd. 4. 41).

THE APOCRYPHA. 111

Greek philosophy, of sacred learning and the highest cultivation which heathendom could shew. "They help to unfold the process of preparation by which Graeco-Jewish thought and language grew to be the chief instrument, in the writings of the Apostles and in the preaching of the early Christians, for the spread and development of a new and a universal religion. They illustrate the condition of the Jewish people, their habit of thought, their literary taste and skill, their mental training, their historical judgment at or about the Christian era."*

(iv.) We may add that their quotations from the Canonical Books of the Old Testament, quotations made from the Septuagint Version of those books, form a testimony in themselves to the completion of the Canon and to the age of the earliest Greek Version of its contents.

* Ryle, as above, p. 182*b*.

CHAPTER XII.

HISTORICAL OR QUASI-HISTORICAL BOOKS.

1. The Third Book of Esdras.

ITS TITLE.

THE Third Book of Esdras is the title given in our Sixth Article to the book which stands first on the list there given of received Apocrypha. This title it takes from the numbering in the Vulgate,* which calls our Ezra and Nehemiah the First Book of Esdras and the Second Book of Esdras respectively.

On the other hand, the Septuagint † combines our canonical Books of Ezra and Nehemiah into one book, which it calls the Second Book of Esdras, and places in front of them the one with which we are now dealing—perhaps as taking up the history at an earlier point ‡—under the title of the First Book of Esdras. As we shall presently be comparing the Greek text of this book with the form in which large portions of it appear in other parts of the Septuagint Version, it will be convenient to adopt for our present purpose the Septuagint nomenclature.

St. Jerome,§ while rejecting the two Apocryphal books of Esdras, and calling them dreams,|| shews that the former (the subject of our consideration at present) was found in the LXX. of his day, while he also says that Ezra and Nehemiah

---

* It may be noted that this book is wanting in Codex Amiatinus and elsewhere.
† And so the Old Latin. See Sabatier, *Bibliorum sacr. Latinæ versiones antiquæ*, Rheims, 1743.
‡ The reign of Josiah. See below.
§ *Præfatio Hier. in Ezram.* Migne, *Patrologia* xxviii. 1403a.
|| *Somnia*, a name more appropriate, as we shall see later, to what the Sixth Article calls "The Fourth Book of Esdras."

HISTORICAL OR QUASI-HISTORICAL BOOKS. 113

"even among the Hebrews,"* were combined into one book. He further speaks of the variations of text which characterized the MSS. of this book—a statement which is amply borne out by those still extant.† We may add that the Council of Trent (1546 A.D.), in defining the Canon of Scripture, omitted this book, whether as unaware that it existed in Greek, or as being determined by the authority of St. Jerome.

PARALLELISM TO CERTAIN PARTS OF CANONICAL SCRIPTURE.

We find that the book, with the exception of one section (chaps. 3, 4, 5. 1–6), runs on parallel lines with certain parts of 2 Chronicles, Ezra, and Nehemiah. A conspectus of the parallel portions here follows :—

1 Esdras 1. 1–58.	2 Chron. 35. 1—36. 21.
„ 2. 1–15.	„ 36. 22 ; Ezra 1. 1–15.
„ 2. 16–30.	Ezra 4. 7–24.
„ 5. 7–73.	„ 2—4. 5.
„ 6. 1—7. 15.	„ 5. 1—6. 22.
„ 8. 1—9. 55.	„ 7. 1—10. 44 ; Neh. 8. 1–13.

In Ezra 4. 1–6 is related the opposition of the Samaritans which followed immediately upon the return from Babylon (538 B.C.). There then follows the section (vv. 7–24), which deals with Samaritan hostility to the Jews about the middle of the following century :‡ while thereupon (Ezra 5. 1, etc.) we are immediately brought back to circ. 521 B.C. (the second year of Darius), when the work was resumed. In the further displacement in 1 Esdras we see still more strongly emphasized the juxtaposition of the events of this section with those of the

---

* et apud Hebræos.
† For the probable cause of the omission of the book from the Codex Friderico-Augustanus (Sinaiticus) see Lupton, Speaker's Commentary, "Introduction to First Esdras," p. 1.
‡ See Ryle, Ezra, etc. ("Cambridge Bible for Schools"), pp. xvi., 64 ff.

Return, which had taken place not very much short of a hundred years earlier.*

From this it appears (*a*) that chapters 3, 4, 5. 1–6 form the only original section of this book as compared with the others; (*b*) that on the whole the chronological order of events corresponds in both columns, with one single exception, consisting in the removal of Ezra 4. 7–24, already, in all probability, out of its order in time in the latter book, and placing it in a position at least as unsatisfactory.

Source of the Book.

The fact of the agreement in subject-matter, and to a large extent in language, between this book and parts of our Old Testament Canon, gives a peculiar interest to the enquiry—to what cause or causes we may ascribe the divergencies in detail which exist throughout these common portions. It must be remembered that we have no Hebrew original to which to refer. It is left to us, therefore, to conjecture either (i.) that the Greek text of 1 Esdras represents a lost Hebrew original (whether connected or not with the existing Massoretic text), or (ii.) that it is based upon the LXX. or some other Greek text of 1 Chronicles, Ezra, and Nehemiah, and that the variations are intentional or accidental modifications of the language of those books.†

Those who accept the former of these two hypotheses as the correct one will account, of course, for the variations as being the more or less faithful reproduction of the Hebrew, of which

---

* *See* Lupton, *op. cit.*, p. 25, for a clear statement of three theories which have been suggested to account for the difficulties in the history contained in this section of Ezra.

† Such cases as that in 1 Esdras 8. 44, where the proper name Λααδαῖον (A Δολδαῖον) and in the next verse Λοδαίῳ (A Δολδαίῳ) occurs. while in 2 Esdras 8. 17 no name is found, are too rare to build upon them with any confidence the theory that 1 Esdras is based upon a translation other than that which has come down to us as the LXX.

they are a translation. The further question would then arise, What is the value of that Hebrew original preserved for us (on this hypothesis) in an indirect form? Have we here a more trustworthy narrative than is contained in the Hebrew which has been actually handed down to us in the corresponding parts of the Jewish Canon?

If, however, an examination of the variations be such as to lead us on the whole to the decision that the readings of this book have the less claim of the two to be considered trustworthy, we thereby so far discredit the supposed Hebrew original, which belongs to the former hypothesis. If, further, in our examination we see reason to believe that some of the variations in 1 Esdras are such as might naturally arise out of the corresponding Greek readings in the Canonical books, but that the converse does not hold good, we shall have advanced far towards a decision that the belief in a lost Hebrew original for this book is untenable, and that the second of the above hypotheses is to be adopted.

A careful comparison of the two Greek texts appears, at least as far as the earlier part of the book (**1. 1—2. 15**) is concerned, to point clearly to the acceptance, in a modified form, of the second rather than the first hypothesis. It is true that, as the list A will shew, there is a good deal to be said for the other view. In fact, there is one species of variant which appears plainly to indicate some acquaintance, whether direct or indirect, with a Hebrew original (the existing one or otherwise), viz., the occasional translation of Hebrew words (see *e.g.* note on 1 Esdras **8. 46** in the A class), when the corresponding passage in the Canonical book has only transliterated the Hebrew. We can hardly however admit, as supporting this side, those cases (of frequent occurrence throughout the book) in which the language differs from the other Greek text by the substitution for an easy or common word of a rare or difficult one, or by expressing the sense in smoother or more idiomatic Greek. This, it is obvious, might have taken place on either hypothesis. In the following tables are placed—

(A) *Examples of comparisons which have been held to justify the view that First* [*Third*] *Esdras was not drawn from the Greek version of the corresponding parts of the Jewish Canon, but from a Hebrew original.*[*]

2 Chron. 35. 1 (and throughout the chapter) τὸ φάσεχ (φάσεκ A).	1 Esd. 1. 1, τὸ πάσχα (but this is a very doubtful example).
2 Chron. 35. 9, (καὶ Βαναίας (after χωνενίας.) No corresponding words are found in the Hebrew text.	1 Esd. 1. 9 omits these words.
2 Chron. 36. 22, μετὰ τὸ πληρωθῆναι, but the parallel passage in 2 Esdras (Ezra) 1. 1 has τοῦ τελεσθῆναι. The Hebrew in both places is לִכְלוֹת.	1 Esd. 2. 1, εἰς συντέλειαν, thus amending the Greek of the Chron. to agree with the Hebrew.
2 Esd. (Ezra) 4. 7, ἐν εἰρήνῃ, mistaking the Hebrew proper name בִּשְׁלָם for בִּשָׁלוֹם. Comp. the LXX.'s error in Psalm 75. [76.] 2.	1 Esd. 2. 15, Βήλεμος; thus correcting from Hebrew.

---

[*] In these lists, Codex B (Vaticanus) furnishes all readings not otherwise marked. It is not, however, very trustworthy in these books. *See e.g.* in 1 Esdras Ἰουδαῖοι (for Ἰδουμαῖοι A) 4. 45, ἐπιθύσομεν (for ἐπιθύομεν A) 5. 66. In 8. 6, B has δεύτερος, while A has ἕβδομος, which latter must be right. So again, 8. 7, Ἀψάρας (Ἔζρας A), 8. 60, ἤλθοσαν (εἰσήλθομεν A). So, too, if we adopt B's reading in 5. 70, we must admit a bad solecism in grammar, which the analogy of the rest of the book renders very improbable. There B's βουλὰς has no government, and we must with A read (for δημαγωγοῦντες) δημαγωγίας. Observe, too, that in 2 Esdras B's Θαναναὶ of 5. 3 appears three verses later as Θανθαναί, and in 6. 13 as Τανθαναί. So Βαγασὰρ of 5. 14 is in the next verse Σαρβαγάρ.

2 Esd. (Ezra) 2. 62, μεθωεσείμ. 1 Esd. 5. 39, καταλοχισμῷ.
(מִתְיַחֲשִׂים, the enrolled.)

2 Esd. (Ezra) 6. 11, πληγήσεται „ 6. 31, κρεμασθῆναι (a
(but A παγήσεται), יִתְמְחָא,   very doubtful ex-
let him be fastened.   ample).

2 Esd. (Ezra) 8. 18, σαχώχ „ 8. 46 ἐπίστημονα.*
(שֵׂכֶל understanding).

2 Esd. (Ezra) 9. 1, ὁ Μοσερεί „ „ 66, Αἰγυπτίων.
(הַמִּצְרִי, the Egyptians).

2 Esd. (Ezra) 10. 6. καὶ ἐπορεύθη. „ 9. 2, καὶ αὐλισθείς.
The Massoretic text has
וַיֵּלֶךְ, and he went, but the
Greek of 1 Esdras may
point to a reading וַיָּלֶן,
and he passed the night, and
this may preserve for us a
superior Hebrew text.

2 Esd. (Ezra) 10. 16. καὶ „ 16. ἐπελέξατο αὐτῷ.
διεστάλησαν. The Massoretic
text has וַיִּבָּדְלוּ, and they
were separated. 1 Esdras
suggests another pointing
of the same root with a
slight addition, וַיַּבְדֵּל לוֹ,
and he separated for him-
self.

---

* In this and other instances 1 Esdras is able to translate Hebrew words which are only transliterated in the Greek renderings of the Canonical books. With non-Hebrew words it has not always been so successful, e.g., 2. 15. Βεέλτεθμος, where 2 Esd. 4. 8 has βαδαταμέν. Here both are wrong. The word is a title of Rehum, postmaster, literally "lord of official intelligence." But in 1 Esd. 2. 16, it is translated ὁ τὰ προσπίπτοντα [γράφων], while in verse 21 [Eng. 25] the two methods are combined. See Sayce, Ezra, etc., p. 25.

There is one case which at first may seem to give support to the view that the translator, if he did not actually render from a Hebrew original, was at any rate cognisant of a Hebrew text resembling the Massoretic. In 2 Chron. 36. 10 the Hebrew calls Zedekiah brother (instead of uncle) of Johoiachin. The Greek there substitutes for "his brother" ἀδελφὸν τοῦ πατρὸς αὐτοῦ. 1 Esd. 1. 44 (Eng. 46) omits mention of the relationship altogether. This, however, looks rather as if the Hebrew and Greek of the Chronicles passage were both glosses. This seems more probable than that the writer of 1 Esdras, knowing the discrepancy, avoided the difficulty by omission.

(B) *Cases which seem to justify the view that the text of 1 Esdras is based upon the existing Greek version, or some kindred Greek version of the Hebrew.*

2 Chron. 35. 4, διὰ χειρός (בְּמִכְתָּב, *according to the writing of.*)

1 Esd. 1. 4. κατὰ τὴν μεγαλειότητα.

This rendering has no sort of connexion with the Hebrew, whereas it may easily have arisen out of a misunderstanding of the force of χείρ. For χείρ taken in the sense of *power, greatness*, comp. 2 Esd. 8. 22 = 1 Esd. 8. 52 (ἰσχύς).

2 Chron. 35. 12, εἰς τὸ πρωί, בָּקָר, *oxen*, read as בֹּקֶר, *morning*.

1 Esd. 1. 10. τὸ πρωϊνόν.

This is almost decisive in itself against a Hebrew source. It is extremely unlikely that two independent versions would

HISTORICAL OR QUASI-HISTORICAL BOOKS. 119

2 Chron. 35. 13 εὐοδώθη (altered later in Vatican MS. to εὐωδώθη). Hebrew is יְבַשְּׁלוּ, *and in the pans.* This was misread.

1 Esd. 1. 11. μετ' εὐωδίας. The Hebrew in no way lends itself to the mistake, which on the other hand involves a very slight misreading of the Greek word, with, it is true, a considerable change in sense.

2 Chron. 35. 22, ἐκραταιώθη, הִתְחַפֵּשׂ, *disguised himself.*

1 Esd. 1. 26. 'ἐπεχείρει.

2 Chron. 36. 6, καὶ ἀπήγαγεν (ἀνήγαγεν, A) Heb. has *to cause (him) to go.*

„ 38 καὶ (but A omits καὶ) ἀπήγαγεν.

It should be observed that, as has been already said, the examples in B are all drawn from a comparison between the last two chapters of 2 Chronicles and that part of 1 Esdras which was parallel with them. For those parts which correspond to sections of Ezra and Nehemiah no such clear examples in support of a Greek source appear to be forthcoming.

(C) Examples of the substitution of an easier or less Hebraic word or form, or of a mode of expression considered more suitable or conforming better to Greek idiom.

2 Chron. 35. 5, hard to construe.

1 Esd. 1. 5, simplifies.

2 Chron. 35. 7, ἀπήρξατο (similarly in *vv.* 8, 9).

„ „ 7, ἐδωρήσατο (similarly in 8, 9).

2 Chron. 35. 13, καὶ ἔδραμον (וַיָּרִיצוּ) softened down in 1 Esdras 1. 11 to καὶ ἀπήνεγκαν.

2 Chron. 35. 22, Νεχαώ. 1 Esd. 1. 26, Ἰερεμίου (it was not considered suitable that a heathen king should give God's message).

„ „ 24, ἀπέθανεν. 1 Esd. 1. 29, μετήλλαξεν τὸν βίον αὐτοῦ.

„ „ 25, ἐπὶ τῶν θρήνων. 1 Esd. 1. 30, omitted, owing to absence of dirge spoken of from the only book of the name known to the writer.

2 Chron. 35. 26. The sentence with νόμῳ Κυρίου, altered in 1 Esd. 1. 30 to avoid the difficulty.

2 Chron. 36. 14. The sentence made to run more smoothly in 1 Esd. 1. 47.

2 Chron. 36. 19, βάρεις. 1 Esd. 1. 52, πύργους.

2 Esd. 1. 3, τίς . . . . ; 1 Esd. 2. 3, εἴ τίς ἐστιν (smoothing away the Heb. idiom).

„ „ 4, λήμψονται αὐτόν. (יִנַּשְׂאוּהוּ). 1 Esd. 2. 6, βοηθείτωσαν αὐτῷ. So in same verse ἀργ. put after, instead of before, χρυσ., and τοῦ ἑκουσίου (הַנְּדָבָה) changed to idiomatic Greek, as in v. 8 also.

1 Esd. 2. 12. Individual items are altered to improbable figures (e.g. 1000 golden cups instead of 30), in order to make them agree with the total. This is a clear indication, as far as it goes, that adaptation has been at work in this book, as it stands. If we

were to suppose a Hebrew source, it would so far discredit that source, as compared with the Massoretic text. The discrepancy in both Hebrew and Greek of 2 Esd. 1. 11 is probably to be set down to an early corruption in some of the numbers.

2 Esd. 4. 9, Δειναῖοι κ.τ.λ. — 1 Esd. 2. 16 omits the various Samaritan tribes, perhaps as not appealing to the interest of Alexandrian Jews of that age.

„   „ 18, φορόλογος. — 1 Esd. 2. 22, ἐπιστολή, as the usual and non-technical word. So τῶν γραφέντων in v. 25. So also φορ. of 2 Esd. 5. 5 is avoided in 1 Esd. 6. 6.

„   2. 43, οἱ Ναθεινίμ. — 1 Esd. 5. 29, οἱ ἱερόδουλοι.*
„   „ 68, ἑτοιμασίαν. — „   „ 43, τόπον.
„   3. 7, ἐπιχώρησιν. — „   „ 53 [Eng. 55] πρόσταγμα (simpler word).
„   6. 5. — 1 Esd. 6. 25. The last part of the v. is a good specimen of expansion and smoothing.
„   7. 13, solecism in grammar. — 1 Esd. 8. 10, solecism removed.†

---

* 1 Esdras is fond of ἱερὸς in compounds, e.g. 1. 3, 14 (comp. 6. 25 with 2 Esd. 6. 5); and in 8. 5 (ἱεροψαλτῶν) as comp. with 2 Esd. 7. 7.

† On the other hand, a reading in 1 Esd. 9. 14, ἐπεδέξαντο, is difficult to harmonize with the context, and not found in 2 Esd. 10. 15. Schleusner (*Lex.*) suggests, however, to amend to ἐπελέξαντο, *co-operated with.*

It should be added that, although the general character of the Greek of 1 Esdras is as we have mentioned, yet it contains several instances of difficult or comparatively rare words which do not find a place in the parallel passages. Such are ἀπηρείσατο (as against ἔδωκεν of 2 Esd. 1. 7), 1. 39, 2. 9, 6. 17,* χάρα ?=χάραγμα, *money*, 5. 55, ἐπικοιμώμενα, *lying as an incubus on*, 5. 69 [Eng. 72], found in 1 [3] Kings 3. 19 in the literal sense, μεταγενέστερος, 8. 1; so Symmachus in Ps. 47. (48) 14.

We have naturally been unable to take any account hitherto of the section 3. 1—5. 6, inasmuch as it has no parallel in the Jewish Canon. The story of the three youths' competition with Darius as judge may be of Persian origin. Ewald† finds traces of it in the earliest of the Sibylline Books (181-143 B.C.). It does not afford us any real help towards the determination of the date. That its language here would be tinctured with Hebrew idiom might naturally be expected, in whatever country it may have had its origin. The passage (5. 1-6), which is obviously inserted in order to smooth the transition to the subsequent narrative, is somewhat more Hebraic in tone.

To conclude, it would seem that the hypothesis that 1 Esdras is based upon a Greek, but emended from a Hebrew, source, is that which best satisfies the somewhat conflicting evidence above summarised.

THE RELATION OF JOSEPHUS TO THIS BOOK.

It has been maintained that a strong argument for the superiority of this book as an historical record when compared with the corresponding parts of the Canonical writings

---

* We may note its occurrence in the LXX. of Dan. 1. 2.
† *Abhandlung über* . . . . *der Sibyllinischer Bücher*, p. 36.

consists in the freedom with which so learned an historian as Josephus makes use of it. He had naturally, it may be said, full opportunity of knowing what trust might be placed in its statements, and was surrounded by critics who would not fail to discredit him, if he were to employ what was recognised at the time to be an untrustworthy source for his narrative. Moreover, the Septuagint, the established version of his day, is that which he habitually quotes elsewhere. May not then the Greek of First Esdras be the real LXX., which has somehow been since deposed, and another version which accords more with the Massoretic text (compare the case of the Greek versions of Daniel) substituted?

It is true that Josephus in his account of the restoration of the theocracy* conforms to the order of events as given in 1 Esd. 2. 15—5. 6.† Nevertheless, he at least shews that he is not disposed to accept precisely the kings of Persia as given in 1 Esdras. For Artaxerxes (1 Esd. 2. 16) he substitutes Cambyses, thus giving the historical order, Cyrus, Cambyses, Darius. "He removes the further historical stumbling-block of the Greek Ezra [1 Esd. 5. 7-10], of Cyrus reappearing after Darius, by doing away with Cyrus in this place and making the return of the exiles first take place under Darius .... a narrative is thus concocted, which differs still more widely from actual history than that of the Greek Ezra itself."‡

Again, in one or two cases Josephus agrees with the Hebrew Book as against 1 Esdras. For ἑπτακοσίους (1 Esd. 1. 9) he has, with 2 Chron. 35. 9, πεντακοσίους,§ and instead of the confused statement in 1 Esd. 1. 38, he agrees with the account as given 2 Chron. 36. 4.||

---

* *See* Schürer, *op. cit.*, II. iii. 179.   † *Ant.* xi. 1, etc.
‡ Schürer, *ibid.*, 180.   § *See Ant.* x. 5. 2. || *Ibid.*

Lastly, he makes assertions drawn from neither the Hebrew nor the Greek Ezra ; *e.g.* :

(*a*) He says Zerubbabel returned from Jerusalem to Babylon, and, as a matter of personal friendship, was made by Darius one of his body-guard ; *

(*b*) He says that the Jews refused the Samaritans' offer of help in temple-building on the ground that the former had received their permission from Cyrus and from Darius ; †

(*c*) He makes the story of 1 Esd. 3 to run more smoothly by giving a reason for the competition of the three youths.‡ According to his account the king, being wakeful, began to talk with his attendants and proposed to them the trial.

On the whole we may conclude that the comparison of Josephus' narrative generally with that of the Old Testament as represented either in its Hebrew or Greek form, does not warrant us in concluding that he would necessarily abstain from making use of such a book as our Greek 1 Esdras, even supposing it to be outside the Canon of his day.

The smoothly flowing Greek would naturally attract such a writer, as well as the occasions on which it removed difficulties in the parallel passages of the other books.

PLACE AND TIME OF COMPOSITION, AND AIM OF THE WRITER.

None of these points can be decided with anything like certainty. The book was at any rate in existence in Josephus' day ; but how much sooner ? The story of Zerubbabel and the others (chaps. 3, 4) bears some resemblance, as has already been said, to a Sibylline composition of the 2nd cent. B.C. It also somewhat resembles a story concerning Jewish elders at the Egyptian court in the time of Ptolemy

---

* *See Ant.* xi. 3. 1. † *Ibid.* xi. 4. 3. ; comp. Ezra 4. 3. ‡ *Ibid.* xi. 3. 2.

Philadelphus, related in the work of the Pseudo-Aristeas.* That work is probably not to be placed before 100 B.C. If a knowledge of it is implied by the form in which the story appears here, this would determine us for a date not earlier than the first century B.C. Such an acquaintance with the Aristean tale is, however, by no means certain. Moreover, scholars generally attribute 1 Esdras to a date somewhere within the first century before Christ.

If we consider ourselves justified in looking for traces of an earlier origin, we find such, as Dr. Lupton † points out, in the events which were taking place in Egypt and Syria between 170 and 160 B.C. Antiochus had sacked Jerusalem, and many natives had taken refuge in Egypt, which already, as we know, had a large Jewish population. Onias, son or grandson of Onias III. the high priest who was slain by his brother Menelaus in 171 B.C., had taken refuge there. He found dissensions prevailing among his countrymen. He, as the lawful successor to the high-priestly office, formed the idea of providing a bond of union in the shape of a temple which should take the place of the desecrated Sanctuary at Jerusalem. He obtained from Ptolemy Philometor and Cleopatra ‡ a site on which stood the ruins of a temple of the sun at Bubastis, and, availing himself of the remnants of the old building, he carried out his purpose, using however, we learn, instead of the seven-branched candlestick, a lamp "shedding a golden radiance," hung by a chain of gold from the ceiling. This detail, as well as the adaptation of a heathen temple to his purpose, seems, as Lupton says, to shew his desire to accommodate his new place of worship to Egyptian ideas. Herodotus describes the joyous pilgrimage to the festival of Bubastis.

---

* Gallandi, *Bibliotheca Vet. Patrum*, ii. 791 ff., Venice, 1766.
† *Speaker's Comm.*, *ibid*. 11 ff.
‡ *See* Jos. *Ant*. xiii. 3. 1.

It is natural to suppose that Onias would desire to retain some of the attractions of the older worship of the place. The writing of 1 Esdras may have been connected with this aim. "In judging of its origin, we must fix our attention on the features it presents most distinct from the Old Testament version of the same story. And these, if we omit for the moment the episode in 3, 4, are the incidents described by the writer, as marking the reception by the Jews of the news of the king's favour, and the starting of the convoy homewards . . . . suggestive rather of the Egyptian festivals than of the return from the Babylonian captivity." He also remarks that a narrative emphasizing as 1 Esdras does, the beneficence of foreign kings in contributing to the work of restoration of the Temple, and telling also of Josiah, slain in an invasion of Syria by the Egyptians, would have a special interest under such circumstances as those mentioned above.

However this may be, Alexandria is plainly a probable place for such a work to appear, when we consider the large Jewish element among the cultured population, as well as the excellence of the Greek in which the book is written. Further, the passage (4. 23) "a man taketh his sword, and goeth forth to make outroads and to rob and to steal, and to sail upon the sea and upon rivers," has been thought to point to an Egyptian origin.*

The aim of the book may have been accordingly—

(*a*) Whether in connexion with the above-mentioned events or not, to glorify the Law, and at the same time win the favour of some foreign power. This harmonizes with both the commencement and the close of the book; but in saying this, we

---

* Note the use of ἀλήθεια = the Thummim, 1 Esd. 5. 40, and contrast the rendering by τέλειος in 2 Esd. 2. 63. The LXX. always, except in the passage just named, has ἀλήθεια.

must not overlook the fact that the end, as we have it, is abrupt.*

(*b*) To give in language more nearly approaching to a classical model, the story of the Return.

(*c*) To glorify Zerubbabel. This would seem a precarious hypothesis. It is true that, as the book now stands, Zerubbabel is the hero of the episode of chaps. 3, 4. But when we proceed to the connecting link (5. 1–6) between that story and the remainder of the book, we gather that it was his son Joachim (5. 6) who is there given as the speaker, and so that the word Zerubbabel of 4. 13 may be a gloss. It is of course possible that the section, in the form presented to us, may in this point betray two recensions, the successful competitor being in the one case the father, in the other the son. The writer had got hold of the tale, and in order to introduce it, compiled the rest of the book. We may at any rate, with Schürer,† believe that "he certainly discovered beforehand" this portion, as it is at variance with the general narrative.

On the whole, we cannot do better than accept the conclusion of Bertholdt (*Einleitung*, iii. 1011),‡ "He intended to compile from older works a history of the Temple from the last epoch of the legal worship to its rebuilding and the restoration of the prescribed ritual therein." For the abruptness of the conclusion of the book, as we have it, we cannot account.

2. Judith.

The very slenderest acquaintance with the history of those Eastern empires with which the Jews were brought into contact is sufficient to shew us that this book is nothing more

---

* This is plain from the Greek, though it does not appear in the versions.
† II. iii. 179. ‡ Quoted by Schürer *ibid*.

than a romance. The opening words date the story as belonging to "the twelfth year of the reign of Nebuchadnezzar, who reigned over the Assyrians in Nineveh, the great city: in the days of Arphaxad, who reigned over the Medes in Ecbatana." *

It is needless to say that Nineveh was the capital of the Assyrian Empire as such, the city of Sennacherib and Assurbani-pal, and that in Nebuchadnezzar's time the Assyrian Empire was at an end and Babylon had become the seat of rule. Arphaxad is known to us only as the name of a country or race. † There is no support for it, either within or without the Old Testament, as the name of a king of Media. The "twelfth year" may, as is pointed out in the *Speaker's Commentary*, ‡ possess a claim, though at best but a shadowy one, to have some point in its present connexion. "The twelfth year of Nebuchadnezzar of Old Testament history was the fourth of Zedekiah, the last king of Judah (*see* Jer. 32. 1). Now in that year the kings of Edom, Moab, Ammon, Tyre, and Sidon, sought to induce Zedekiah to join in a general revolt against Babylon (Jer. 27. 3, compared with 28. 1). The time would be judged favourable, if Nebuchadnezzar were engaged elsewhere, say in Media." The chronology is so hopelessly at variance with facts that the writer, having thus opened by virtually dating his story at a period anterior to the overthrow of the Southern Kingdom and deportation of Zedekiah to Babylon, proceeds without any misgivings a little later § to say that the children of Israel "were newly come up from the Captivity, and all the people of Judæa were lately gathered together: and the vessels, and the altar, and the house, were sanctified after the profanation."

---

* Judith 1. 1. † Gen. 10. 22, 24; 11. 10-13.
‡ *Ad loc.* § Judith 4. 3.

The time intended to be pictured is thus shewn to be soon after the return of the exiles. That the story, however, could not in fact be referred to so early a time was plain even to later Jewish tradition, which makes Judith the sister of Judas Maccabeus, and the daughter of his brother John.*

It is difficult to fix the time of composition within any precise limits. It seems clear at any rate that the work is of a decidedly pre-Christian date. Volkmar † indeed maintains that the real reference is to events in Trajan's day (98–117 A.D.), and that the book was composed not earlier than the time immediately following the death of that Emperor. This theory, however, besides other grave objections, ‡ is overthrown by the fact that Clement of Rome (Ep. to the Corinthians lv.), writing in 95 or 96 A.D., § refers to the book ('Ιουδὶθ ἡ μακαρία).

More probable dates suggested are, the war carried on by Jannaeus, ‖ the end of the reign of Demetrius II. (129 B.C.), ¶ the reign of Alexandra (Salome, 79–70 B.C.).** It is probably later than 1 Maccabees, and thus would be at any rate after the death of John Hyrcanus (105 B.C.). A good deal may be said in support of the view that in the heroine of the tale there is throughout an oblique reference of a complimentary character to Queen Alexandra, widow of Jannes, a strong supporter of Pharisaic principles. In her time the high priest and Sanhedrin attained an unusual amount of power, a state of things which is in harmony with the words of Judith 11. 14. Joakim takes the leading place in public affairs, and during this reign more than perhaps at any other time during the

---

* *See* extracts from Jellinek's *Bet ha-Midrash*, translated in *Speaker's Comm.*, "Introd. to Judith," Appendix I.

† *Handbuch der Einleitung in die Apocryphen*. Tübingen, 1860, pp. 337, 375, 403

‡ *See* it dealt with in a long note in *Speaker's Comm.*, "Introd. to Judith" (C. J. Ball), p. 245.

§ *See* Lightfoot's *Apostolic Fathers, S. Clement of Rome*, i. 316 ff.

‖ *See* pp. 66 f. ¶ *See* p. 56. ** *See* pp. 71 ff.

period the people might be said to be living under a theocracy.

In connexion with discussions as to the date and aim of the story special significance has been sought to be attached to the names Joakim,* Simeon,† Arphaxad, ‡ Holophernes.§

We can at any rate with certainty say that the writer has imported the ideas of the Maccabean age into the times in which he has desired to place his narrative. There has been long oppression, and the desire for vengeance consequently burns strong in men's hearts. The Sanhedrin (γερουσία, xv. 8) is referred to. Pharisaic legalism is conspicuous throughout. The utmost importance is assigned to the due performance of ceremonial rites and to the avoiding of uncleanness. Not only are Sabbaths and new moons to be observed with strictness, but also (**8.** 6) the eves of the same (a later development of the law). On absolute conformity to the traditional observances of this nature was to depend the success of Judith's heroic attempt to deliver her nation from the heathen oppressor.

The aim of the book also harmonizes well with the Maccabean period. Danger threatens both the people and their religion. Holophernes' demand was "that all the nations should worship Nebuchadnezzar only, and that all their tongues and their tribes should call upon him as god." ‖ Whether or no this be a veiled reference to the demands of Antiochus

---

* As though indicating the Alcimus of 1 Macc. 7. 5. See p. 44 *supra*.

† As either Simeon of 1 Macc. 2. 1, or Judas's elder brother, see p. 39 *supra*, or Simeon ben Shatach, see p. 65.

‡ As Artaxias of Armenia, defeated and captured by Antiochus Epiphanes (Appian, *Syriaca*, 45. See Diod. ap. Müller, *Fragm.* ii. p. 10: comp. Dan. 11. 40), or Arsaces, Arsacides, Parthian titles.

§ A title of the kings of Cappadocia in the Persian and Greek periods. In the time of Jonathan Maccabeus, 158 B.C., there was a king of Cappadocia named Orophernes: but that name also occurs much earlier in close connexion with the sovereignty of the country, viz. about the middle of the 4th century B.C. See Smith's *Dict. of Bible*, Article " Holophernes," for details.

‖ Judith 3. 8.

Epiphanes and his violent assaults upon the Jewish faith,* we may at any rate say that it is to some such danger threatening the national life and religion that allusion is made. The story may be called a "novel with a purpose," and that purpose, to encourage and sustain the people in their allegiance to the God of their fathers, and in their conformity to the precepts of His Law. It desires emphatically to declare that His highest favour was conferred in times past upon those who had combined minute obedience to the commands of the Torah as interpreted and supplemented by tradition, with heroism shewn in encountering danger and in dealing death and discomfiture to the unbeliever and his host.

We may assume it as certain that the book was originally written in Hebrew. "The language as a whole, the syntactical construction, the mode of presenting events and ideas, the general complexion of the work, so irresistibly suggest a Hebrew original, that as a rule it is easy to divine what the Hebrew must have been." † We may therefore infer that the book is the work of a Palestinian rather than of an Alexandrian Jew, while the same conclusion may be drawn from the nature of the topographical references.

In Origen's time, however, the Hebrew original was unknown.‡ In the Old Latin Version (made from the LXX.) the five MSS. collated by Sabatier § vary quite enough to confirm the statement made by St. Jerome in his preface to the book as to the result of a comparison of the MSS. of that version to which he had access. He rendered according to his own account in much haste, and only in response to an urgent request not to leave the book untranslated. He used a "Chaldee" copy, and whatever was not contained in it he

---

* Comp. Dan. 11. 31 ff.
† *Speaker's Comm.* l.c. p. 214. *See* details in note there.
‡ *Ep. ad Africanum*, chap. xiii.
§ *Op. cit.*, i. 744-790.

disregarded. As in the case of Tobit, which he translated at the same time (see his preface to Tobit), viz. 398 A.D., at Bethlehem, he caused some learned Jew to read aloud the "Chaldee" into Hebrew. From the latter language, as familiar to him, he dictated his version to his scribe. He admits himself that he did not care for verbal exactness in the matter. The task was undertaken reluctantly. His esteem for the book was but slight, and other occupations pressed. The "Chaldee" version which he thus employed may well have been less worthy of deference than he supposed. It is very possible that it was a retranslation from a Greek or Latin text, and thus was merely a version of a version (with an accumulated chance of error) made for the benefit of Aramaic-speaking Jews after Origen's time.*

3. Tobit.

The contrast between this book and that of Judith, of which we have just treated, is of a character to remind us of the change from the turmoil described in the Book of Judges, to the idyllic scenes which we come upon when we turn over the page and find ourselves in the Book of Ruth, claiming, as the latter does in the opening sentence, to relate to "the days when the judges ruled."

In Judith the land is polluted by the presence of an invading force, and the enemy is within a measurable distance of the gates of Jerusalem. It is a time of intense excitement, and one that calls for exceptional daring. The scenes of the Book of Tobit move in a different atmosphere. They have to do with Israelites who belonged to the Northern Kingdom, and lived in the days before Nebuchadnezzar. Moreover, Tobit deals with the conditions of Jewish life in a distant land. Tobit and

---

* See *Speaker's Comm. l.c.* p. 243, note 1.

his family are at Nineveh. They have been taken captive by Enemessar (Shalmaneser), and retained in exile under his successors Sennacherib and Sarchedonus (Esarhaddon). But their surroundings are those of a secure city life, and their virtues are those of peace. As religious Jews of the best type they are law-abiding, charitable, careful to carry out the precepts of Moses, so far as may be possible, and fully cognisant of the duties which home life and mutual relationship involve.

Date.

The political events to which we have just referred determine an anterior limit, while the fact that Polycarp * quotes the book † prevents us from placing it later than the middle of the 2nd century A.D. But within these bounds the most various dates have been assigned, from the 7th century B.C. to a time subsequent to the overthrow of Jerusalem and its Temple by the Romans (70 A.D.), or even to the 3rd century A.D.‡ The internal evidence of the book is at any rate equally opposed to both these views.§

1. In chap. 14, Tobit, when on the point of death, calls together his sons and grandsons and sets before them the future in connexion with the Holy City and the Temple. "Jerusalem," he says, "shall be desolate, and the house of God in it shall be burned up, and shall be desolate for a time ; and God shall again have mercy on them, and bring them back into the

---

* *Ad Philip*, chap. x. Polycarp's martyrdom occurred in all probability early in the latter half of the 2nd century A.D. See " Polycarp " in Smith's *Dict. of Christ. Biog.* for discussion as to the exact year.

† Tobit 4. 11 ; 12. 9.

‡ Kohut thinks that he finds a reference to the first Persian monarch of the Sassanian dynasty (226 A.D.). See Ball in *Speaker's Comm.*, " Introd. to Tobit," p. 157.

§ The minuteness of detail in some places (1. 1, 2; 8. 20; 11. 18, 19,), although supplying in some literary questions an argument for the contemporaneous character of the document which contains them, has not the same force here, as being a common feature of Eastern romance. Compare the same feature in Judith (*e.g.* ch. 1-10).

land, and they shall build the house, but not like to the former house, until the times of that age be fulfilled; and afterward they shall return from the places of their captivity, and build up Jerusalem with honour, and the house of God shall be built in it for ever with a glorious building, even as the prophets spake concerning it."*

If, as the advocates of a very late date maintain, the reference here be to the Roman overthrow of Jerusalem, we must of course admit the time to be at any rate not earlier than 70 A.D. But the words will apply at least as well to the destruction under Nebuchadnezzar, as followed by the Return and building of the Temple of Zerubbabel, "but not like to the former house." † The remainder of the passage quoted seems to shew that Herod's costly and magnificent Temple ‡ was not yet in existence in the time of the writer. Thus we are able to some extent to narrow our limits of time.

2. The general standpoint of the book with regard to religious observances is much of the same as that of Judith. The requirements of Jewish ceremonial are of paramount importance and authority. Daily life is to be controlled by them in all respects. Fasting is enjoined (12. 8), the duty of almsgiving receives special emphasis. In fact, the upholders of a late date dwell upon the earnestness of the way in which this duty is set forth, and the virtue attributed to it. Strong as some of the passages are, which are quoted by them in this connexion, they do not seem to differ from the teaching on the subject which might naturally be found in the Greek period, or even earlier. It is true that in this, no less than in other features presently to be noticed, there is a marked divergence from the tone observed in the Canonical books of the Old Testament. "There may be symptoms of a tendency to formal righteous-

---

* *rv.* 4, 5.   † Comp. Hag. 2. 3; Ezra 3. 12.   ‡ Built 17 B.C.

ness of works, but as yet the works are painted as springing from a living faith."* This will be seen from the following instances. Tobit claims credit for living all his life "in the way of truth and righteousness," and illustrates his claim by reference to his deeds of kindness to his poorer brethren carried away like himself by the Assyrian conqueror.† In his exhortation to his son, he dwells upon the duty of almsgiving in words some of which the Offertory sentences in the Communion Office have made familiar to the ears of English Churchmen.‡ Raphael instructs Tobit, " Good is prayer with fasting and alms and righteousness. . . . It is better to give alms than to lay up gold,"§ while, lastly, Tobit, on recovery of sight " gave alms, and he feared the Lord God more and more, and gave thanks unto him," quoting also in his dying speech the case of Manasses, who by the same means " escaped the snare of death which he set for him." ‖

There are indeed certain strong-sounding statements on this point, viz., " alms delivereth from death " (4. 10 ; similarly 12. 9 adding, " and it shall purge away all sin "). Whatever we may think of the theology of such passages, it appears at any rate probable that they have no reference to blessings to be procured in a future life by deeds of charity in this world.¶ Thus they by no means serve to bring the date of composition of the work in which they occur to the period of Rabbinic fancies coeval with the early centuries of Christianity. It is further plain that in the opinion of the writer of this story, alms, however bountiful, were worthless unless the motive which inspired them was pure. That the good deeds of the guilty or the hypocrite were considered of no avail appears from the charge made by Anna, however unjustly, against her husband.

---

* Smith's *Dict. of Bible*, Article "Tobit" (Bp. Westcott).
† Tobit 1. 3, 16, 17. ‡ Ibid. 4. 7-9.
§ Ibid. 12. 8. ‖ Ibid. 14. 2. 10. ¶ Comp. Dan. 4. 27.

"Where are thine alms and thy righteous deeds, [which profit thee not in the day of thy trouble]? Behold, thou and all thy works are known."*

It may be added, that it is only to be expected that the writer, in dealing with the case of Jews cut off from the possibility of Temple worship and offerings, should insist the more upon the performance of those religious duties which it was still open to them to discharge. Moreover, such language by no means implies that the Temple had been finally overthrown. "Atonement for sin by sacrifice in the Temple was as impossible to the exile in Assyria and Babylonia in the time of Sennacherib and Nebuchadnezzar as it was to the Jew who wept over the desecration consummated by Titus. In both cases a substitute for animal sacrifice was required. . . . . The recognition of a spiritual religion as equivalent and even superior to the purely ceremonial worship dates, not from the first century after Christ, but from the time of the Captivity." †

3. The position given in this book to good and evil spirits falls in with the view that it is to be assigned to post-captivity yet pre-Christian times. There is a considerable development of the doctrine of angels, as compared with the teaching on that subject which we gather from the Old Testament Canonical writings. Raphael seems to eat and drink, has the power to appear and disappear at will (12. 21)—so far we have Old Testament parallels—but further, in accordance with his name,‡ he

---

* Tobit, 2. 14. The words in brackets are supplied by the Hebrew form of the story which, though probably late (*see* below), doubtless here correctly interprets the meaning.

† *Speaker's Comm.*, " Introd. to Tobit " (J. M. Fuller), p. 158. For the illustration which Tobit in his dying speech (14. 10) gives of the duty and the reward of piety, mercy, and charity in the shape of a reference to a story of Achiacharus—a reference which commentators in general have hitherto failed to explain—*see* Dr. M. R. James, in *Guardian*, Feb. 2, 1898. He refers the reader for the story as given at full length to Henry Webber, *Tales of the East*, ii. 53. Edin. 1812. It is shortly to appear under the joint editorship of Mrs. S. S. Lewis (Cambridge) and others.

‡ Divine Healer.

comes as the messenger of heaven to the rescue of the sick and suffering (**3.** 17 ; **12.** 18), he secretly watches the good deeds of the pious (**12.** 12, 13), and brings the remembrance of their prayers before the Holy One (*ibid.*). The more vivid conception of the nature and holiness of God has begun to demand methods of approach through intermediate agencies. Raphael and six of his heavenly associates act as intercessors. They "present the prayers of the saints," and "go in before the glory of the Holy One" (**12.** 15 ; comp. **8.** 15).

Evil spirits, on the other hand, while possessed of power of injury, are checked by the exercise of prescribed means accompanied by prayer and virtue (**6.** 7 ; **8.** 1–3, etc.). When overcome, they are bound by an angel (**8.** 3). Here, as in the case of good angels, the treatment of the subject evidently occupies an intermediate position between the reserve characteristic of the Old Testament Canon and the development of Jewish speculation shortly before, and still more after, Christ.*

4. The limits within which we seek to place the date may be perhaps narrowed, when we notice the many parallels which exist between the Books of Tobit and of Ecclesiasticus. We have referred to the stress laid in Tobit on almsgiving. Equally strong expressions are to be found in the latter work. Such are "almsgiving will make atonement for sins" (Ecclus. **3.** 30), "shut up alms in thy store-chambers,† and it shall deliver thee

---

* See the very elaborate treatment of the subjects of angelology and demonology from the point of view above referred to, in *Speaker's Comm.*, "Introd. to Tobit," Excursus II. (J. M. Fuller). In particular the writer there points out the expansion of Jewish theological opinion on the point in the Book of Enoch (second and first century B.C.), as we shall notice more fully when dealing with that work. He further shows that the teaching of Tobit as to evil spirits suggests contact with Babylonian and Persian conceptions, while even if the name Asmodeus be Persian or Median and not Semitic ("the destroyer"), the details relating to him are closely connected with Assyrian belief. He also shews that the (later) Rabbinnic conception of "Ashmedai" "from its mixture of kindness and mischief, of good humour and cunning (*l.c.* p. 180), differs much from the picture here given of the "king of the demons" (**3.** 8, Aramaic and Hebrew versions).

† *i.e.*, as the Vulgate explains, "in the heart of the poor."

out of all affliction" (**29.** 12 ; *see* also next *v.*), "Brethren and succour are for a time of affliction, and almsgiving is a deliverer above both" (**40.** 24).

The saying, "He that honoureth his father shall make atonement for sins" (Ecclus. **3.** 3), taken along with the mention of "atonement" in the passage just quoted, when compared with such passages as Tobit **4.** 10 ; **12.** 9, helps us to identify both works with the same general period of Jewish thought. Again, the "deliverance" from trouble, *i.e.*, evidently *in this life*, spoken of in Ecclesiasticus, may be taken as a parallel to the passages just now named in Tobit, and as explanatory of the deliverance there referred to. Accordingly, as the date of Ecclesiasticus can be clearly shewn to be not later than the first part of the 2nd century B.C., it follows that the parallel expressions in Tobit cannot be fairly adduced as arguments for placing it in much later times. The *Speaker's Commentary* on this book, from which the above examples are taken,* adds, "Other 'precepts' (Tobit **6.** 15) upon which Tobit lays so much stress, in his advice to his son, and his maxims generally, find frequent place in the chapters of Ecclesiasticus. Devotion to God, purity of marriage, honest dealing towards servants, the right estimate of wealth, the general duty of helping the poor and needy, etc. are forcibly urged by both writers. . . . The date of Ecclesiasticus should therefore throw light upon the date of Tobit."

If on the whole we may not place the book as early as the Persian period, in spite of one or two indications (*e.g.* **14.** 4) which have been thought to tend in that direction, at any rate it may with confidence be determined to be pre-Maccabean. At the same time, bearing in mind that the atmosphere of the story, as we saw at the beginning, is so very different from that which belongs to the romance of Judith, we are perhaps right

---

* P. 161, where see examples of the points of comparison which follow.

in saying that the former must have been written at a time when the Jews had had indeed experience of oppression, but were not yet in anything like imminent danger from a foreign foe.

As to the aim and value of the book; the former of these will have been already gathered from the comments which we have made. The writer desires to exhort his countrymen who are of the "Dispersion." By tracing the character and virtuous life of one living far from Palestine, but maintaining in a distant land the love for Jerusalem and devotion to religious duty, which was incumbent on every Jew, he encourages those in a like position to exhibit, however adverse their condition, similar sentiments and equal fidelity to the faith of their fathers. The book has always been considered as a noteworthy picture of Jewish piety. Placing it within the limits of time which we have already indicated, we possess in it an attractive sketch not only of uprightness and benevolence of conduct, but also of domestic life. "The parting of Tobias and his mother, the consolation of Tobit (**5.** 17–22), the affection of Raguel (**7.** 4–8), the anxious waiting of the parents (**10.** 1–7), the son's return (**9.** 4, **11**), and even the unjust suspiciousness of the sorrow of Tobit and Anna (**2.** 11–14), are painted with a simplicity worthy of the best times of the patriarchs. Almost every family relation is touched upon with natural grace and affection : husband and wife, parent and child, kinsmen near or distant, master and servant, are presented in the most varied action, and always with lifelike power (**2.** 13, 14 ; **5.** 17–22 ; **7.** 10 ; **8.** 4–8 ; **10.** 1–7 ; **11.** 1–13 ; **1.** 22 ; **2.** 10 ; **7.** 3–8 ; **5.** 14, 15 ; **12.** 1–5, etc.). Prayer hallows the whole conduct of life (**4.** 19 ; **6.** 17 ; **8.** 5–8, etc.) ; and even in distress there is confidence that in the end all will be well (**4.** 6, 14, 19), though there is no clear anticipation of a future personal existence (**3.** 6)."*

---

* Smith's *Dict. of Bible*, Article "Tobit" (Bp. Westcott).

When we regard Tobit as a book intended to convey special teaching and edification, and compare it with parts of the Jewish Canon, at least two points of contrast present themselves.*

1. When we ask ourselves, How is the problem of suffering dealt with here compared with the Book of Job? we see that there is a marked difference in treatment. In Tobit, prayer, fasting, and good works are inculcated. If these are observed, all will be well. The matter may be left in God's hands, and He will at once intervene, summoning, if needful, miracle to His aid. In Job, on the other hand, it is seen that the matter cannot thus be settled offhand. The problem is a much more complicated one. Not only may suffering exist in combination with innocence, but that combination is not warranted to be dissolved in a prompt and effectual manner, either by the intervention of supernatural aid or in any other manner. The soul of the afflicted is racked with distress, as his body is with pain. He is left full of perplexity, if not of despair. Deliverance is not to be had at his beck, but only in God's good time, when the sufferer has confessed that his arraignment of the Divine Justice was the utterance of things that he understood not; things too wonderful for him, that he knew not (Job 42. 3).

2. As regards miracles, we cannot of course lay down any hard and fast rule as to the occasions on which Divine interposition may fitly be expected to occur. Nevertheless the character of the miraculous occurrences related in Tobit differs from the presentation of the supernatural as set forth generally in the Canonical writings. The study of miracles in their connexion with special needs, special persons, or special epochs of Old Testament history, serves to convince us

---

* For the thoughts of the next two paragraphs, see Smith's *Dict. of Bible, l.c.*

that it is incongruous that for such persons and in such circumstances as are here depicted, miracles, and in particular miracles of the character of those here alleged, should be permitted to occur.

In all ages of the Church the beauty of the story has procured it favour. Luther's words* have often been quoted "Is it history? then it is a holy (*feinheilig*) history. Is it fiction? then it is truly beautiful, wholesome, and profitable fiction, the production of a skilled poet." From the Church of England it has met with special honour. One of her Homilies † even refers to 4. 10, as the teaching of the Holy Ghost in Scripture. In the unrevised Lectionary it was read from the evening of Sept. 27 to Oct. 4. We find in one of the petitions of the Litany an adaptation of the Vulgate version of 3. 3 ("Remember me, and look on me, take not vengeance on me for my sins and mine ignorances, and the sins of my fathers").

Similarly, in the preface to the Marriage Service, we have an adaptation of the Vulgate of 6. 17; while (as has been already remarked) two of the Offertory Sentences are taken from this book (4. 7-9).

PLACE OF WRITING AND ORIGINAL LANGUAGE.

These two questions are connected in such a way that our inability to answer the former leaves intact the obscurity which from other causes rests upon the latter problem. The book professes to be written in Assyria. That it was actually written (*a*) in some country further east than Palestine, (*b*) in Egypt, (*c*) in Palestine itself, are theories which have all had their advocates. And corresponding to these three views are the theories as to its primary form, whether Aramaic, Greek, or

---

* Preface to Tobit in his translation of the Bible.
† *Of Almsdeeds*, second part, towards the beginning.

Hebrew. For a very full discussion of the whole subject the reader may be referred to the *Speaker's Commentary*. *

The following is a brief summary of the case. There are extant two forms of the text in Hebrew. Both of these may for our present purpose be dismissed from further consideration, as it is clear that neither of them represents the original form of the book. The Codex Sinaiticus, closely allied to which is a form of Old Latin text, as given by Sabatier, † and two other texts ‡ represent the Greek form of the book. Further, there is a Syriac version, based upon the Greek. But St. Jerome in his preface to the Book of Tobit states, in relating his method of procedure, his use of a "Chaldee" manuscript. § Such a MS. has only lately been forthcoming for us. It agrees on the whole with the (Greek) Sinaitic Codex. But the question still remains, Is one derived from the other, and, if so, which can claim the priority? Now the Greek text (in agreement in this respect with the Syriac and the Old Latin) when speaking of Tobit uses the first person from the beginning of the book as far as 3. 6, and afterwards the third. The "Chaldee" and the Vulgate employ the third person throughout. In such a case the presumption is that uniformity is the result of the desire for smoothness, and so probabilities point to the harsher form as the older. If then we are to admit the claims of our existing "Chaldee" version to represent the original, it can only be by considering it as the descendant of an earlier "Chaldee" text which used both persons in the above-mentioned manner. Moreover, it was evidently believed in St. Jerome's time (he himself, no mean critic, sharing that belief) that the Greek or Latin texts extant were unsatisfactory as compared with the "Chaldee."

---

* "Introd. to Tobit," Excursus I.   † *Op. cit*, i.
‡ Viz. that of the Vatican and Alexandrian Codices and the text of certain cursive MSS.
§ *See* p. 132 *supra*.

It is often possible to decide by internal evidence the question whether a Greek text is or is not a translation from a Semitic original. No doubt on this point could exist when we examine *e.g.* the Greek of 1 Maccabees or Ecclesiasticus, or, speaking generally, of the LXX. of O.T. Books. The abundant use of constructions and idioms suggested by a Hebrew original determine the matter beyond controversy. But as we saw in dealing with First [Third] Esdras, it is not always so obvious. And this is the case here. The Greek version, in the opinion of some, furnishes clear proof of its Semitic source, in that of others the direct reverse. But the majority of critics agree to uphold a Semitic original. If this be granted, and that the work was therefore composed in Palestine, it will be further probable that that original was Hebrew somewhat Aramaicised. On this last point, however (viz. the amount to which Classical Hebrew was thus diluted), in the absence of any clear indications as to date, we cannot speak with confidence.

4. The Books of Maccabees.

Besides the two books of the Apocrypha which appear under this title, there are three others, which have never found admission to the Canon, called respectively the Third, Fourth, and Fifth Books of Maccabees. It must not, however, for a moment be supposed that the two, much less the five books, which derive their name from the Maccabean family, form a chronological sequence after the manner of the Books of Kings or Chronicles. " If the historic order were observed, the so-called *third* book would come *first*, the *fourth* would be an appendix to the *second*, which would retain its place, and the *first* would come last." *

---

* Smith's *Dict. of Bible*, Article " Maccabees, Books of " (Bp. Westcott).

To this we may add that the Fifth Book above referred to would also with a fair probability retain its position, chronologically speaking. It is, however, a compilation from the First and Second Books, supplemented by Josephus. The history contained in it begins with the attempt of Heliodorus (*see* page 28), ends with the birth of our Lord, and is of no independent historical value. Putting this last aside therefore, a brief justification of the above suggested change of order is found in the periods of time which the four books respectively cover, or (in the case of the Fourth Book) in the nature of the work itself. This will appear, when we mention that the Third Book is devoted to a narrative of events which are by way of having long preceded Maccabean times properly so called, and that the Second Book also commences its story a few years earlier than the opening of the main account as given in the First Book. The Fourth Book, while relating in common with 2 Maccabees one of the most stirring incidents of the contest (the death of Eleazar, and of the seven brothers and their mother), proceeds to make use of the story as the basis of a philosophical discourse.

Although, therefore, from the point of view of the historical sequence of events, the order of these books, as commonly numbered, is not in strictness accurate, we may well be content to leave that order unchanged, not only from considerations of convenience, but also because it so happens that the present order appears to coincide both with their respective dates of composition (so far as these can be ascertained) and their comparative value.

We may now proceed to notice the books in detail.

The First Book of Maccabees.

The book relates the history of the most stirring times in the post-Captivity period. It covers a space of 40 years (175–

135 B.C.), and gives us the account (*a*) of the successful revolt under the noble and unselfish Judas Maccabeus, (*b*) of the continuance of the struggle under his brave but less scrupulous and more self-seeking brother Jonathan, (*c*) of the consolidation and ordering of the state thus delivered, a work carried out by Simon, who appears perhaps, if we look at him carefully, as the noblest of the three brothers. The book presents us with a remarkable picture of heroic and at the same time skilful patriotism, advancing against great odds to the rescue of a nation from grievous oppression, and further exhibiting itself in wise counsels and well-considered and successful political dispositions. "The history, in this aspect, presents a kind of epic unity. The passing allusion to the achievements of after times (16. 23, 24) relieves the impression caused by the murder of Simon. But at his death the victory was already won : the life of Judaism had mastered the tyranny of Greece." *

The arrangement of the matter is orderly and well proportioned. A short introductory notice (1. 1–9) describes the establishment of Greek dominion in Asia generally, and so, in particular, in Palestine. Then follow in detail the action of Antiochus and his sympathisers in Judea, the revolt under Mattathias, and the conduct of affairs under his three sons just named. There is one insertion of the nature of a parenthesis, descriptive of the Roman power, as viewed by a Palestinian Jew of the period (8. 1–16).

The narrative, thus well-ordered and marked by a sense of proportion,† appears in almost all cases trustworthy. Not only does it receive a general support from secular historians,‡ where their paths cross that of the writer, but the internal

---
* *Dict. of Bible*, ii. p 171.
† The account of the exploits of Judas, although occupying but a small space in the whole period treated of, yet is dealt with at a length suited to its comparative importance (3. 1–9. 22).
‡ Polybius, Appian, and others.

evidence points to the same conclusion. He is careful to date important events from the Seleucid era (312 B.C.). The miraculous element is conspicuously absent (contrast the abundant display of it in the Second Book when dealing with the same events), and there is a general soberness of style, which betokens truth. We observe no hesitation in recording the defeats and defects of the people, their misdeeds, and their despondency. Abuse is not poured upon the enemies of the Jews. It is quite exceptional, when Antiochus himself is called "a sinful root" (1. 10). The writer refrains from reference to the profligacy of Alexander Balas, when opportunity presented itself for so doing. Nor are the Syrian generals or other opponents of the Jews spoken of with anything like severity.

At the same time, we can here and there detect failures in strict accuracy.* Where the writer is speaking of matters relating to foreign nations, his information is not always to be accepted. His account of Alexander the Great as appointing his successors (1. 6) is clearly unfounded, and the same may be said of such statements for example as that the Roman Senate consisted of 320 persons, that they sat every day, and that the Romans committed "their government to one man year by year, that he should rule over them." † These mistakes, it need hardly be said, in no way weaken the testimony which the book bears to the value of the writer's evidence when it has to do with matters with which he was naturally familiar.

STYLE.

Speaking generally, the character of the composition is that of a plain, straightforward narrative, uninfluenced by art and by attempts at adornment. From time to time, however,

---

* Reference has already been made to this feature as regards numbers, *e.g.* 7. 46; 11. 45-47.
† 1 Macc. 8. 15. 16.

especially in chaps. **1–7**, we find exceptional passages. The writer's feelings here lead him into flights of rhetoric, as he warms with the contemplation of the nature of that which he is recording. The account of mourning in Israel when Antiochus rifled the Sanctuary (**1**. 25–28, 37–40) is a case in point, and others occur in subsequent chapters. The only such passage found later than ch. **7** is in **14**. 8–15. Specimens again of poetical language are the lamentation of Mattathias (**2**. 7–13), his dying words (**2**. 49–68), and several passages in chaps. **3, 4, 7**. From the general features of both the earlier and later portions of the book it may safely be inferred that it is the work of one and the same man throughout. As evidence of this commentators have pointed to the uniformity of style, minuteness in the matter of dates, and the careful abstinence from the use of the Divine Name.

Place, Sources, and Date.

We should naturally think of Palestine as the country in which would first be put into writing a history of events such as are here recounted. When we add to this the consideration that the original language of the book was almost certainly Hebrew,* we may safely accept that country as the place where it first saw the light. At the same time we may feel assured that no long interval elapsed before the Jewish colony in Egypt would demand and receive a Greek translation of a work to them of such thrilling interest.

As regards sources (besides those which may be alluded to in **9**. 22), the writer quotes various original authorities in the shape of speeches and letters. Doubtless in the case of some of these the substance is all that has been preserved, and we

---

* *See* remarks on the language later.

may well assume the existence of that amount of manipulation of such sources which was considered permissible by ancient historians. We must also remember that, even granting their substantial accuracy, many of them must be from the nature of the case versions of versions, *i.e.* rendered first into Hebrew by the writer, and then into Greek by the translator of the book. Further, it has been thought that the fact, just now noticed, of the presence of a considerable amount of rhetorical and poetical matter in the account of the achievements of Judas, as compared with the scantiness of such passages in later parts of the book, points to the use of some earlier narrative of the exploits of the great Maccabean leader. But it has been sufficiently answered that the most heroic deeds contained in the history " were those of Mattathias and Judas: the latter phases of the war were comparatively commonplace. Thus the style merely varies with the subject-matter." *

For the determination of the date we have evidence which enables us to fix tolerably narrow limits. On the one hand, the writer speaks of a monument which Simon on his accession (143 B.C.) erected to the memory of his father and brethren, adding that it was to be seen " unto this day " (**13. 30**). Even allowing for the unsettled state of the country, and the consequent violence which such an erection might meet with, the expression has been thought to imply that at least thirty years may well be supposed to have intervened. Such a supposition would shew that the book was not written earlier than 113 B.C. On the other hand, the terms in which the writer refers to John Hyrcanus (**16. 23, 24**), evidently the reflection of those in which deceased rulers are spoken of in the Books of Kings and Chronicles, are thought to indicate that the book was not written during that ruler's lifetime (ob. 105 B.C.). This,

---

* *Speaker's Comm.*, " Introd. to 1 Macc." (G. Rawlinson), p. 380.

however, is not a certain inference, and the author's statement in the same passage that the doings of Hyrcanus were " written in the chronicles of his high priesthood, from the time that he was made high priest after his father," may be meant to assign the reason why it was not thought necessary to continue a narrative of events the official record of which was now available. We have, however, a clear ulterior limit of date to guide us. The book was certainly written before the capture of Jerusalem by Pompey (63 B.C.). At no time subsequent to that event could there have been so complete an absence of hostile feeling towards Rome. The tone of ch. 8. 12–16 is clearly not that of one acquainted with the bloodshed and generally stern treatment meted out at that time to his countrymen.

Estimate of its Value, as Compared with Canonical Books.

The writer was clearly an orthodox Jew in all respects. He had the utmost reverence for the Law, ceremonial as well as moral, and deplored all violations of its commands, the desecration of the Sabbath, the eating of unclean meats, as well as the pollution of the altars, and the idolatry practised by many of his countrymen. In spite of the calamities, civil and religious, which marked so great a portion of the period described in the narrative, he recognises the guidance of Divine Providence throughout. Nevertheless his way of dealing with the providential element as overruling the affairs of the Chosen People is different from that to which we are accustomed in the historical books of the Old Testament. Not only have we none of the miraculous element, which enters so freely into the story of the same events in 2 Maccabees, but there is a less explicit reference of success or failure to God's disposition of the affairs of men. Thoroughly religiously-minded as the writer is, he is evidently reticent upon matters of faith, partly, perhaps, by nature, partly from training and circumstances. A remarkable feature of the book is the absence from his narrative of the name of God, an absence amounting in some cases to an absolute awkwardness in expression. Where necessary, the word "heaven" or the like is the substitute. It has been thought that this is not merely a forecast of the Rabbinic refusal in later times to pronounce the specially Sacred Name,* inasmuch as the Maccabean writer equally avoids all names for the Supreme Being. It may probably be connected with a fact which we notice in his pages, and which stands in strong contrast to the Book of Enoch and the "Psalms of Solomon," dating, as we shall see, from about the same period as the book we are now considering. While they are full of the strongest Messianic hopes as regards the uplifting of the nation and its deliverance from long oppression, this book, on the contrary, while recognising (9. 27) that it was long "since the time that no prophet appeared unto them," merely looks forward † to the coming of the prophet who shall decide such questions as how to deal with the stones of the altar which had been profaned in the persecution of Epiphanes, or impose permanent regulations for the civil and ecclesiastical government of the Jewish state. One would have thought that the successful struggle against external tyranny and oppression would, in this writer as in the other cases just referred to, have kindled a more fervid expression of Messianic expectation. But it is not so. "Like the Book of Esther, its greatest merit is that it is throughout inspired by the faith to which it gives no definite expression, and shews in deed, rather than in words, both the action of Providence and sustaining trust in His power." ‡

Ceremonial observances, as we are aware, had begun to loom large in the minds of many at this time. In the minutiæ of

---

* "Jehovah." † 4. 46; 14. 41. ‡ *Dict. of Bible*, ii. 174.

outward cleansing there came to be a tendency to dwell less upon the need of purification of the heart. It is instructive to note the contrast between the teaching of the prophets of Old Testament days and the scribes who had now succeeded them as the guides of the people. "The consciousness of sin and the sense of penitence grew continually weaker in the religious life of the nation, and are virtually absent from the prayers put into the mouths of the Maccabean leaders." *

LANGUAGE.

Testimony, external and internal, combines in pointing to a Hebrew original. Origen,† enumerating the Old Testament Books by their Greek and Hebrew titles, calls this Book Σαρβὴθ Σαβαναιελ, clearly the transliteration of a Hebrew title.‡ St. Jerome, the other Hebraist among the Fathers, says :§ "The First Book of the Maccabees I found in Hebrew : the Second in Greek, a fact which can be shewn also from its style." Hebrew more or less influenced by Aramaic words and idioms is the language which a Palestinian Jew would naturally use. In fact Palestine, as far as we know, produced no Greek book at this time. The style thoroughly bears out St. Jerome's testimony. It is more strongly Hebraic than can be readily accounted for by such influence of Aramaic upon Greek idiom, as occurs, *e.g.*, in New Testament books. Further, certain passages are quoted,‖ where difficulties exist, only explicable on

---

* *Cambridge Bible for Schools,* "1 Macc. *Introd.*" p. 47, where the contrast in this respect is pointed out between this book and Nehemiah (1. 6, 7; 9. 2, 3, 16, etc.), and Daniel (9. 3-20), the last named book not in this point at any rate indicating the Maccabean date which is claimed for it by many.

† In Eusebius, *Hist. Eccles.* vi. 25.

‡ The sense is obscure. It has been variously explained as (*a*) the prince of the house, which God has raised up; (*b*) the sceptre (*i.e.* government) of the prince of the sons of God; or, perhaps best, (*c*) as a combination of two alternative readings, viz., prince of the *house* of God, and, prince of the *sons* of God.

§ *Prol. Gal.* to Kings.

‖ *e.g.* 6. 1; 11. 28; 14. 5.

the hypothesis that they are errors arising in the course of translation from one to the other language.*

The Second Book of Maccabees.

The earlier part of the book is by no means homogeneous with the main narrative. In chap. 1. 1–9, and 1. 10—2. 18, we are given two letters supposed to be written by the Palestinian Jews to their co-religionists in Egypt, inviting them to attend the festival of the "Dedication," and to shew thereby their sympathy with the victories of Judas Maccabeus, commemorated at that feast. The letters are clumsy forgeries, such as were numerous at that period in the literary society of Alexandria. Thereupon follows a Preface or Introduction (2. 19–32) to the history which follows. With chap. 3. 1 the main part of the book commences, and relates the history of the period from the attack upon the Temple by Heliodorus, the minister of the Syrian monarch Seleucus IV. (ob. 175 B.C.) to the victory of Judas Maccabeus over Nicanor (160 B.C.). It describes, often with much amplitude of detail, the persecution by Antiochus Epiphanes, the Maccabean struggles and successes, and the continuation of the contest to the time just mentioned.

Sources of the Book.

Besides the letters above referred to, a lost work by a certain Jason of Cyrene in five books furnished the writer, as he tells us himself (2. 23), with the materials which he has thus abridged. Traces have been found of the fivefold division of the original in the shape of a phrase seeming each time to mark the close of a section of the narrative (3. 40 ; 7. 42 ; 10. 9 ; 13. 26 ; 15. 37). It has been conjectured that Jason is to be

---

* Both books of Maccabees are absent from the Vatican MS. (B). The 2nd book also lacking in the Codex Sinaiticus.

identified with the son of Eleazar, mentioned (1 Macc. 8. 17) as sent to Rome on a mission by Judas, after he had overthrown and slain Nicanor. This would fall in with the cessation of the history at that date, as Jason's design in writing may have been to give only those events which took place while he was still not more distant at any rate than Egypt from the scene of the contest. However this may be, we may well suppose that Jason, a Cyrenian by birth, lived and wrote in Alexandria, where he would find a large public interested in such a work, in the shape of the Jewish community in that city.

Date.

If we allow a space of not less than twenty years between the composition of Jason's work and the abridgement which we are now considering, even so, inasmuch as we are unaware of the time at which that work was composed, we cannot speak with any kind of certainty as to the date of the abridgement. The latest event mentioned in 2 Maccabees itself (**1. 10**), if the reading there "fourscore and eighth" (R.V.) be correct, is in the year of the Seleucid era corresponding to 124 B.C. If, however, we should read there * *forty-eighth,* then the latest date mentioned in the book is that which occurs three verses earlier (**1. 7**), which corresponds to 143 B.C. On the other hand, some would place Jason's history as late as 100 B.C., with a corresponding shifting of the date of the epitomised work.† If we enquire as to the sources from which Jason himself derived his materials, the general character of the narrative will perhaps help us to answer.

---

* With Ewald, supported by two MSS.
† The supposed references in the Epistle to the Hebrews (11. 35, "not accepting their deliverance." Comp. 2 Macc. 6. 21 ff., 7. 24 ff.) may be only to the tradition and not to the actual book. Josephus seems to have been unacquainted with 2 Maccabees. Not so apparently Philo, *Quod omnis probus liber* (Mangey's ed. ii. 459). See Schürer, *op. cit.,* II. iii. 214. However, it was in any case written before the destruction of Jerusalem (*see* 15, 37).

CHARACTER OF THE NARRATIVE AS COMPARED WITH THE FIRST BOOK.

We here notice first (in connexion with the remark at the end of the last paragraph) that in the parts of the history which are covered by both books in common, there is in this book, speaking generally, a greater copiousness of detail, combined with much inaccuracy and exaggeration. The miraculous element, conspicuously absent from the First Book, here abounds. Divine interpositions on the side of the Jews are of frequent occurrence. In many cases the numbers mentioned are evidently greatly exaggerated. These are precisely the features which would arise if we suppose that Jason took his narrative from the oral accounts given by eye-witnesses, but possibly in some cases passing through several stages before reaching him. As Schürer remarks : * "The unhistorical notice, **15**. 37, that after the victory over Nicanor Jerusalem remained in the hands of the Hebrews, can indeed only have been written by one at a great distance from the events. But, on the other hand, this scarcely affects Jason, but his epitomiser."

It will be seen from what has been already said, that in the matter of trustworthiness this book compares unfavourably with the preceding. Nevertheless, in several cases it gives us details which we have no reason to doubt on points which have not been dealt with in the earlier book.† And in any case it supplies us with valuable information concerning that period for which it is our sole authority, viz., the few years which preceded the reign of Antiochus Epiphanes (3. 1—4. 6).

The style of the book is also in strong contrast with that of the earlier one. In the main it is marked by a display of rhetoric such as doubtless approved itself to the readers for whom

---

* *Op. cit.*, II. iii. 213.   † *e.g.* 10. 12, 13; 12. 3-5; 14. 19-26.

it was intended. False antitheses, farfetched similes, and elaborately wrought sentences are of frequent occurrence, not only in that portion of the work which is avowedly taken from Jason, but in that much smaller portion (2. 19-32, 15. 38, 39) which we may assume to be the writer's unaided composition. We may thus conclude that proportionate to the extent in which these same features present themselves in the main part of the narrative may be held to be the degree in which the writer has worked up, and not merely reproduced, the materials furnished him by the earlier author. Examples and passages where in all probability we have Jason's own style, as indicated by the above-mentioned test, are **3.** 4, 5, 7-11, 35-40 ; **4.** 3-10, etc.

Although rhetoric and a striving after effect are prominent features of the style, there are yet passages which exhibit the utmost roughness. They can only be likened to hasty notes, taken down with the intention to expand them later, or to the crudest efforts of a tyro in literature.

Religious Character of the Book.

The writer is an orthodox Jew, who, if he writes from Alexandria, by no means desires to put forward the possession of a temple at Leontopolis as an excuse for slackness in the duty of going up to Feasts at Jerusalem (1. 9, 18). In fact, it is his strong feeling on this point which forms the only reason apparent for his prefixing to his history such irrelevant matter as the letters which compose the opening sections of the book. His reverence for and admiration of the Temple and all things and persons belonging to it is very conspicuous, both from the epithets of honour which he so frequently bestows upon it (**2.** 19, 22 ; **3.** 12 ; **5.** 15, etc.), and from his full accounts of the attempts made to rifle it of its treasures (**3.** 6-35; **4.** 32, 39;

5. 15-21), and its deliverance on more than one occasion (10. 1-8; 14. 31-36 ; 15. 17-36).

We have already spoken of his readiness to introduce miraculous manifestations of Providential care. His readiness also, in contrast to his predecessor, to mention the name of God, is in harmony with the care with which he points the moral of his story, by shewing that signal punishment is the lot of the wicked, that the sufferings of the holy are for chastisement and purification, that in any case they may look forward to a joyful resurrection (7. 9, 14 ; 12 43), and that even in this life God maintains their cause and grants them prosperity as a consequence of holiness of living and devotion to His cause. The dead, too, may obtain advantage from the prayers of the living (12. 44).

Language.

There can be no question in this case of a Hebrew original, except possibly in the case of the two letters (1. 1—2. 18). Hebraisms are of rare occurrence. Greek idioms abound, although there are many words unknown to classical Greek, and many others employed in new senses.*

The Third Book of Maccabees.

This and the Fourth Book need not long detain us. The Third Book deals with a visit of one of the Ptolemies to Jerusalem, his violation of the sanctity of the Temple, the supernatural punishment which came upon him, his consequent hatred of the Jews, and attempt to exterminate those who

---

* For lists see *Dict. of Bible,l.c.* (reproduced in *Speaker's Comm.*, " Introd. to 2 Macc.." p. 540). For conspectus, with dates, of the comparative length of the periods covered by the two books, see Chronological Scheme of the History contained in 1 and 2 Maccabees, with references arranged in parallel columns, in *Speaker's Comm., l.c.,* p. 546. N.B.—In that conspectus opposite the date 151-150 B.C. read for " Demetrius " Alexander.

lived in Egypt, the answer to prayer, the melting of the king's wrath, and the destruction which, intended for themselves, overtook their enemies. The king to whose reign the story attributes these events is Ptolemy IV. (Philopator, 221–205 B.C.). The only foundation for the narrative, however, is furnished us by Josephus, who * tells a somewhat similar story (without any such amplitude of detail), as referring to Ptolemy IX. (Energetes II. or Physcon, 146–117 B.C.). A festival, stated by him to have been instituted in commemoration of this deliverance,† doubtless points to the substratum of fact, whatever it was, upon which the legendary matter contained in this book was based.‡

The book was most probably written in Alexandria. The date is quite uncertain. While the 1st century B.C. is very possible,§ others ‖ have seen a hidden reference to the times of Caligula (37–41 A.D.).

Perhaps the most interesting feature in connexion with the book as regards our present purpose is the fact that it " offers an instructive contrast to the Book of Esther, with which it is closely connected both in its purpose and in the general character of its incidents. In both a terrible calamity is averted by faithful prayer; royal anger is changed to royal favour; and the punishment designed for the innocent is directed to the guilty. But here the likeness ends. The divine reserve, which is the peculiar characteristic of Esther, is exchanged in 3 Maccabees for rhetorical exaggeration: and once again the words of inspiration stand ennobled by the presence of their later counterpart." ¶

---

* *C. Apion.* ii. 5. † Mentioned also in 3 Macc. 6. 36.

‡ Dr. Mahaffy, however, (*Empire of the Ptolemies*, p. 269) considers that this historical substratum has to do with the reign of the earlier of the two Ptolemies mentioned.

§ Not earlier, for the author is acquainted (6. 6) with the Greek additions to Daniel. *See* below.

‖ *e.g.* Ewald, *History of Israel*, v. 469.

¶ Smith's *Dict. of Bible*, Article " 3 Maccabees " (Bp. Westcott), p. 179.

The Fourth Book of Maccabees.

So far as it is true that this book deals with the causes of the persecution by Antiochus, and relates the deaths of Eleazar and the rest, its claim to the title is valid. Nevertheless a large part of it differs much from the other books in subject-matter, being an application of these events to the purpose of encouraging the readers to emulate the virtues of the sufferers. It points out the nobility of martyrdom for a righteous cause, the stern force of duty, the power of reason, and holds out clearly the hope of rewards and punishments in a future life in accordance with men's conduct here.

It is composed in vigorous but very ornate Greek, and contains many peculiar but well formed words.

It was evidently written during some troublous time, and it has been conjectured that its date is circ. 67 A.D. when, under Vespasian, there began to be realised the impending overthrow of the Jewish state. At any rate it was written before the destruction of Jerusalem.

As regards the Fifth Book of the Maccabees it does not seem needful to add anything to what we have said above in the sentences of general introduction. *

5. The Rest of the Chapters of the Book of Esther.

These additions consist of further details, intended to be fitted into different parts of the story of Esther, as given us in the Canonical work of that name. When we examine them in detail, as given in the English versions, we find that, besides their position, grouped together as a separate work, there is also much disorder apparent in the earlier part of the arrange-

---

* For these books in an English dress the reader may be referred to Cotton's *The Five Books of Maccabees*, Oxford, 1832.

ment. For this disorder the Greek version is not responsible. The history, as given there, is continuous and complete, making a consistent narrative. But St. Jerome, after translating the Canonical book from the Hebrew into Latin, appended these additions, which he had found in the Greek, but not in the Hebrew. He began with that which forms the opening additional matter in the English (10. 4–13), and placed it in its natural order as a continuation of the last part of the Hebrew book.

Next after it he put the note which has been thought to supply the date of the Greek version (Eng. 11. 1), and then arranged the remaining additions in order, with indications where they were to be respectively inserted. These indications were in the course of time swept away, and the arrangement in the English editions is the result.

It seems scarcely possible to doubt that these additions are considerably later than the Hebrew text, and they are not translated from a Semitic original. In support of the opposite opinion a somewhat fanciful conjecture has been adduced. It is supposed that the great popularity of the festival of Purim, and the emphasis laid upon the ritual observances in commemoration of the Jewish deliverance from Haman, had early called for a fuller description of the circumstances of its origin, to be used for public reading in the synagogues. To that end, the additional chapters were written, some even said by Mordecai himself.* But (it is continued) the grosser part of the festal observances was overdone, and the excesses indulged in demanded the abbreviation of the record, and the elimination from it of the name of God, as unfit to be on the lips of men at a time when free rein was given to carnal pleasures. From this there results the Hebrew Esther in contrast to the

---

* Arguing from Esth. 9. 22, 23, a very insecure foundation for the opinion.

longer form of the book. The conjecture has little or no trustworthy support.*

The last words of 11. 1,† whatever may be their exact sense, have plainly no reference to the translation of the whole of these pieces into Greek. St. Jerome denies their existence in Hebrew, and the character and idiom of some of them is utterly unlike a version from an original in that tongue.

Date.

In the fourth year of the reign of Ptolemy and Cleopatra, Dositheus, who said he was a priest and Levite, and Ptolemy his son, brought the epistle of Purim here set forth, which they said was the same, and that Lysimachus the son of Ptolemy, that was in Jerusalem, had interpreted it." ‡

This extract from the "additions" is by no means so explicit as its wording might at first suggest. We have to choose among four Ptolemies, each of whom had a queen or queen-mother named Cleopatra. Probably, however, Philometor (182–146 B.C.) is the king here meant. The "Epistle of Purim," may have been brought for use in the temple erected in his reign for Jewish worship at Leontopolis. If so, the "fourth year" was circ. 177 B.C. But, further, it is by no means clear what it was that Lysimachus had interpreted. The words may be meant as a guarantee which the learned of Palestine were alleged to have been willing to give for the genuineness of these "additions," or, as translated from a Hebrew original, they may only indicate that Lysimachus verbally explained discrepancies, real or apparent, between details as related here and in our Canonical form of the book.§ In

---

* *See* the evidence for it stated in *Speaker's Comm.* "Apocrypha," i. 362 ff.
† The verse will be noticed immediately in connexion with the question of date.
‡ 11. 1.
§ *e.g.* Haman's nationality. In 16. 10, he is a Macedonian.

either case the value of the testimony is further impaired by our uncertainty as to its date.

Whatever may be the history of the "additions" in these respects, we may well conclude that they were admitted to the Canon of the Alexandrian Jews (less rigidly conservative as regards the limits of Scripture than their Palestinian brethren), owing to the interest felt in the period with which they dealt, from the desire to emphasize the care which God exercised over His people in the land of the stranger, and perhaps also in order to compensate by the frequent introduction of God's name for its conspicuous absence from the older book. Josephus seems to have accepted not only these* but some other additions as well to the Hebrew form of the story, as his account contains further particulars, e.g. additional passages read to Ahasuerus from the chronicles of the kingdom.

6. Additions to the Canonical Book of Daniel.

The tendency to the construction of stories with a moral or religious purpose (Haggadah) from time to time exhibited itself in a special way: viz. by fastening on some stirring expression in the Scriptures, and by the exercise of that fancy which converts the abstract into the concrete. Thus some striking personality in history, or the obscure allusion to persons or events more than half forgotten, or the desire to make the deeds or powers of the owner of a name correspond with its real or supposed derivation, set the imagination to weave a story on the basis thus suggested.

The three short Apocryphal books, which are included under the above description, form specimens of fiction which has had this tendency for its genesis. We now proceed briefly to deal with them singly.

---

* *Ant.* xi. 6, 1, etc.

(I.) The Song of the Three Holy Children.

Three Old Testament passages suggest themselves, any or all of which may possibly have been in the mind of the writer when he was led to compose this song.* Various passages in the Talmud shew the hold which a story of the kind had upon the Jewish mind, and how men went back in fancy to the days of Abraham himself for a conspicuous example of this form of attempted compulsion to idol-worship, inflicted upon the godly at the hands of the unbeliever, as well as the display of the frustration of his design, and the thanksgivings of the faithful at the open demonstration of the protection exercised by the Almighty over His chosen.†

The hymn has been used in the Christian Church since the 4th century, and although it has been charged with vain repetition, monotony, and dulness in its constant refrain "praise and exalt him above all for ever" (Rev. Vers.), yet it may be well answered there is a certain effectiveness in the very recurrence, likened, as it has been, to the beat of the wave on the shore, and suggesting "to the imagination the amplitude and splendour of God's world, and the sublimity of the universal chorus of praise." ‡

(II.) The History of Susanna.

This and the following "addition" may be said to deserve that title more accurately than the preceding, as they do not claim to form an integral part of the history as related in the Canonical Daniel, but are rather of the nature of appendices.

---

* Ps. 66. 12 ("We went through fire," etc.), Is. 43. 2 ("When thou walkest through the fire," etc.), Zech. 3. 2 ("Is not this a brand plucked out of the fire?").

† For details see *Speaker's Comm.*, "Apocrypha," ii. 306 f.

‡ *Speaker's Comm., l. c.* (C. J. Ball), p. 307. For the question of the original language of the three stories, additions to the Book of Daniel, see remarks on the last of them (Bel and the Dragon), p. 165 *infra*.

Much has been written as to the purpose with which this story was composed, and the sources from which it may be drawn. Jewish tradition, according to Origen, identifies the two elders with the false prophets Ahab and Zedekiah,* and Susanna's husband Joakim with Jehoiachin (the last king but one of Judah) in the time of his captivity at Babylon. Various passages in later Jewish writings, given at length in the *Speaker's Commentary*,† are considered by him to throw light upon the tale, so far as it concerns the conduct of the two elders, while he considers the main purpose of the romance to have been the support of Pharisaic principles on the subject of the execution of false witnesses, as opposed to the more merciful view of the Sadducees.‡ According to him, therefore, the book is the product of the time when the struggle between the two parties as to this point was at its height (94–89 B.C.), viz. during the rule of Alexander Jannaeus, and in support of the views of Simon ben Shatach. § "The contrast is between two kinds of criminal procedure, which are represented, not by a dry general description, but by a concrete instance of their actual working." ‖

Others ¶ prefer simply to see in the story a further illustration of the wisdom ascribed to Daniel. "The Judgment of Daniel," as one of the titles by which the book was known, accords with this view. The last two verses in the LXX. (62, 63) seem to regard the work as written for the purpose of glorifying youth at the expense of age, and in order to maintain among them the spirit of wisdom and piety.**

---

* See Jer. 29. 20–23.
† ii. 325. Mr. Ball adduces as his authority for the elaboration of his view Brüll, in the *Jahrbücher für Jüdische Geschichte u. Literatur*, Frankf. a. M. 1877.
‡ See p. 73 *supra*.
§ See *Pirke Aboth*, i. 9.
‖ *Speaker's Comm.*, l. c., p. 328.
¶ Bp. Westcott in Smith's *Dict. of Bible*, Article "Daniel, Apocryphal additions to."
** For comments on the original language see the next notice.

(III.) The History of Bel and the Dragon.

As in the case of the first of these pieces illustrative of the Jewish Haggadic literature, so here the story may be founded upon a too literalising interpretation of passages in Jeremiah relating to the overthrow of Babylon, "He hath swallowed me up like a dragon, he hath filled his maw with my delicates," "I will do judgement upon Bel in Babylon, and I will bring forth out of his mouth that which he hath swallowed up," "his molten image is falsehood and there is no breath in them. They are vanity, a work of delusion : in the time of their visitation they shall perish."*

The Babylonian captivity seems to have been a period on which the mind of the Jew loved in later days to dwell. Stories of God's care for His people, the contrast between His omnipotence and the futility of idol-worship, the marks of His favour, as shewn to His faithful followers in that season of national depression—all such narratives found a wide circle of appreciative readers, and doubtless did not lose in the telling.

It is doubtful to what extent Babylonian myths on the subject of dragons and sea monsters may have influenced in this case the form of the story. It has been connected by some † with the myth describing the overthrow by the Solar god Belmerodach of Tiamat, who represented the powers of darkness or chaos.

The legend, though obviously without any claim to represent authentic history, is an interesting specimen of the tales which grew up round the figure of Daniel in the Jewish mind.

---

* Jer. 51. 34, 44, 17, 18.
† See *Speaker's Comm.*, "Apocrypha," ii. p. 346 ff., for illustrations from these sources.

The title in the LXX., which tells us that the work is "from the prophecy of Habakkuk son of Joshua, of the tribe of Levi," probably arises from the part that is played in the story by the prophet Habakkuk (*vv*. 33 ff.).

LANGUAGE.

Here we may consider jointly this and the two preceding narratives. It may be at once admitted that the Greek in all three has more or less of an Hebraic colouring. This, however, is not decisive. The phraseology of Alexandrian Jews (supposing the books to have received their present form in that great centre of literary effort) would naturally be in many cases influenced by the idioms of their sacred national tongue, even where it had ceased to be at all familiar to them as a written or spoken language. In order to determine the question whether the Greek form is original or a translation from Hebrew or Aramaic, it is therefore necessary to find such decisive proof as is afforded, *e.g.*, by errors which can only be supposed to arise in the course of rendering from the one language into the other, as, for instance, by the confusion of two similar Hebrew words, or of two meanings belonging to the same word.* And it appears that of these no certain specimens can be produced.

We must therefore have recourse to other considerations. Although it seems possible enough that such tales might first assume a written form among the Jewish circles in Egypt, yet it is very improbable that they would not likewise exist in a tongue available for Palestinian readers and hearers, and there seems an inherent probability that in the latter country they would be current at an earlier date.

Again, the fact that in the "Song" the names of the three appear in their Hebrew forms (Azarias, etc., not Shadrach, etc.),

---

* As in the cases we noticed, when dealing with First [Third] Esdras.

is, so far as it goes, an argument for the Greek being a version of an Aramaic original.

It has also been suggested * that it is improbable that the LXX. translator of Daniel would incorporate with his version of a Hebrew and Aramaic work pieces which, so far as he knew, existed only in Greek. The conjecture therefore presents itself that these Greek additions to the Canonical Daniel may represent further pieces of the Aramaic Book of Daniel which is supposed by some to be the source of the non-Hebrew parts of that Book, and to have been then introduced to fill the place of lost portions of an originally complete Hebrew work.

The names of the trees furnish a special argument in favour of a Greek original for the history of Susanna. Mr. Ball, however, points out that this by no means amounts to positive proof. He shews that it is quite possible in Hebrew, by careful choice of names of trees together with terms expressing the kind of punishment to be inflicted, to produce corresponding plays upon words, and that therefore those of the Greek text are far "from constituting an insuperable objection to the theory of a Hebrew original." †

As Origen remarks,‡ all three books are to be found in two Greek recensions, viz. the LXX. and Theodotion. The latter differs from the former but slightly in the Song, considerably in the two latter pieces. St. Jerome admits the Greek additions from Theodotion, marked as such, into his translation of Daniel, but he is careful to declare his opinion with regard to the non-canonicity of all three books.

---

* But the force of the suggestion is much impaired by the fact that the additions to the Book of Esther (see p. 159) are almost certainly not taken from a Hebrew or Aramaic original.
† *Speaker's Comm.*, "Apocrypha," ii. 324.
‡ *Epist. ad Africanum*, chap. ii. (Migne, *Patrol.* Gr. xi. 52).

CHAPTER XIII.

OTHER PSEUDEPIGRAPHIC ADDITIONS TO THE CANONICAL LITERATURE.

1. The Book of Baruch,* with the Epistle of Jeremiah.

THE Book of Baruch consists of two parts: (*a*) an introduction (1. 1–14), followed by a confession of sin (1. 15—3. 8); (*b*) an exhortation and prophecy (3. 9—5. 9).

The introduction gives with sufficient clearness the date which the work claims for itself, viz. "the fifth year" from the date when "the Chaldeans took Jerusalem, and burnt it with fire" (1. 1). This can only refer to the taking of the city in the 11th year of Zedekiah (588 B.C.), there being no mention of burning in connexion with an earlier capture. Two questions at once arise: (i.) Are we to accept this as the genuine date of the book, and consider it to be the work of Jeremiah's faithful companion? (ii.) Is the book, as we have it, one continuous work, or composite?

Answering the latter question first, we plainly see that there is an abrupt transition from (*a*) to (*b*), as above. Moreover, the style † changes as well as the subject. While (*a*) has a strong Hebraic complexion,‡ so that a good case may be made out for considering it a version from a Hebrew original, (*b*) is

---

* It will be seen that the conclusion to which we have come as to date would in strictness place this book outside the period we have set ourselves. Inasmuch, however, as there is not an absolute consensus of opinion on the point, we have thought it well to include it.

† The names for God are distinct in the two parts. See this worked out in *Speaker's Comm., l. c.,* p. 253.

‡ For instances in proof of this see *Speaker's Comm., l. c.,* p. 249.

much freer from Semitic idiom, and may safely be considered as having had a separate existence and authorship.

As regards the former enquiry, it may be urged on behalf of the genuineness of the book that there is no reason to deny that Baruch went from Egypt, where we leave him and Jeremiah (Jer. 43. 7), to Babylon before the date mentioned.

On the other hand, there are plain indications in (*a*) that it belongs to a later time. One such it will suffice to mention. In 1. 11 Nebuchadnezzar and "Baltasar" (Belshazzar) "his son" are spoken of as reigning jointly. Even though we were to consider Belshazzar to have been descended in the second generation from Nebuchadnezzar, through the daughter of that king,* it is impossible to believe that a resident in Babylon at the time stated could have spoken of them thus. Anyone who wrote of Belshazzar in these terms must have lived long after the Return of the exiles.†

In (*b*) also there are signs of a much later date. The words in 3. 10 ("thou art waxen old in a strange country") could not be employed as early as the fifth year after Zedekiah had entered on captivity. We are able, however, to put the matter more definitely. There is a close resemblance between Baruch 4. 36—5. 9, and the 11th of the "Psalms of Solomon." Both are in close connexion with passages in the LXX. of Isaiah and Jeremiah : yet a close examination makes it appear that they are not taken independently from these common Canonical sources, and further that the Baruch quotations or adaptations are later, as being based upon those of the "Psalms" in question. The latter are dated between 70

---

* See Driver, *Lit. of the O. T.*, Edinburgh, 1897 (6th ed.), p. 499, on this view.

† Those who make Daniel to be a book dating from the time of the Maccabees would derive an argument to the same effect from the correspondences between Daniel and Baruch. See especially Dan. 9. 7-10, compared with Baruch 1. 15-18, in which the Daniel passage is clearly the original, not the derived. On this last point see Pusey, *Lectures on Daniel*, p. 362. London, 1868 (2nd ed.).

and 40 B.C.:* it follows that this part of Baruch is posterior to that date.

Looking again at the evidence afforded by subject matter and style, we conclude that the mention of Babylon and foreign rulers is a veiled reference to the Roman overthrow of Jerusalem, and consequent break up of the nations.

And this will be true of the first, as well as of the second part of the book. "The analogy of 4 Esdras and the Apocalypse of Baruch reminds us that the Chaldean invasion and capture of Jerusalem were the accepted historical types of the final overthrow by the Romans." † Thus the object of the writer was to warn and encourage his countrymen after that final overthrow. According to the manner of writers of the time, he attributed his sentiments to a well-known name, feeling that the thoughts he penned were in substantial harmony with those of the person in whose mouth they were placed.

The book shews an absence of originality. It lacks the genuine ring of a prophet's voice. It draws much from Deuteronomy, Isaiah, Jeremiah, Daniel, and others of the Canonical writings. Yet it has at least the distinction of being the only book in the Apocrypha which is modelled upon the *prophetic* utterances of the Old Testament, and both in the faithful setting forth of the nation's sin and punishment, and in the cheering hope of deliverance with which the writer concludes, we see at any rate a later reflection of the days when the voice of the true prophet had not yet ceased to be heard in the land.

The Jews held the book in but slight esteem. ‡ When it began to be in frequent use in the Christian Church from the

---

* For full discussion of the relationship between the passages above referred to, see Ryle and James, *Psalms of Solomon*, Cambridge, 1891, p. lxxii. ff.

† Smith's *Dict. of Bible*, Article "Baruch," 2nd ed., 1893, p. 361*a*. This view seems decidedly preferable to that which would place the first part of Baruch about the close of the Persian period.

‡ For the doubtful character of the statement in the Apostolic Constitutions on this point, see *Dict. of Bible, l. c.*, p. 359.

days of Irenaeus and onwards, it was often quoted as the work of Jeremiah. Its inclusion with that prophet is probably the reason why it was not mentioned in the list of Apocryphal Books in the first (Latin) edition of the 39 Articles (1562).

The Epistle of Jeremiah,

Forming the last chapter of Baruch, represents the prophet as addressing "them which were to be led captives into Babylon by the king of the Babylonians, to certify them, as it was commanded him of God."* The composition of it was probably suggested by the letter spoken of in Jer. 29. 1, and, on the principle already noticed, the writer placed in the mouth of Jeremiah sentiments which he knew to be in harmony with his genuine utterances, perhaps also realising that it was safer thus to veil, under the name of an ancient prophet and the sufferings of a much earlier time, references to the troubles which in his own day affected his countrymen. Accordingly he borrows from Jer. 10. 1-16 as well as from other Old Testament passages.

There is a supposed reference to the Epistle in 2 Macc. 2. 1, 2, but as the writing there referred to is said (*v.* 4) to have also contained the prophet's directions with regard to the tabernacle and the ark, it would seem that the connexion is only fanciful. The "setting up" and "putting down" of kings is spoken of in the Epistle (*vv.* 34, 53, 66), and has been thought to indicate a date in the times of the later kings of Egypt and of the Seleucid dynasty.

The Epistle is divided into sections by a frequently recurring burden or refrain, "they are no gods, etc." It was doubtless written in Greek, there being no marks of a translation.

---

* Baruch 6. 1.

2. The Prayer of Manasses.

It is possible that here, as in the last case, a passage of Canonical Scripture may have supplied the basis for an apocryphal addition. Manasseh's repentance, not recorded in the history of the Book of Kings, is told in the parallel part of the Chronicles.* In particular the king "prayed," and it is added that his prayer, together with other circumstances, is "written among the acts of the Kings of Israel." †

The Greek betrays no sign of being a translation from a Hebrew original. Still, it is of course not impossible that it might be derived, with perhaps several intermediate Haggadic links in the chain, from the prayer which we may suppose to have been in the hands of the Chronicler when he recorded the repentance of the king. The Talmud has many references ‡ to Manasseh's history, adducing him as a typical example of the efficacy of repentance, although elsewhere declaring that he was one of three kings who should have no place in the world to come.

---

* 2 Chron. 33. 10–13. † *Ibid.* 18.
‡ See these in *Speaker's Comm.,* l. c., p. 363 f.

CHAPTER XIV.

GNOMIC AND PHILOSOPHICAL WRITINGS.

IT has been asked whether the Hebrew nation could rightly be said to have in their literature anything which might be called philosophy. The answer will depend much on the meaning which we assign to that word. If all that we understand by it be the effort to classify facts, to arrange given *data*, material or mental, in an orderly manner—in a word, to generalise, the Jewish claim is established. They, like other nations, generalised. They were not devoid of the universal instinct of mankind, so far as it is not borne down by the cravings for the supply of primary physical needs, to examine into the constitution of things within and around them, to group the facts of existence, and reduce confusion to order, miscellaneous facts to underlying principles, chaos to cosmos.

There was, however, as between the Jewish and the Greek philosophy, an essential difference in the manner of grappling with the problems which presented themselves. The Greek began with the world, and worked backwards towards the elementary principle, or First Cause. When that elementary principle was reached, it might indeed go by the name of God, but it was in fact either a Deity wholly outside and careless of the world, or one who was virtually identified with it. The Jew, on the contrary, starts from the other end. For him God is neither unconcerned with the world, nor immanent therein. He works in the world, although distinct from it. All branches of knowledge, as all created things, arose and exist by His will, as the sole Creator and Ruler of the world. In framing into wise saws or proverbs the results of human experience, in setting forth maxims of worldly prudence or enforcing moral lessons, or dealing with any other of the problems of human life, the Jewish teacher adopts a basis of monotheism.

Moreover, God has revealed Himself *in His Law*. That Law is immutable, and is absolute in its claims to obedience. Its authority is to be assumed. It contains, explicitly or by implication, all truth.

In accepting, however, the Law as foundation, the teachers with whom we are dealing were quite separate as a body from either priest or prophet. The three classes are carefully distinguished in the language placed in the mouths of those who desired to silence by force Jeremiah's warnings and rebukes. "The Law shall not perish from the priest, nor counsel from the wise, nor the word from the prophet." * "The wise," in this special sense, were by no means confined to the Jewish nation.†

The nature of this teaching is brought before us more or less fully in several books of the Old Testament Canon (Proverbs, certain of the Psalms and Job, Ecclesiastes) as well as in the Apocryphal Book of Ecclesiasticus. All these are distinctly national in their type, and so bear little or no trace of the influence of non-Jewish culture. With the Book of Wisdom the case is different. In it there are manifest indications of Greek philosophy, as we shall see presently in more detail. Accordingly in these two Apocryphal Books, Ecclesiasticus and Wisdom, we have conspicuous examples respectively of the Palestinian and the Alexandrian Wisdom; in other words, we have in the one the teaching of "the wise" in its purely Jewish form, in the other the blend wrought by the skilful combination of this with an eclectic teaching drawn from the schools of Greek philosophy.

---

* Jer. 18. 18.   † *See* 1 Kings 4. 30 : Jer. 49. 7 : Obad. 8.

Varied in their subject matter as are the above-named portions of Canonical and Apocryphal writings, there is one problem (to which we have already referred, when dealing with the Book of Tobit) that is common to them all—the problem of human suffering. The fact was plain that, exceptionally perhaps, but yet undoubtedly, in some cases the wicked prosper, the righteous are afflicted. It is interesting to note the different ways in which these writings deal with that ever-recurring difficulty. For this purpose we must try to place ourselves at a pre-Christian point of view. For writers of that time (with the partial exception of the author of the Book of Wisdom) this life was practically all. If the thoughts ever went further, it was only to rest upon a dim vision of an unknown beyond, a shadowy existence at best, a sleep, or a colourless prolongation of consciousness. Starting with this assumption, they had to assume also that it was in this life that the divine principles of justice were vindicated. If there was, as there must be, a law by which rewards and punishments were meted out to the righteous and the sinner, there was no room to place their operation elsewhere than in the visible world.*

At first apparently this view was regarded as satisfactory. Israel sinned and was punished for its sin, or it repented and accordingly prospered. But soon facts came into collision with the theory, both as regards the nation and individual lives. This discovery was not made as soon as would appear to us natural and inevitable. In our complicated state of society the misdoings of one class act upon others in a way that was not felt in the simpler relationship of those days. The interweaving of interests among various grades and occupa-

---

* Sanday (*Inspiration*, Bampton Lectures, London, 1893, p. 205) points out that "it was because within the sphere of revelation the sense of the presence of God was so full and so intense, that this life only seemed to suffice and it did not seem necessary to fall back upon a further life to come."

tions was practically unknown. And thus, for a while at least, the simple theory above mentioned remained unquestioned.*

We can see that it was in accordance with Providential dealings with Israel that it should be so. They thus had impressed upon their minds the truth that God was a moral Governor, and that in some way, though not in so obvious a one as they at first supposed, His general government of the world, and in particular of the Jewish nation, took cognisance of human character and actions.

This period, illustrated in the Book of Proverbs, may be called that of the acceptance of principles without recognition of exceptions. But the exceptions forced themselves into notice, and especially in the times which followed the Return. Harsh treatment by one foreign foe after another was inflicted on the nation as a whole. If any distinctions were made, it was the righteous, the faithful adherents of the Law, that fared worst. "It was the very cream of the nation that suffered the severest calamities." And so in the case of individuals. "The wicked were many times observed to be prosperous, and on the other hand the righteous were plagued every day. The first side of the difficulty is treated in such Psalms as **17, 37, 49, 73**, and others: the second side in the Book of Job."

The reply as there given was, in the main, that divine Justice would be shewn forth later, but still *in this life*. The adversity of the upright was temporary. The riches of the ungodly would make to themselves wings, and calamity would overtake him. And as facts still opposed themselves from time to time to any such absolute rule, the date for the justification of Divine Providence shifted itself nearer to the end of life.

---

* *See* remarks on the view of the question taken in the Book of Tobit as compared with Job, p. 140 *supra*.

The wicked should at any rate shew, by special sufferings or other misfortunes attendant upon his death bed, that a course of sin was not to find absolute impunity.

It is clear that the writer of Ecclesiastes had perceived even this solution to be inadequate. Without any definite substitution of another, he yet points to the omnipotence of God and the littleness of man. Quiescence in the face of the problems of existence—submission and the performance of duty —this is "the whole of man." *

In the two Apocryphal Books with which we are now to deal the old question presents itself. In neither of them does a forecast of the Christian solution of the difficulty shew itself with anything like clearness. Yet in both a new element appears in the answer attempted. In Ecclesiasticus, while the Almighty power of God and the insignificance of man reappear in the discussion, the writer further suggests that even though the wrong-doer himself escape the just consequences of guilt, they are inflicted on his children after him, and thus subsequent generations, as bearing the iniquities of their fathers, establish the truth of the righteous dealings of God with men. †

In the Book of Wisdom, we shall see a somewhat nearer approach to a Christian solution. A kind of immortality is foreshadowed by the writer, yet it is hard to grasp its exact significance. In due course we shall note his teachings on the subject. In this as in other points the two Books (Ecclesiasticus and Wisdom) represent, as we have already said, respectively the strictly national, and the blended Hellenic and Jewish teaching, in this form of literature. ‡

---

* Eccles. 12. 13.
† For references *see* next section.
‡ For many of the above thoughts *see* A. B. Davidson's papers on *The Wisdom of the Hebrews*, *Expositor*, xi., xii., (1st series), from which the two quotations on p. 175, are taken (xii. 440 ff.).

A.—Ecclesiasticus; or, the Wisdom of Jesus the Son of Sirach.

Title.

The designation is not intended as that of the author, but is used to describe the work itself,* a " Church-book," as denoting that it was used either in the services of the Church, or for the instruction of catechumens (though not, strictly speaking, Canonical), or perhaps in order to distinguish it from the Book of Proverbs, which was sometimes called " Wisdom." The popularity which Ecclesiasticus early acquired may account for the restriction of the name " Church-book " to this one member of the group similarly admitted to public use. St. Jerome tells us † that the original Hebrew title was Proverbs, and it may well be that a further reason for giving the name Ecclesiasticus to the " Wisdom of the Son of Sirach " was to avoid confusion with the " Wisdom of Solomon."

Name and Circumstances of the Writer.

In chap. 50. 27 he calls himself " Jesus the son of Sirach . . . . of Jerusalem." ‡ "The son of Sira" (Sirach is a corruption, appearing first in the Greek version) is his title in later Jewish writings. The word does not occur in them in any other connexion. It has been variously interpreted as "thorn," "hedge of thorns,"§ "coat of mail " or "cuirass." ‖

The very improbable conjecture has been hazarded ¶ that he was high-priest in succession to Simon II., and that he held office for six years. There is more to be said for the belief

---

* Non auctor libelli, sed scripturæ qualitas."—Ruffinus, *Comm. in Symb.* § 38.
† *Praef. in Libr. Sol.* Migne, *Patrol.* ix. 1212.
‡ Some MSS. add Eleazar after Sirach (so Rev. Vers.), but this may only be in connexion with the belief that he was a priest. *See* below.
§ Edersheim in *Speaker's Comm., l.c.,* p. 3.
‖ Schürer, *l.c.,* p. 25.
¶ Syncellus, *Chron. ed. Dindorf,* i. 355.

that he was simply of priestly descent. In his praise of famous men he devotes seventeen verses to the celebration of Aaron, while even Moses is not given more than five. His references are frequent to the office of priest, and to sacrifices.* Still these indications fall far short of demonstration, and we must remember one feature of that time, which those who made him a high priest may have failed to realise, viz., that quite apart from the priesthood there was a class of learned men (*Chakhamim*) to whom a work like this might most naturally be referred.

At any rate the writer does not appear to have been a physician (as some have thought, in consequence of his praise of that profession in chap. **38**), still less an agriculturist or craftsman.† Clearly he held a prominent position in the state.‡ He had been a traveller for the purpose of enlarging his views, and he recommended this form of education, adducing his own case to shew that the process need not lead to any loosening of religious convictions.§ It is probably for deliverance from the danger which befell him in the course of his journeying ‖ that he gives thanks in the beginning of chap. **51**.

Date.

This has been the subject of much discussion, although, as we shall see, there should be no real doubt on the matter.

The Prologue,¶ written by the grandson of the author, and prefixed to his Greek version of his grandfather's work, tells us that he found the book in Egypt, and translated it in "the eight and thirtieth year . . . . when Euergetes was king." That this means in the 38th year (not of the translator's age, but) of the reign of Euergetes may be taken as highly probable,

---

* *e.g.* vii. 29–31. † See *e.g.* 38. 25–30.
‡ See 38. 24, 33; 39. 1–5. § See 34. 11; 39. 1–4.
‖ See 34. 12. ¶ Viz. the second of the two given in the A.V.

in spite of the peculiar character of the Greek expression. Exact parallels, where there can be no doubt of the sense intended, are found in the LXX.*

There was, however, more than one Ptolemy who bore the name Euergetes, viz., Ptolemy III. (= Euergetes I., 247–222 B.C.), and Ptolemy VII. (= Physcon, Euergetes II., 171–116 B.C.), who during the first twenty-five years of his reign ruled jointly with his brother.† Since of these two the latter alone reigned long enough to satisfy the statement in the Prologue to Ecclesiasticus, there can be no hesitation in deciding that the book was translated about the year 132 B.C. If so, we are justified in assigning to the original work a date about 60 years earlier, *i.e.* a few years before the outbreak of the Maccabean persecution. We may notice that troubles from foreign oppressors were already impending,‡ if not actually present. §

It might also be supposed that the mention in chap. 50. 1 of "Simon the high-priest, the son of Onias" (to whose praise the greater part of that chapter is devoted), would be a material help in establishing the date. There were, however, two high-priests of the name, and each happens to have been son of an Onias, viz., Simon I. (310–290 B.C.) and Simon II. (circ. 219–199 B.C.). ‖

Edersheim¶ strongly maintains that the former of the two is the person commemorated in Ecclesiasticus, urging among other arguments (*a*) that Josephus (*Ant.* xii. 2. 5 ; xii. 4. 1) refers to

---

* *See e.g.* Hag. 1. 1 ; 2. 1 ; Zech. 1. 7 ; 7. 1.
† We know otherwise that he was in the habit of reckoning his reign as commencing with his joint, and not his sole, rule.
‡ *See* chap. 35 and 36.
§ *See* 45. 26 ; 50. 22–24.
‖ Authorities differ as to the exact limits of his period, as well as on the question to which of these two the name *Tsaddik* properly belongs. *See* Dr. C. Taylor, *Pirke Aboth*, Cambridge, 1897 (2nd ed.), p. 12, note 2.
¶ *Speaker's Comm.*, "Introd. to Ecclesiasticus," p. 7, ff.

him as "the Just"; (*b*) that a book like Ecclesiasticus, if written at the later of the two dates, must have contained distinct marks of the strong hostility which had by that time arisen between the religious conservatism of the *Chasidim* and the Hellenizing party.

On the whole, we may, without hesitation, follow the obvious sense of the date above referred to, as given by the translator in the Prologue. It is true that on this hypothesis the writer of the book lived at any rate on the verge of troublous times. Devotion to Jewish forms of worship, as well as religious vitality, were in danger of succumbing to the advancing influence of Greek customs and Greek art. The author himself was not one whose outlook suffered in width through lack of knowledge of men and countries. In his travels he had become familiar with the ways of other nations than his own. He has "seen the religious observances of foreigners and heathens, but has kept himself wholly pure from alien taint, and honours the God of his fathers with an intelligent worship which rests not on mere outward observances but on the devotion of the heart (5. 5, 6; 7. 9, 10; 35. 1–7)."[*] Although, as we have just said, we do not trace in the book anything like acerbity of party feeling on the subject of the relaxation in Jewish customs and ways of thought, yet it is plain that the author desired to uphold with all earnestness the authority of the Law and the prophets. Simon II., who meets with such encomiums, was himself unable effectually to resist the advancing tide. In the historical sketch of the times we have seen that two of his sons, Jason and Menelaus, were strong supporters of Hellenism. Accordingly, therefore, our author, according to his grandson's statement,[†] "when he had much given himself to the reading of the Law

---

[*] W. J. Deane in *Expositor*, 2nd ser., vi. 334.   [†] Prologue to Ecclus.

and the prophets, and other books of our fathers, and had gotten therein good judgment, was drawn on also himself to write something pertaining to learning and wisdom, to the intent that those which are desirous to learn, and are addicted to these things, might profit much more in living according to the law."

CHARACTERISTICS OF THE BOOK.

1. *In form.*—The parallelism of clauses, by way of comparison or contrast, which is characteristic of proverbial and poetic literature in Hebrew, is so prominent a feature of the book that no examples need be quoted.

On the other hand, in the form of this book as compared with Proverbs we find a marked distinction. In the latter there is for the most part no attempt at classification of matter. Sayings dealing with the most distinct subjects follow each other without there being any aim at arrangement of material. On the other hand, in the Wisdom of Sirach * we find a considerable amount of grouping of this kind. *See* chaps. **22, 23**, for examples, where sayings relating to "good and bad children," "the character of the fool," "friendship," etc.,† follow in orderly succession.

The main divisions of the book are these: (*a*) Wisdom, doctrinal and practical **(1—43)**; (*b*) the praise of famous men **(44—50)**. The Appendix was perhaps put on as an after-thought **(51)**.

2. *In substance.*—The opening words of the book, "All Wisdom cometh from the Lord, and is with Him for ever," give us the author's subject and the sense in which he understands it. Wisdom with him includes both speculation and practice. To know God, to acknowledge him as Creator, Ruler,

---

* As was perceived as long ago as the time of the introduction of the headings at certain points in the Greek text.
† *See* Cheyne, *Job and Solomon*, London, 1887, p. 183.

and Preserver, to recognise him as the source of morality, and the sole object of men's worship—this is the duty of all. On the other hand, wisdom is that which enters into and inspires the every-day existence of man. Every relationship, association, occupation in life calls for the exercise of wisdom, if its duties are to be effectively carried out. The king, the worshipper, the counsellor, the physician, the parent, the handicraftsman, the labourer in the field, equally need to know and fulfil its commands. The author's researches into past history and his personal experience alike shew that wisdom is to be the guide of life.

Wisdom is not personified, or viewed as in any way separate from God. In the view of Sirach "Wisdom, as the active principle in creation, was poured out upon the earth, and in measure imparted to all nations (1. 9, 10, 15; 24. 3–7). But it was concentrated in the revealed Law of God, and became permanently resident in Israel." *

Thus the teaching of Ecclesiasticus is, as we have said, of a decidedly Palestinian type.†

The problem involved in the prosperity of the wicked was one which presented itself to the writer as to other thoughtful men of those times. When emphasizing the relation between piety and prosperity, he evidently from time to time felt the need of accounting for the exceptions. Moreover, how is it that one man differs from another in his opportunities, or in his capacity for realising spiritual things? He answers by reference to God as omnipotent, and irresistible. To His omniscience the solution of such matters must be left. ‡ "All the

---

* *Speaker's Comm.*, l. c., 11.

† For a criticism of the views of those who contend for a more or less conspicuous Alexandrian element in this book, see Drummond, *Philo-Judæus*, London, 1888, pp. 147 ff.

‡ See 16. 26; 23. 20; 33. 10-13; 39. 20, 21. Nevertheless man is possessed of free will and is responsible for his actions (15. 14-17).

works of the Lord are good."* Moreover, "although the righteous may suffer—since suffering is the common lot—yet their sorrows are not like those of the wicked, and they have also both immediate and final consolation under them."† The reward for good or the punishment for bad deeds may come late, but will surely fall on the evil doer or on his children. ‡

TEACHING AS TO THE UNSEEN AND A FUTURE LIFE.

There is not very much reference to angelic agency (**17. 17**; **48. 21**; comp. **39. 28** ff; **45. 2**). The author's one mention of Satan (**21. 27**) is interesting, as it seems to shew a tendency to a rationalistic identification of the devil with a man's depraved will.

There is no indication of a Resurrection. If the soul exists at all in Hades, it is in a state of eternal sleep. Immortality can only be found in the permanence of that which a man leaves behind him—his possessions, or his posterity, or posthumous fame. § There is no definite Messianic hope, the only approach to it being a somewhat obscure reference to the future work of Elias (**48. 10**), who should "turn the heart of the father unto the son," and "restore the tribes of Jacob." The object of expectation can scarcely be called in any true sense a Messianic kingdom, inasmuch as there is no trace of a king. That Israel should be established as a powerful nation pre-eminent among the peoples of the earth—this seems the utmost aspiration of the sage.

Interesting and important as the book is, there is an inferiority in the position which it takes up when compared with the books of Canonical Scripture. For one thing the writer seems less independent in his tone. He is deeply read in the Sacred

---

* 39. 33.   † *Speaker's Comm., l. c.*, p. 15.
‡ 11. 26.   § *See* references in *Speaker's Comm., l. c.*, p. 16.

Writings, and so connects his sayings with the great names of the historical past. His claim is less to add than to develop and interpret. He prays for a renewal of the inspired and accredited messengers of old.* He himself brings no fresh contribution, but expounds the principles and duties which underlie the course of life.

Moreover a certain worldliness is perceptible in his teaching. His apophthegms from time to time are framed with regard to the promptings of earthly prudence.† It has been remarked that there is now and then a self-consciousness, and an eye to effect upon others, marking the advice which he tenders. In spite, however, of such occasional blemishes, he often anticipates the moral teaching that we find in the Gospels, and notably that in the Epistle of St. James.

Language.

Although the Greek translator's prologue, already referred to, left no doubt that the book was composed in Hebrew, nothing beyond fragments of the original had survived in the form of quotations more or less accurate by Rabbinic writers. St. Jerome ‡ possessed a Hebrew copy, but for the purposes of his Vulgate he simply adopted the Old Latin. In the 10th century we have traces of its being known, but thenceforward even such distinguished Rabbis as Rashi and Maimonides had no first-hand acquaintance with it.

Many will be aware of the important series of discoveries by which a large portion of the original text has recently been brought to light. In May 1896, Mr. (now Dr.) S. Schechter,

---

* 36. 15, 16.   † 12. 2 ; 13. 9 ; 22. 23 ; 31. 12-29.
‡ *See* his prologue *in Libr. Sol.* He also speaks of the book as "doubtful," while the Canonical Scriptures are "sure," and says (in the words which form the basis of those in the 6th Article of the Church of England) that it should be read "for the instruction of the people, not to support the authority of Ecclesiastical doctrines."

Reader in Talmudic in the University of Cambridge, recognised some Hebrew writing * as a part of the long lost text (**39. 15—40. 7**). The leaf formed one of a collection of MS. fragments acquired in Palestine by Mrs. Lewis (who had some time previously brought to light the MS. of the Curetonian text of the Gospels, found by her in the Convent on Mount Sinai). Soon afterwards, in a box of Hebrew and Arabic fragments, acquired through Prof. Sayce by the Bodleian Library at Oxford, there was found another portion of the original text, forming a continuation of Mrs. Lewis's leaf, and running as far as **49. 11.** † Later still, Dr. Schechter has succeeded in obtaining, from the Genizah ‡ at Cairo, together with many other literary treasures, a considerable part of the rest of the Hebrew text of this book.

The language is on the whole classical Hebrew, specially as regards its syntax. "The vocabulary has a mixture of late or Aramaic words or expressions, such as might be expected from the date at which the author wrote." §

The two chief versions are the Greek, which has always been known, and the "Peshitto Syriac, an independent version of the original, of uncertain date and origin."‖

The correspondence of the newly-discovered original text with those versions "changes in almost every line, agreeing in some places with the Greek, in others with the Syriac. In other places, again, it agrees with *neither* of these versions, omitting whole clauses which are to be found in both the

---

* Dating, according to Dr. Schechter, from the 11th or early in the 12th century.

† *See* the Hebrew text together with the early versions, and an English translation, etc. by Cowley and Neubauer, Oxford, 1897, followed shortly afterwards by an English translation, with Auth. Vers. in parallel columns, from the same editors.

‡ The word is used to indicate a storehouse of old or disused MSS. or books in connexion with a synagogue.

§ Cowley and Neubauer, *op. cit.*, p. xiii.

‖ Smith's *Dict. of Bible*, Article, "Ecclesiasticus."

Greek and the Syriac, or offering new readings which have been either misunderstood or misread by the translators." *

VALUE.

The book is one which, had it stood alone, would doubtless have attained to a higher degree of importance in the general mind than it now possesses. It has inherent claims which raise it above the average level of the Apocrypha, and we may well suppose that only the fact that it forms one of a group which on the whole are of lower merit than itself, will account for the comparative neglect which it receives.

1. It gives a picture of Jewish thought, manners, and religion at a time of which we have otherwise but little knowledge in these respects. By its comments on practical wisdom, and its rules for the guidance of men's conduct in the various departments of human activity we are brought to some extent into touch with the beliefs, interests, and prejudices of Ben Sira's day.

2. It forms a prominent connecting link between the Canonical Books of the Old and New Testament. Problems were rising up and demanding an answer, which the older Revelation did not supply. Individual, as opposed to national, life was taking a more prominent place in the thoughts. What was the relation of the personal soul to God? What were to be a man's rules of conduct in relation to his fellow men, to those of low as well as high degree, what was the moral bearing of the increasing complication of human interests—those were questions that began to demand an answer. Old forms of religious belief had shewn or were shewing themselves inadequate to meet the advancing complexity of circumstances. The leading intellects of the day realised that Greek civilisation

---

* Schechter in *Expositor*, July, 1896, quoted by Cowley and Neubauer, *op. cit.*, p. xii.

was become a potent factor, and that the world was a larger thing than it had seemed to their fathers. The book represents what was perhaps the last great effort to grapple with the problem on the basis of thorough loyalty to the traditional beliefs and practices of Judaism. Not till two centuries later were the gathering perplexities to be resolved by the foundation of the kingdom in which there should be " neither Greek nor Jew." The book indicated, as no other does, the transition from the tradition of the past to the revelation yet future.*

The Wisdom of Solomon.

This book, " the most beautiful and important work of Jewish Alexandrianism " † deals in the main with the doctrine of Wisdom in its various aspects.

How is the Wisdom here treated of to be defined? Primarily, it denotes the attribute of God, abiding in Him, but manifested in His works, animate or inanimate alike, the Divine nature, as supramundane, being through Wisdom enabled to connect itself with the world of matter. As the writer waxes warm in his subject, he seems to conceive the Divine Wisdom, emanating from God and employed in the Creation and maintenance of the world as though it were, if not a separate existence from God, yet something to be regarded as separable. It is perhaps going too far to say that he actually personified the Wisdom,‡ of which he gives a description in such noble language.§ But in the poetical treatment of his subject he lays stress upon a thought which had its providential share in

---

* For correspondences between Ecclesiasticus and (*a*) Proverbs, (*b*) the Greek of certain Psalms, (*c*) St. James, see *Speaker's Comm.* l.c., pp. 21 f.: also for passages connecting the book with Koheleth (Ecclesiastes), see C. H. H. Wright, *Ecclesiastes*, p. 41, London, 1883.

† Dean Farrar in *Speaker's Comm.*, " Introd. to Wisdom," p. 407.

‡ The passages which might seem to support such personification are 16. 12; 18. 15.

§ 7. 22--8. 1.

the preparing of men's minds for the fuller revelation of Him who was "of one substance with the Father," and "by whom all things were made."

But man as a sentient part of God's creation is given a share of the wisdom of His Maker. Man's wisdom thus derived is of two kinds, speculative or theoretical, and practical. Under the former heading come, as branches of knowledge, theology (**8.** 4), history and prophecy (**8.** 8), science (**7.** 17–21). Under practical we may place virtue (**8.** 7), and handicrafts (**14.** 5).*

So far we may observe considerable resemblance between the teaching of this book and that of the Son of Sirach. But when we look more narrowly at the methods of treatment pursued by the two writers, we perceive the contrast to which we have already adverted. While both cling closely to the Law of their fathers, the author of Wisdom has added to distinctively Jewish learning an acquaintance with external systems of philosophy. He has studied the Revelation given in the Law and the Prophets in the light of Persian and Greek wisdom, and thus he exhibits something of the character more fully shewn us in Philo, the Alexandrian. "On one side he is a Jew, on the other a Greek philosopher." † He does not, it is true, seek, like Philo, to allegorize Old Testament history, in order to suit the tastes of a non-Jewish reader, but yet in the freedom with which he handles the Old Testament, in availing himself throughout the later portion of his book of the Midrashic traditions which had grown up around the Sacred narratives, as well as in the knowledge which he shews of Greek philosophical systems, he exhibits a method of blending

---

* The above classification is taken, with modifications, from the *Speaker's Comm.*, " Introd. to Wisdom," p. 419. See a full analysis of the book from this point of view by Bp. Westcott, Smith's *Dict. of Bible*, Article, " Wisdom of Solomon," p. 1779.

† Schürer, *op. cit.*, II. iii. 228.

Hellenistic with Jewish teaching, which made in subsequent times considerable advance.

JEWISH CHARACTERISTICS.

(i.) *In form.*—Here we may notice the balancing of clause against clause, and frequent antitheses (*e.g.* 13. 18, 19), the many Hebraic phrases, especially in the earlier chapters, his preference for the simplest connecting particles, as well as the use of Old Testament expressions and thoughts, and in particular the adaptation of his book to the style of the earlier writings claiming to come from the wise king.*

(ii.) *In substance.*—In the warning against ungodliness, and especially in the long discourse on the evil of idolatry in chap. 13. and onwards, the writer describes the contrast between idolaters and the followers of Wisdom, and illustrates his theme from Old Testament history.

HELLENISTIC CHARACTERISTICS.

(i.) *In form.*—The writer shews a remarkable mastery over the Greek language in the development which it had attained in his day. His skilfully elaborated sentences (*e.g.* 12. 27), his use of purely Greek turns of phrase, figures of speech, and allusions,† his abundant vocabulary coupled with a grasp of the language sufficient to construct for himself (apparently) fresh compounds without any violation of principles—these, as well as the rhetorical skill shewn by him in the later chapters of his work, all mark him as one who was thoroughly conversant with the language in which he wrote.

(ii.) *In substance.*—Greek philosophy has in various ways moulded the writer's thought, and influenced his teaching.

---

* Solomon's authorship is only suggested (7. 1-21 ; 8. 10-16, and especially 9. 7, 8), not stated, in the body of the work.

† *e.g.* 2. 8; 4. 2; 8. 4; 13. 15; 14. 1. Comp. the Sorites as a Greek form of logical argument, in 6. 17-20.

From the Stoics he learned the enumeration of the four cardinal virtues, "soberness and understanding, righteousness and courage" (8. 7). From Plato he drew his teaching in 8. 20, which implies the pre-existence of souls. His doctrine that the soul is weighed down by a corruptible body and by its earthly tabernacle (9. 15), is evidently drawn from non-Jewish philosophy, and there are various other signs in the book of his obligations to similar external sources.*

FOR WHAT READERS INTENDED.

According to chapter 1. 1 ; 6. 1, ff. the author addresses himself in this book to the kings and judges of the earth, warns these potentates of the folly of ungodliness, tells them the meaning of true Wisdom, and inculcates its cultivation. On the other hand, the frequent references to the history contained in the Jewish Scriptures suggest that the writer had his own countrymen in view, and if so, we may suppose that he was addressing himself to those who, whether in Egypt or elsewhere, gave signs of falling away from the faith of their fathers and adapting themselves to Gentile customs and beliefs inconsistent with Judaism. Thus the substance of the book indicates that " its warning and instruction are addressed to heathen-minded readers, whether these are by birth Jews or heathen." †

LANGUAGE.

As we have already pointed out, the language, although in general excellent Greek, has to some extent an Hebraic character. The general structure, however, makes it absolutely certain that it is not a translation from the Hebrew.‡

---

* *e.g.* to Epicurean teaching (2. 6-9), and to the followers of Euhemerus's view as to the origin of certain kinds of idolatry (14. 15-17).

† Schürer, *op. cit.*, II. iii. 231.

‡ The same is shewn by the abundant assonances and paronomasiae found in the Greek.

If this view needed further confirmation, such might be found in the fact that "the book contains unequivocal traces of the use of the LXX. where it differs from the Hebrew . . . . and this not in direct quotations, where it is conceivable that a Greek translator might have felt justified in adopting the rendering of the version with which he was familiar, but where the words of the LXX. are inwrought with the text itself." *

We may safely say that the hypothesis of a Hebrew original would never have found the smallest favour, had it not been for the ascription of the book to Solomon. But probably even the writer never intended to be taken *au pied de la lettre*, and merely meant that his words were in consonance with those handed down to his times as the utterances of the reputed parent of this kind of teaching in Israel. †

PLACE OF WRITING, DATE, AND AUTHORSHIP.

Probabilities point very plainly to the Egyptian origin of the book, and thus to a Jew living in Alexandria as its author. Palestine seems excluded not only by the familiarity with Greek philosophical systems, above referred to, but also by the writer's having at least some acquaintance with various sciences (**7.** 17–20; **8.** 8), with art (**14.** 14, 18; **15.** 4, 5), with Egyptian animal worship (**15.** 18), and in particular with the manufacture of idols of gilt clay, as carried on in that country.

The question of the date is a much more difficult one to determine. In any case it cannot be prior to the LXX. translation. We have already observed the use made here of that version, and we may further remark that in **15.** 10

---

* Smith's *Dict. of Bible*, l. c., p. 1781, where illustrations are given.
† Compare comments on the authorship of the Book of Baruch, p. 169, *supra*.

the writer quotes the Greek of Isa. 44. 20 ("his heart is ashes"). It is held by some that the book was composed in Christian times,* and was consequently subsequent to, or coeval with, Philo. It has even been held that Philo was himself the author. Considerations of language, style, philosophy, and treatment of Scripture make this last supposition utterly unlikely. Moreover, although there is doubtless a certain amount of resemblance in the method of treating the Old Testament narratives, so far as the introduction of traditional or Midrashic material, yet the manner in which Philo allegorizes away the Mosaic account in order to make things palatable for his readers, no less than his doctrine of the Logos as constituting the link between God and the world, seems to stamp him as the later of the two writers. The conceptions which had already clustered round Wisdom would later pass to the Logos, and in so doing receive a further development.

Aristobulus, the "teacher" † of Ptolemy Philometor (182-146 B.C.), has been conjectured to be the author. But the prosperous condition of the Jews at that time agrees ill with the indications of trouble and persecution contained in this book. ‡

Again, it has been maintained, but on very insufficient grounds, that the work is by Apollos (written before his conversion). §

It seems thus impossible to determine with any probability the name of the writer, or, as regards date, to go much beyond what we have said above, observing once again that at any rate it bears traces of a period of persecution such as the

---

* Dean Farrar (*Speaker's Comm.*, l. c., p. 422) places it "probably in the decade after the death of Christ." If, as has been conjectured, it belongs to the days of persecution under the Roman Emperor Caligula, 14. 16-20 may then refer to his attempt to place a statue of himself in the Temple.
† 2 Macc. 1. 10.   ‡ *e.g.* 2. 10; 3. 10.   § See *Speaker's Comm.*, l. c., p. 411.

Egyptian Jews underwent in the times of Ptolemy Philopator (222–205 B.C.), and Ptolemy Physcon (146–117 B.C.).*

OBJECT AND VALUE.

(i.) The writer, whatever attractions Greek philosophical speculation had for him, was a firm upholder of the Law. He evidently considered no censure too severe for those who, like Jason and Menalaus,† forsook their allegiance to the customs of their fathers, and scorned or even persecuted those who continued faithful.‡ Thus he set forth the folly and iniquity involved in the idolatry of the non-Jewish world, and especially in those forms of it which came under the observation of Jews living in Egypt: and thus he seeks to check waverers, to rebuke apostates, and to convince any heathen readers of their duty to become proselytes to Judaism.

(ii.) He desires to console those of his countrymen who remained faithful in the midst of persecution. He points to the happiness and blessing procured by the pursuit of wisdom in this life, and, although there is no trace of the Christian doctrine of the Resurrection of the body, it is hard to believe that such a passage as chap. 3. 1–9 does not definitely indicate the belief that for the God-fearing man there is a life of conscious happiness beyond the grave, where the inequalities of earth will be redressed.§ When Wisdom (the writer would say) is thus fraught with blessing to all who will embrace her, the folly as well as wickedness of the sceptical tendencies of the day are manifest.

---

* But reigning jointly with his brother for 25 years previous to the earlier date.
† See p. 31, *supra*. Jason is called "that ungodly man" in 2 Macc. 4. 13.
‡ 2. 10–20.
§ See especially v. 7, and compare 1. 15; 2. 22, 23; and other passages. In 8. 13. on the contrary, the "immortality" *may* mean no more than the "eternal memory" (in the hearts of subsequent generations), which holds the corresponding position in the parallel clause.

Value.—(i.) The book shews us* the kind of answer to the ever-recurring problem of the distribution of human happiness and suffering which commended itself to a pious Alexandrian Jew, learned in the philosophical systems which found favour in his day, yet faithful to his traditional beliefs.

(ii.) It has furnished us with more than one expression, the beauty of which has secured for it a permanent place in Christian thought. Such are "the souls of the righteous are in the hand of God," † a hope "full of immortality," ‡ "Thou sparest all : for they are thine, O Lord, thou lover of souls." §

(iii.) The preparation which this book unconsciously makes for the teaching of the New Testament is illustrated by its introduction of words expressing the virtues of faith, hope, and love, united as these are in the teaching of St. Paul,‖ St. Peter,¶ and the Epistle to the Hebrews.**

(iv.) The book marks the highest point of religious knowledge attained by the Jews in the period between the close of the Old Testament Canon and the beginning of the Gospel dispensation.

It sets forth, though with a certain amount of inconsistency, a future retribution of the wicked, consisting, according to 1. 11, of annihilation, according to another passage (4. 18–20), of conscious anguish. It approaches the truth of an individual

---

* *See* above. † Wisd. of Sol. 3. 1.
‡ *Ibid.* 3. 4.
§ *Ibid.* 11. 26, A. V. The Greek corresponding to "lover of souls" is one of the few instances in which the writer uses a word in a sense wholly different from that belonging to it in the classical period of the language, viz. in this case *lover of life, cowardly.*
‖ Rom. 5. 1–5; 1 Thess. 1. 2, 3.
¶ 1 Pet. 1. 21, 22.
** Heb. 10. 22–24 (R. V.). For these three characteristic moral conditions, thus grouped, and generally typical of the Christian life, *see* T. B. Strong's *Christian Ethics* (Bampton Lectures for 1895), pp. 79 ff. London, 1896.

immortality beyond the grave (2. 23 ; 6. 19 ; 8. 17 ; 15. 3) ; it expresses the nature of God as being predominantly "love" (11. 26 ; 11. 10) : it represents love as the final law of creation (7. 22, 23 ; 11. 24, 26).*

(v.) By the personification of Wisdom, which is set forth, even if it be only as a poetical figure, in this book, it prepares the way for the Christian realisation of the mediatorial office of the Son of God. "In its picture of the righteous sufferer it almost attains (however unconsciously) to a prophetic picture of the death of Christ" (2. 13–20),† and the ideal thus framed "helped the early Jewish-Christian Church to get over the stumbling-block of the Cross, and to recognise in Jesus the fulfilment of the long anticipations of a yearning world." ‡

INFERIORITY TO THE CANONICAL BOOKS.

In spite of what has just been said, there are obvious points in which the teaching of this book falls short of that given elsewhere in the Old Testament, as well as of the book which most closely resembles it in the New, viz. the Epistle to the Hebrews.

While the existence of sin is clearly recognised, and there is even the identification of the tempter of Gen. 3 with the devil, as the one by whom death entered into the world,§ there is scarcely any hint of sin in its character of a universal malady, or as affecting in any degree those who had given themselves to wisdom as their guide.‖

Again, when we compare it with the above-named New Testament Epistle, we find that the latter "is incomparably more logical, more truthful, more original, and more rich in

---

* Farrar, *op. cit.*, p. 408 f. † *Ibid.* ‡ *Ibid.* p. 420.
§ 2. 23, 24. ‖ Only in 15. 2.

divine instructiveness than the best efforts of the pseudo-Solomon."*

Lastly, it contains no indication of a personal Messiah. Israel should have universal dominion over other nations, and with that dominion the worship of the God of Israel should supplant idolatry throughout the world—this was the extent of the Messianic hope—at best a kingdom without a king.

---

* Farrar *op. cit.*, p. 407.

CHAPTER XV.

POETIC LITERATURE.*

Canonical Post exilic Psalms.

IT is clearly impossible to discuss here with anything like adequacy the question whether any Psalms are to be reckoned as composed after the Exile, and, if such be found, to what dates they respectively belong. In the few pages that follow we shall only attempt (*a*) to point out the inherent difficulties which present themselves in dealing with the subject; (*b*) to comment upon the probability that some Psalms are post-exilic; and (*c*) to notice a few prominent Psalms which have been placed by some critics as late as the days of the Maccabees.

DIFFICULTIES IN DETERMINING THE DATES OF INDIVIDUAL PSALMS.

These arise (i.) from the nature of the Canonical Psalms; for utterances which take the form of prayer, of lamentation, of thanksgiving, are to a large extent of so general a character as to be appropriate to the various experiences of individual souls in very different periods, as well as to the circumstances of a nation at more than one epoch of its history; (ii.) from the brevity of many of the Psalms, for if, as we have seen, it be sometimes hard to fix the date of a book of the size of Wisdom, or even Tobit, how much more in the cases we are now dealing with; (iii.) from the fact that, just as has happened with the

---

* With regard to the poetic fragments embodied in Judith (16. 2-17), Tobit (13), Ecclesiasticus (51), it does not seem needful to add anything to what has been said in commenting on those books.

hymns of later days, the language of various Psalms has been modified in more ways than one, either in order, we may suppose, to adapt them to some new occasion, or from other causes. Psalm 19 is a case in point. The two subjects with which it deals, viz., the glory of God as manifested in Nature and in the Law plainly indicate the union of two different compositions, so that *vv.* 7 ff. may be taken as a subsequent addition. For similar signs of *editing* we may compare the many slight variations which occur in Psalm 18 as compared with the form which it assumes in 2 Sam. 22. So Psalms 14 and 53, substantially identical, vary in slight details, and the same may be said of Psalm 70, as compared with 40. 13-17, and 108, which is made up of 57. 7-11, followed by 60. 5-12.

A similar inference may be drawn from the occasional occurrence of breaks in the alphabetical sequence of verses, or half verses, or of larger portions in an acrostic Psalm.* So great is the lack of completeness from an acrostic point of view in the case of Psalms 9, 10 (properly to be reckoned as one Psalm) that it is impossible to recover the original form.

The Book of Psalms, as is well known, is to a large extent made up of groups formed by earlier collections. Of these there are three principal ones, corresponding to (*a*) Book I. (Psalms 1—41), (*b*) Books II. and III. (Psalms 42-89), (*c*) Books IV. and V. (Psalms 90—150). But although on the whole it may be said that the order of the Psalms corresponds, though very roughly, with their dates, yet there are many obvious exceptions, earlier Psalms being placed in later books, and *vice versâ*. Accordingly this fact, together with our uncertainty as to the time when these various compilations were made, gives us good cause to hesitate before assigning precise dates with anything like confidence.

---

* Such Psalms are 9. 10, 25, 34, 37, 111, 112, 119, 145.

The Existence of Post-Exilic Psalms.

There is no reason for doubting, but on the contrary we have fair grounds for an *a priori* belief, that such may exist in the Canon. Just as the stirring events in pre-exilic times were the occasion of sacred poetry, so too the sufferings of the Exile, the enthusiasm of the Return, and the varying fortunes of the nation in post-captivity days under Persian, Egyptian, and Greek rule, and the revival of the national spirit under the Hasmonean family, might well be expected to produce sacred poems of a lyrical character or otherwise. The hints which various Psalms give us in the subjects with which they deal, and their vivid expression of the feelings and emotions of their day, lead us to the same conclusion. To this, *e.g.*, we are pointed by the references to attacks on the Temple, as well as to persecutions on account of religious fidelity. Again, when we find passages uniting the expression of abhorrence for idolatry with a claim to national innocence in this respect, and the assertion that the sins of the people in their collective capacity now lie altogether in the past, such sentiments suggest to us a period in the history subsequent to the monarchy. Once more, the contrast which from time to time appears * between the saints, the righteous, the meek, the upright of heart, and the wicked, transgressors, violent men, best fits the day when the heathenism of powerful neighbours or the influence of external customs caused defections in the ranks of the writer's own countrymen, and produced apostacy from the God of Israel and His traditional worship. Such Psalms are the utterances of spiritual faith contending with oppressors from within as well as from without the nation, and in their material helplessness and sufferings maintaining their constancy to Jehovah, and pleading for support and deliverance.

---

* *e.g.* 34. 21 ; 37. 14, 17, 38, 39 ; 79. 2 ; 147. 6.

We may add that the insertion of individual Psalms in the collection, even as late as Maccabean times, is not necessarily inconsistent with the closing of the Canon at an earlier period.*

On the other hand, while it seems clearly established that Psalms of exilic and post-exilic times form part of our collection, it is difficult, if not impossible, to point to any which may be said to be of certainly Maccabean date. We proceed to notice a few to which that date has been attributed.

Psalms alleged to be of Maccabean Date (168 B.C. and onwards).

The following (among others) have been adduced with confidence, 30, 44, 60, 74, 79, 83, 113—118, 149. We proceed to notice these singly.†

Psalm 30.—The title, "A Psalm ; a Song at the Dedication of the House," suggests, as well as earlier possibilities, the Festival instituted by Judas Maccabeus (165 B.C.).‡ But this seems a slender foundation on which to build anything like certainty. Even if we grant that the liturgical use of the Psalm belongs to that particular " Dedication," as opposed to an earlier one, for example, that of the second Temple (Ezra 6. 16), it does not follow that that was the date of its composition.

Psalm 44.—The Psalm clearly applies to a period of national disaster, and apparently (*v.* 22) of persecution even to death for conscience sake. So far, the days of Seleucid oppression form an eminently suitable conjecture. But (*a*) even the defenders of a Maccabean date find a difficulty in agreeing upon any

---

* *See* remarks on this point on p. 105.
† For the substance of the comments on Psalms 30—83 I am indebted to the Introductions to those Psalms in Dr. Kirkpatrick's contribution to the *Cambridge Bible for Schools and Colleges.*
‡ *See* p. 43, *supra.*

particular occasion to which it may refer;* (*b*) it occurs in a collection of Psalms which bear evidence, in the way of musical titles † and otherwise, of an early date; and (*c*) it "produces a strong impression that it belongs to the time when Israel had still an independent existence as a nation, and was accustomed to make war upon its enemies." ‡

Psalm 60.—It is enough to say here that the chief ground for attributing this Psalm to the Maccabean time is its similarity to that with which we have just dealt. §

Psalms 74 and 79.—These may be treated together. They both describe scenes which certainly bear a strong resemblance to those of the days of Antiochus Epiphanes' persecutions. Israel was grievously oppressed, and had become the scorn of neighbouring nations. Her Temple had been burnt. The bodies of the slain were left unburied. The LORD seemed to have permanently cast off His people.

Clearly the two occasions to which such a state of things can be referred are the destruction of Jerusalem by the Chaldeans (586 B.C.) and the persecutions of Epiphanes. In favour of the latter are urged (*a*) the correspondence between these Psalms and various details mentioned in the Book of Maccabees; ∥ (*b*) the words "there is no more any prophet"; ¶ (*c*) the existence of synagogues; ** (*d*) the fact that the persecution is a *religious* one; †† (*e*) the expression "they have set up their ensigns for signs."‡‡

---

* See Kirkpatrick, *l.c.*, for objections to each of the occasions suggested.
† Obsolete long before Maccabean days, and to the LXX. translators often absolutely meaningless.
‡ Kirkpatrick, *l.c.*, p. 236. See in *v.* 9 the reference to the overthrow of the *army*. If the Psalm be not Maccabean, it would thus appear to be thrown back to the days of the Monarchy.
§ Comp. especially *v.* 10 with 44. 9.
∥ 1 Macc. 2. 6 ff.; 2 Macc. 8. 2 ff.
¶ 74. 9. Comp. 1 Macc. 4. 46; 9. 27; 14. 41.
** *Ibid.* 8. †† *Ibid* 10, 18, 22. ‡‡ *Ibid.* 4.

In reply it may be said that a date about fifteen or twenty years after the destruction of Jerusalem by the Chaldeans will equally well suit (*a*) and also (*d*), for all wars against the Chosen People were in a way religious wars. It will also suit (*e*), and is not against (*b*), for Jeremiah and Ezekiel may have been dead. As to (*c*), the LXX. translated the word " synagogues " otherwise, viz., *solemn feasts* (the cessation of which is also bewailed in Lam. 2. 6).

Moreover, (1) on the later occasion the Temple itself was not burnt, nor the city actually laid in ruins ; (2) there was no *prolonged* desolation (three years only elapsed before the Temple was re-dedicated) ; (3) " the mockery of the neighbouring peoples was a conspicuous feature at the time of the destruction of Jerusalem (Ps. 137 ; Ezek. 25. 3, etc.) ; " * (4) " The parallels with Jeremiah, Lamentations, and Ezekiel are at least as striking as those with 1 Maccabees."†

Psalm 83.—In this, Moab, Edom, and other enemies of Israel combine against them. It has been supposed that the reference is to the expression of hostility on the part of "the Gentiles," when they heard that Judas Maccabeus had set up the altar and restored the sanctuary.‡ But to mention only two objections to such an identification, Moab had ceased to exist as a nation, and there is not any mention of an alliance in the Maccabees passage. It should be added that there is no period in Jewish history known to us with which the position of affairs, as indicated in this Psalm, is in complete correspondence. It is therefore very possible that it refers to some sudden danger, which either from its transitory character, or for some other reason, has not been recorded.

---

* Kirkpatrick, *op. cit.,* Introd. to Ps. 74.
† *Ibid.* He adds examples of the former class.
‡ 1 Macc. 5. 1 ff.

Robertson Smith * refers the three Psalms which we have last noticed to the rebellion in Persian times under Artaxerxes Ochus (circ. 350 B.C.), when many Jews were punished for the part which they had taken, by being transported to Hyrcania.† Our knowledge, however, of the circumstances of this revolt, as of much else in the post-captivity history of the Jews, is too slight to warrant us in considering this view as by any means a certainty. The case is somewhat different with certain Psalms which appear in the latest groups (Books IV. and V. 90—150), though even there an assignment to the Maccabean period is more or less conjectural. Such Psalms are, for example, 113— 118 (the Hallel),‡ 149.

In general we may further say, that if any Psalms were added in Maccabean times, then, on the supposition (see Prologue to Ecclesiasticus, and p. 105, supra) that the Canon was closed, it is difficult to conceive of such Psalms being inserted here and there, and not rather placed as a supplement. Moreover, if the LXX. was then completed, there is the further improbability that the Egyptian Jews should have conformed precisely in this respect to the action of their co-religionists in Palestine.

To sum up therefore :

It is not impossible that there should be Psalms of an actually Maccabean date.§

But (a) in considering the probabilities of each case, we must remember that a Psalm composed in reference to an earlier epoch

---

* *The Old Testament in the Jewish Church*, pp. 207 f., 438 f. London, 1892 (2nd ed.).

† Euseb. *Chron.*, *Anno* 1658, *Abr.* referred to by Rob. Smith, *op. cit.*, p. 438, where he gives arguments for the above-mentioned opinion.

‡ Songs of *praise*, sung at the chief annual feasts.

§ It is noteworthy that we find as early a commentator as Theodore of Mopsuestia (see Dr. Swete's Article in Smith's *Dict. of Christian Biography*, iv. 939) holding that certain Psalms refer to that period. He, however, considered that they did so *prophetically*.

might very likely be used, with or without change, for a later occasion of a like kind.

(*b*) At the time when the Septuagint translation of the Psalms was made—and we may infer from the Prologue to Ecclesiasticus * that that had then taken place—the Psalter, as we have it, had been completed long enough to hold an authoritative position.†

Thus it follows that, even though certain Psalms may have been introduced into the collection as late as 165 B.C., it must have been finally closed " within a few years at most after this great event. From the time of Hyrcanus downwards the ideal of the princely high priests became more and more divergent from the ideal of the pious in Israel, and in the Psalter of Solomon (about 50 B.C.) we see religious poetry turned against the lords of the Temple and its worship."‡

Psalms of Solomon, otherwise called Psalms of the Pharisees.§

Of the double title which belongs to this collection of Psalms, the former part is probably of late origin, and at any rate has no claim whatever to be taken seriously by us. The alternative heading, Psalms of the Pharisees, will be presently shewn perfectly to accord with the internal evidence of the work itself.

Comparing among themselves the 18 Psalms which form the collection, we find that there is sufficient similarity in

---

* (Circ. 130 B.C.) *See* pp. 178 ff. *supra*.
† Even though we were to grant that the LXX. Psalter is not to be dated earlier than 100 B.C., it seems difficult to believe that the many intervening steps (*see* them enumerated by Dr. Sanday, *Inspiration*, Bampton Lectures, London, 1893, pp. 271 f.), some of them involving considerable spaces of time, can be included within a period of about 70 years.
‡ Rob. Smith, *op. cit.*, p. 211 f.
§ The substance of the following pages is little more than a selection and condensation from the very full Introduction to be found in the edition of this book by Drs. Ryle and James, Cambridge, 1891.

character and contents to justify us in concluding that all belong to the same age or generation, if not to the same author, such differences in style as exist being easily referable to differences in subject matter.

DATE.

This we gather with virtual certainty from the contents of several of the series,* and in particular from the allusions contained in Ps. 2. In the midst of prosperity and outward piety, war suddenly approaches in the shape of an army led by a stranger from a remote country, and preparing to attack Jerusalem. The rulers receive him with acclamation; but after he has thus gained an entrance to the city resistance arises from some internal quarter; he overthrows fortifications by the use of the battering-ram; the Temple and the Altar are desecrated by the presence of the Gentile invader. A bloody massacre follows; many exiles are carried off to "the bounds of the West" (17. 14); even the rulers are led captive and insulted. But the profanity of the stranger meets with speedy retribution. He goes to Egypt and is slain "upon the mountains,"† while his body is cast to the waves and there is none to bury him. ‡

This picture can only refer to the capture of Jerusalem (*a*) by Titus (70 A.D.), or (*b*) by Antiochus Epiphanes (170 B.C.), or (*c*) by Pompey (63 B.C.).

But the two former occasions are excluded by the subsequent fate of the conqueror, as well as by several other points in which the correspondence between the Psalms and the actual history fails. Thus there can be no doubt that the reference

---

* Pss. 1 ; 8 ; 17. 1-22.

† But possibly we should read "borders" (the Greek words differing only by a smooth and rough breathing), though the latter sounds rather prosaic, and it is more likely that the original writer may intend an allusion to the elegy in 2 Sam. 1. 19, etc. ("high places").

‡ The above particulars are gathered from Pss. 1 ; 2 ; 8 ; 17

is to the last named.* Pompey was "the mighty striker," (8, 16), having just overthrown Mithridates. The peaceful reign of Alexandra was barely over, when his attack came. The brothers Hyrcanus II. and Aristobulus II. were rivals for power, and were both in Jerusalem. The former admitted "the stranger": the latter resisted from within the Temple precincts, and, after the scenes of blood above-mentioned, was subjected to the mockery of the great nation of "the West" as he graced Pompey's triumph at Rome. The conquering general entered the Holy of Holies—an act of ignorant profanity which according to Jewish belief brought him in due course to a dishonoured end (2. 30).†

Pompey's death took place in 48 B.C. This date thus supplies a *terminus ad quem* for at least that Psalm (2) which relates it. Cæsar's triumph over his rival in the contest for the world's dominion, and the favour shewn by the former towards the Jews, seem reflected in the tone of several of the Psalms, in the shape of enthusiastic joy at Pompey's fate and the expectation of coming glory to the Jewish nation.

We may thus place the Psalms as a whole between the years 70 and 40 B.C.

Social and Religious Condition of Judea.

The picture given us by the "Psalms of Solomon" in these respects is in the main as follows:—

The successes of the Hasmonean princes in war brought about a renewed tendency to the cultivation of Hellenistic

---

* A fourth possibility, viz. that Herod (being an Idumean) is referred to, as one who was a "stranger to our race" (18. 9), is precluded by many considerations. Although it is true that he laid siege to Jerusalem, and at the beginning of his reign slew many of the Sanhedrim, he was more of a diplomatist than a warrior, made it his general policy to conciliate the prejudices of the Jews, did not carry them away to the West, and finally, did not meet with an end like that of Pompey.

† Pompey's mangled remains were in fact buried in haste by his freedman, but comp. Lucan, *Pharsalia*, x. 380 f. "tumulumque e pulvere parvo Aspice Pompeii, non omnia membra tegentem."

customs and modes of thought, while the growing prosperity of the Palestinian Jews was not without its influence in the same direction. But the stricter party, the Pharisees, objected to wars entered upon for aggrandisement, resented the granting of the high priesthood to the Hasmonean family, and maintained, in the true spirit of the ancient Theocracy, that the Jewish kingdom should not be of an earthly character.

Thus the ruling family naturally tended to side with the opposite party, the old aristocracy of Sadducean leanings. We have already dealt with a quarrel between John Hyrcanus (*ob.* 105 B.C.) and the Pharisees, the civil war that followed his reign, and the turn of good fortune which befell the Pharisees under Alexandra (78-69 B.C.).* Their ascendancy was ensured by the overthrow of Aristobulus II. and the establishment of his brother Hyrcanus II. as ruler and high priest. It was under such circumstances that these Psalms were written, and their Pharisaic origin is plain from the following considerations:—

(i.) They divide the nation into "righteous," or "saints," and "sinners," or "transgressors," charging the latter (the Hasmonean family) with usurping the throne of David (17. 5, 8) and the high priesthood (this last is clearly meant in 17. 6).

(ii.) Those who minister in holy things are careless, and guilty of ceremonial uncleanness (1. 9, etc.: *see* specially 8. 13). †

(iii.) The Theocracy is emphasized (2. 34, 36, etc.).

(iv.) "Righteousness" is signalized by care to fulfil the ceremonial law (3. 8-10, etc.), as well as by a spiritual worship.

---

* *See* pp. 62-71.
† For development of these two points, *see* Ryle and James, *op. cit.*, pp. xlvii. f.

(v.) National disasters are deplored, not as checking political aspirations, but as the necessary consequence of the sins of which the nation has been guilty, and which thus have drawn down the Divine vengeance (2. 1, 15, 16, etc.).

(vi.) The true Israelite (as opposed to "them that live in hypocrisy in the company of the saints," 4. 7) must abide in humiliation and prayer * God's appointed time for shewing mercy (7. 9 ; 15. 1, etc.).

(vii.) There shall be a Resurrection to life when the Lord visits the earth with judgment (3. 16, etc.).

(viii.) The doctrine of angels is at least once referred to (17. 49).

(ix.) The Messiah in God's good time shall come, a descendant of David. He shall overthrow Gentiles and "sinners" (Sadducees), bring back the "Dispersion," and re-establish the glory of the Holy City and of the Temple worship. The Gentiles shall become tributary and proselytes. His rule shall be spiritual, holy, wise, and above all things just.†

The Messiah, called in these Psalms by the title "Christ," ‡ is to be "the Son of David." This is a return to the conception of the prophets (*e.g.* Hag. 2. 21–23). Zechariah (6. 11–13) emphasized the priestly side of the conception. So it is *Jeremiah* who appears in a dream to Judas Maccabeus (2 Macc. 15. 12–16). In Ecclesiasticus (48. 10) it is *Elijah* who is to "restore the tribes of Jacob." *Now* the house of *David* reappears.

The Messiah is God's vicegerent upon earth. He unites the offices of king and high priest ; but he is not divine.

---

* Contrast the subsequent violence of the Zealots.
† For references *see* Ryle and James, *op. cit.*, pp. lii. ff., of which the above is a brief abstract, and for the next three paragraphs *see ibid.*, pp. liv. ff.
‡ "Not a characteristic title of the promised Saviour in the O. T.," Bp. Westcott, *1st Epistle of St. John*, p. 189, quoted by Ryle and James, p. liv.

It is specially noteworthy that the personal character * of the Messiah is brought out so clearly in these Psalms. Not a hundred years before, the Pharisaic teaching dwelt simply upon the duties of fulfilling and disseminating the Law, and made little or no attempt to indicate with any definiteness the nature of the future greatness of Israel. But Maccabean heroism had rekindled Jewish aspirations for a monarchy, and the Pharisees found that their only way of gaining a hold upon the people generally was to encourage those aspirations, and, by pointing out the failure to realise them on the part of the ruling house, to secure to their side patriotic enthusiasm by promising a universal dominion under a king of Davidic lineage and unexampled glory.

Style, and Connexion with other Literary Remains of this Period.

These Psalms can claim no high degree of poetical merit. They are in the main simple in their style, and shew great familiarity with the Old Testament, a familiarity indicated not only by quotations, but still more by the adoption of its phraseology. Most nearly approaching them "in style and character are the hymns preserved in the early chapters of St. Luke's Gospel (**1.** 46–55, 68–79 ; **2.** 10–14, 29–32), which in point of date of composition stand probably nearer to the Psalms of Solomon than any other portion of the New Testament." †
They allude frequently, but as a rule indirectly,‡ to Old Testament history.

There are a good many cases of agreement in language or thought with Ecclesiasticus, but where there is an actual

---

* The 17th of these Psalms is the earliest passage where this is plainly declared in the post-biblical literature of *Palestine*. (Enoch, I. xc. 37, 38 is vague.) A Sibylline fragment, on the other hand (*Orac. Sibyll.* iii. 652 ff. 125–100 B.C.), sets forth the teaching of *Alexandrian* Judaism on this point.

† Ryle and James, p. lx.   ‡ 9. 1, 17 ; 17. 5, form exceptions.

correspondence of expression "the agreement is generally to be explained by some passage of Scripture from which both writers have borrowed."*

Authorship, why ascribed to Solomon.

Three reasons may be assigned :—

(*a*) Certain parts of the work were thought to fit in naturally with Solomon's circumstances or position. Ps. **17**, *e.g.*, has a certain likeness to the 72nd of the Canonical Book, and as the latter bears the title *Psalm of Solomon*, the former, and with it the rest of the collection, may have been ascribed to his authorship.

(*b*) Some passages may have suggested it by their resemblance to the style of the Book of Proverbs (*e.g.* **4**. 4–6 ; **5**. 15–20, etc.).

(*c*) As Solomon was son of the king whose name was associated with the Canonical Psalter, and moreover had himself been declared (1 Kings **4**. 32) to be the author of "a thousand and five" songs, it may have been conjectured that these were some of that number.

In any case it appears to be only copyists or translators who are responsible for the ascription of these Psalms to his authorship.

Place and Object.

"The prominence given to Jerusalem makes it probable that our Psalms were composed by a Jew (or Jews) residing

---

* Ryle and James, p. lxiii. For the influence which these Psalms have been thought to exercise on the Book of Enoch, the Book of Jubilees, and other writings, *see ibid.*, lxv. ff.; also pp. lxxii. ff. for discussions on the connexion between Ps. 11. and Baruch 4. 36—5. 9, in their references to the LXX., the decision that the Baruch passage is the later of the two, and the resulting inference (for date of Baruch *see* p. 168 *supra*) that the Psalms of Solomon had been turned into Greek some considerable time before A.D. 70, thus assuming "new importance, as monuments of Hellenistic Greek of the first century, and as most likely anterior in date to the whole New Testament literature."

in the capital. 'The Holy City,' or 'The City of the Sanctuary' (8. 4), is in the Psalmist's estimation the centre of the universe."*

The object, as we have already seen, was earnestly to protest, from a political and religious standpoint, against Sadducean teaching and practices.

LANGUAGE.

If these Psalms were composed, as we have just seen reason to believe, in Jerusalem, it follows that Hebrew, rather than Greek, would be their language, the more so, when they owe their origin to so strongly national a party as the Pharisees, and further, may have been intended (though of this we cannot feel at all sure) for liturgical use.

Other circumstances, which point to the same conclusion, are as follows :—

(i.) Occasional obscurities in the Greek, which can best be accounted for on this hypothesis.

(ii.) The simplicity of structure and lack of variety in the way of particles, which is characteristic of translations from Hebrew.

(iii.) Difficulties in the rendering of tenses, on account (apparently) of their use in Hebrew being attended by peculiarities well known to students of that language.

(iv.) The frequent omission of the substantive verb (which is a Hebrew idiom).

(v.) What appear to be duplicate renderings of the same original expression, or words added by the translator to make the meaning clearer.

It should be noted that correspondence in point of language between the LXX. version and quotations of the Old Testament

---

* Ryle and James, p. lviii. *See* further illustrations there.

in these Psalms by no means militates against the above conclusion. A translator familiar with that version would naturally make use of it.

Date of the Greek Translation.

Baruch, ch. 5, which, as we have noticed, may be taken as a later expansion of the 11th Psalm of this collection, is quoted by Irenaeus (*ob. circ.* 202 A.D.), and must therefore have existed for some time previously. It may accordingly be concluded that the Greek form of these Psalms is not later than the middle of the 1st century A.D.

If the work contains traces of Christian influence, it is clear that the above date would be a somewhat early one to assign. But the two chief instances which have been held to indicate a Christian hand are not decisive. One is the expression "the Lord Christ,"[*] an expression occurring more than once in the Old Testament (as well as twice in the New, viz. in Luke 2. 11; Col. 3. 24), and not therefore a characteristically Christian phrase. The other is a word [†] which has been taken (but without sufficient grounds) as relating to the Second Advent, or to the pre-existence of the Messiah. Had those Psalms been really subjected to Christian revision, we may feel assured that they would exhibit much more distinct traces of Christian doctrine.

For five "Odes of Solomon," three of which are clearly of Christian time, while two *may* be Jewish, as well as for certain other pieces, as to whose date little can be determined, though they " resemble rather markedly the general tone of the Psalms of Solomon," see Ryle and James, *op. cit.*, Appendix (pp. 155 ff.).

---

[*] χριστὸς κύριος (17. 36).   [†] ἄναξις (18. 6).

CHAPTER XVI.

APOCALYPTIC LITERATURE.

WE may preface our separate comments upon individual books by some general remarks on apocalyptic as distinct from prophetical writings, (i.) in their general point of view, and (ii.) in certain characteristic details.*

(i.) A prophecy is primarily *spoken*, and retains much of this character after it has been committed to writing. We seem to see the attendant gestures. The illustrations which accompany it are not of the nature of narrative, but rather historical representations of what is passing before our eyes, upon which the prophet makes his commentary. Further, the tone is that of exalted feeling, whether it be sorrow, humiliation on account of sin, eager expostulation, righteous anger, or thankfulness, joy, ecstatic contemplation of the Divine Glory. We are not permitted to forget the oft-recurring " Thus saith the LORD." The prophet is pre-eminently Jehovah's messenger.

The apocalyptic style, on the other hand, is that of a writer, not of a speaker. There is comparatively little variation of tone, as the vision or series of visions is recorded. Whatever be the interest excited in the mind of the reader by the scenes exhibited to him, he feels all the time that it is by their inherent power and vividness, and not by any rhetorical

---

* For fuller treatment of most of the points which hereafter follow, *see* J. E. H. Thomson, *Books which influenced our Lord and His Apostles*, Edinburgh, 1891.

embellishment or poetry of diction, that his attention is riveted.*

(ii.) Differences in detail.

(*a*) The great ruling powers which had successively included Palestine within their vast dominion had not been without their permanent effect upon the nation. Babylon, Persia, Greece had succeeded in impressing upon the minds of Jews that the world was considerably greater than they once thought it. Their point of view, almost in spite of themselves, became shifted from their own country as the centre of all things. They began to realise the width of civilisation and the culture which was possessed by non-Jewish peoples. And with this came the disposition to recognise God's dealings with the world as a whole, to contemplate history as the unfolding of the Divine plan from the beginning, to mark the succession of world-powers, and to look for the consummation of the whole drama of humanity as something that each seer would fain expect to take place in the near or immediate future, when Israel should obtain her rightful position among the kingdoms, and the descendants of those who had oppressed them acknowledge in word and deed the supremacy of Him who is worshipped at the Temple in Jerusalem.

Thus the tendency of an apocalyptic writer was to give a sort of universal history from the time of the person whose name he assumed for purposes of authorship, but dealing more minutely with the history of the Jewish nation. The narrative grows in fulness as it approaches his own times, which naturally loom large before his mental vision; when suddenly our power of identifying the events to which he refers with those preserved by other records of the time, fails us, and we con-

---

* In Zechariah we have a connecting link between the two, prophecy so called and vision being both of them characteristic features in his writings.

clude that the rest is of the nature of prophecy, which has been falsified by the actual course of things. A common feature is that the author expects the end of the world, or the Messianic kingdom to arrive very soon after the time at which he writes.

It will follow that the date of an apocalyptic book of this nature will fall " between the latest event clearly described in it and its first unmistakable break from the actual facts of history." *

(*b*) Much as the Jews had learnt from Greece and its philosophy, and perhaps most of all from that of Plato, they yet in one respect at least clung to their own traditional ideal as opposed to his conception of the perfect state. The republic, the form of government, which he considered to represent political perfection, must, from the nature of it, be of no great dimensions. As a scheme of representative government was a creation of much later days, it was necessary for Plato's ideal that all the citizens should be able to meet for deliberative and legislative purposes in their Ecclesia. But the Jews' ideal had always been a different one. A ruler, either Divine, or human as representing the Divine, a Theocracy, or a monarchy bearing a sacred character, this was the type firmly established in the nation's affections, and lending itself by its principle of paternal government to a dominion unrestricted by geographical limitations. Such a kingdom was the ultimate issue towards which the visions of apocalyptic seers led up. It was the consummation of the series of events which constituted the Divine ordering of the affairs of men for the ultimate glory of Jehovah as set forth in the exaltation of His chosen people.

(*c*) The long troubles which befell the nation have their reflection in this branch of literature.

* Thomson, *op. cit.*, p. 398.

They were oppressed by conqueror after conqueror. They were despoiled of their goods by excessive imposts. They were carried captive to distant regions. They were subjected to famine and distress by the arbitrary action of the satrap, or king, or prince, or victorious general. From time to time their Holy City was sacked, their Temple and altar desecrated, their most sacred rites made the sport of the conqueror.

Accordingly the visions dwell upon material as well as spiritual prosperity in the days to come. It is true that the promises of superabundant plenty may be meant, in part at least, in a figurative sense, but doubtless the literal signification of the words is not to be excluded. Moreover, Israel shall have cause to exult over their foes. The tables shall be turned on the conqueror and the oppressor. The words "Vengeance is mine and recompence," * had not yet been emphasized by an Apostle. And so we read; "But all those who ruled you, even they shall be delivered over to the sword." †

(*d*) One of the many connecting links which this literature affords between the Old Testament and the New is found in the frequent references to angels, one distinctive feature, however, as compared with inspired books, consisting in the readiness to name these celestial beings, which is shewn to its greatest extent in the Book of Enoch. In Daniel, as in the New Testament, we learn the names of two, Michael and Gabriel. In Tobit we are told of another, Raphael. In Enoch, Phanuel is added to these. In Daniel, "princes" (angels) are appointed as guardians of certain nations. In Enoch, seventy shepherds (angels) appear as ruling over Israel. In Daniel and in Enoch alike we read of another class of

---

* Deut. 32. 35, quoted Rom. 12. 19; Heb. 10. 30.
† *Apocalypse of Baruch* (probably however of post-Christian date. *See* below) 72. 6.

angels, called "watchers." * Babylonian idolatry may well have furnished the occasion upon which in the Providence of God the doctrine of angels and their ministry as exercised in behalf of men began to be developed. To the elaborate hierarchy of gods now arose as a counterpart an elaborate hierarchy of angels, "who would defend the worshippers of Jehovah from the power of these gods of the nations." †

(e) The doctrine of final judgment, and of rewards and punishments in the next world, comparatively obscure in the prophetic books of the Old Testament, had evidently now come to be a very real part of the Jewish popular faith. We may contrast in this respect the poetic picture of the descent of the king of Babylon into Sheol,‡ with the elaborate account of the fallen angels in the Book of Enoch, and the state of the lost as described in the Apocalypse of Baruch (48. 38, 39).

The writings of the period which in whole or in part are extant under this head may be classified in accordance with the main purposes which their respective authors seem to have had before their minds, viz. :—

(A) those in which the aim was to represent to the Gentiles the excellence of Judaism as the one true religion, and the danger of neglecting its claims to acceptance; in other words, those in which is discernible a proselytizing or propagandist aim; and

(B) those which in their composition had regard to the encouragement and warning of the writer's co-religionists, pointing out for their edification the judgments that should come upon the wicked, and the final blessedness of the righteous.

The chief extant literature of the former character consists of the Sibylline Oracles. Under the latter heading we may

---

* Comp. *Testaments of the XII. Patr.* Reub. 5; Naph. 3.
† Thomson, *op. cit.*, p. 211.   ‡ Isa. 14.

place the Book of Enoch, the Book of Jubilees, the Apocalypse of Baruch, and the 2nd [4th] Book of Esdras.

(A) The Sibyllines.

"The Sibyl was in heathen antiquity 'the semi-divine prophetess of the orders and counsels of the gods concerning the fate of cities and kingdoms.' She was distinguished from the official priestly order of prophets by representing a free and non-official prophetic power, being indeed first of all a personification of the Deity as revealing itself in nature."*

At first there was supposed to be but one Sibyl, who moved from place to place. Afterwards as many as ten were enumerated.† In Asia Minor and Greece, Sibylline verses were possessed and circulated privately only. In Rome, on the contrary, a collection was kept, and from time to time officially consulted, in the Capitol. It consisted of about a thousand verses which had been got together to replace those which were said to have been first obtained by Tarquinius Superbus, and which perished in the burning of the Capitol, 83 B.C.

From the secrecy which belonged to these as well as to any private collections, it followed that they possessed the charm which appertains to the mysterious, and further, that they could conveniently be added to at pleasure. Accordingly, when it occurred to the Jewish mind to make use of this mode of propagandism, it was an excellent method to hit upon for bringing about the desired result. Later, Christians took up the same idea, and through them the pre-Christian oracles as well have been transmitted. The original form invariably used was that of Greek hexameter verse. Fourteen books of this nature have been handed down to us.

---

* Schürer, *op. cit.*, II. iii. 271 f.
† So Varro in Lactantius, *Div. Inst.* i. 6. (Migne, *Patrol.* vi. 141).

"The collection *as we have it is a chaotic wilderness*, to sift and arrange which will ever baffle the most acute criticism. . . . Such being the nature of the whole, it is not possible always to distinguish with certainty between Jewish and Christian matter."*

The third book contains the oldest portions, dating in all probability from Maccabean days. Passing by the lines 1–96, which are clearly out of place, we may summarise the contents of the rest of the book, in three divisions, as follow :—

(i.) (lines 97–294) The Tower of Babel, Confusion of Tongues, and Dispersion. Rule of Chronos, Titan, and Japetos. Quarrel between the first two, contest between their descendants, and destruction of both races. Thereupon ensue the kingdoms of Egypt, Persia, Media, Ethiopia, Assyria, Babylonia, Macedon, Egypt again, and Rome. Prophecies of the Sibyl as to those later sovereignties. In the reign of *the seventh Egyptian king of Greek descent*, the chosen people of God shall grow strong and teach all men how to live aright. Judgments are foretold for the kingdoms of the world. This division closes with an historical sketch and laudation of the Jewish people.

(ii.) (295–488) Disconnected judgments on Babylon, Egypt, etc., and on individual towns, islands, and countries. A promise of prosperity and peace in Asia and Egypt.

(iii.) (489–807) Oracles relating to Phœnicia, the Greeks, and others. Encomiums on Israel, which shew the idolatry and licentiousness of the nations of the world. Exhortation to conversion, and warnings of judgments on the ungodly, specially on Greece, with promises of the blessedness of the Messianic kingdom.

* Schürer, *op. cit.*, p. 276.

One link connecting the three groups is a reference occurring in all of them * to the time of Ptolemy VII. (Physcon).

DATE.

The last named circumstance is a clue to the date of these groups, which (apart from interpolations) constitute the oldest portion of the oracles. Ptolemy Physcon reigned conjointly with his brother Philometor, from 170–154 B.C. Thereupon he underwent a period of banishment, but returned after his brother's death, and exercised sole rule from 146 to 117 B.C. The expression used of him in line 608 may indicate youth, either in years or in sovereignty,† and thus might refer to either the earlier or the later of these two periods. The second, however, is the more likely in itself, and is confirmed by allusions to the destruction of Carthage and of Corinth (146 B.C).‡

Apparent references to Antiochus Epiphanes and some of the subsequent Seleucid kings, ending with the rule of the intruder, Trypho (146–139), suggest the date circ. 140 B.C. *Roman* times at any rate are precluded. The nation which the oracle looks for as the destroyer of the Temple is *Libya*.§

This book shews acquaintance with the Book of Daniel.‖ It is itself quoted as early as the *Chaldaica* of Alexander Polyhistor (80–40 B.C.).¶ There is a doubtful quotation by Clement of Rome (*ob.* circ. 97 A.D.) : several certain ones by his namesake of Alexandria (born 150–160 A.D.), and numerous references in Lactantius (*ob.* 325 A.D.).

Other portions of these oracles are also of pre-Christian origin. Such are (*a*) certain fragments which stood at the

---

* 191-193, 316-318, 608-610.
† βασιλεὺς νέος, *young* king, or *new* king.   ‡ 484 ff.
§ 324, 328 f. Lines 464-470 may well indeed relate to Roman times, but they are held to be a later insertion.
‖ 388-400.   ¶ *See* Euseb. *Chron.* ed. Schoene, i p. 23.

beginning of the prophecy,* and which are now placed accordingly (though not occurring in the manuscripts of the Sibyllines) in front of the First Book as an Introduction. They probably † formed the original opening of the Third Book (which we have just been discussing), and by their earnest propagandism and denunciation of idolatry, bring out as clearly as any of these writings this special feature of the Sibylline branch of apocalyptic literature : (*b*) (**3.** 36–92) a passage which is shewn by its allusions to belong in point of date to the triumvirate of Antony, Octavian, and Lepidus,‡ and to the female sway, to which all the world shall yield obedience.§ This fixes the time as 40–30 B.C. (*c*) Certain portions of the Fifth Book, which may *possibly* be of pre-Christian authorship.||

(B) **Other Apocalyptic Literature.—The Book of Enoch.**

The characteristic feature of this book, as compared with other writings of the same class, is its hopefulness, and joyful anticipation of the overthrow of the wicked earth-rulers, and the establishment of peace and prosperity for Israel under Messianic sway.

The book is of interest, not only from its contents, but also through its being (apparently) quoted in the New Testament.¶ The Book of Jubilees ** draws largely from it, and so do Tertullian and other early Christian writers. It is twice quoted

---

* *See* Theophilus, *Ad Autol.* ii. 36. (W. B. Flower, London, 1860).
† *See* Schürer. *op. cit.*, p. 283.
‡ *See* line 52.
§ Cleopatra. *See* lines 75–80. The end of the world is expected in her life time.
|| For particulars as to forged verses under the name of well-known Greek poets, or other spurious compositions or interpolations in genuine works, all having for their object the glorification of Judaism, and the promotion of a belief in the regard paid to it by leaders of Greek culture in former days, *see* Schürer, *op. cit.*, 294–320.
¶ Jude 14. 15.
** *See* next section.

in the Epistle of Barnabas.* After the 8th century all trace of it disappeared till Bruce the traveller brought to Europe three manuscripts of an Aethiopic version, which he had obtained from the Abyssinian Church. A large piece of it is now known in Greek.†

To give even a complete outline of the contents would occupy too much of our space. The book claims to be a record by the patriarch Enoch of visions and other revelations shewn him by angels (chaps. 1—36), while he visits heaven itself. He is further shewn the secret processes of nature, and the abode of departed spirits, righteous and wicked. Chaps. 37—71 consist of three allegories (similitudes or parables). In these he sees the heavenly host, and learns the mysteries of the universe, including secrets appertaining to the celestial bodies and the names of the stars; also the nature of the Messiah and of His mission, and the day upon which He shall judge the world.

Other visions follow, in particular, that of the cattle, sheep, wild beasts, and shepherds, this vision depicting by symbolism the history of Israel down to Messianic times (85—90). To that vision therefore (on the principle noticed on p. 215) we turn for a clue to the date of at least this portion of the book.

Among the subsequent visions which form the conclusion of the book comes an account of events attending upon Noah's birth.

It is generally allowed that the book is not all the work of one author. Also there are many longer or shorter interpolations.

Moreover, although the section entitled "allegories" is in all likelihood pre-Christian,‡ its internal indications of date

---

* 4 and 16. † A. Lods, *The Akhmim Fragment*, Paris, 1892.

‡ Some critics have maintained that the whole of the book, and others that the allegories, are of Christian date, but their grounds are insufficient. *See* Thomson, *op. cit.*, pp. 407 ff. for their arguments.

are by no means such as to ensure unanimity among critics. While generally referred to the 1st or 2nd century B.C., Thomson * would place it as early as 210 B.C.

However this may be, it is plain that the allegories, as compared with other parts, are the production of a different author. In them the use of the names of God, the angelology, the eschatology, and the doctrine of the Messiah, differ essentially from the remainder of the book.†

"Also, instead of its being the wicked and the ungodly in general who appear in contrast to the pious, as is the case in the rest of the book, it is rather the Gentile rulers, the kings and powerful ones of the earth.‡ .... This circumstance serves to explain why it is that in these allegories such decided prominence is given to the Messianic hope."§

Turning now to chaps. 85—90, which are to supply us with our clue to the date, if any portion can do so, we have an historical vision, in which the patriarchal times and onwards are represented under the symbolism of animals, whose colour indicates their character. White cattle and then, from Jacob's time, white sheep denote Israel. Wild animals (Assyria, Babylon, etc.) attack and hurt them. The Lord appoints seventy shepherds (angels) to tend them, and prescribes that only a certain number of the sheep are to be given over to destruction. The shepherds are lax, and are consequently consigned to the place where the fallen angels undergo punishment. After various vicissitudes lambs are born to the sheep, and, further troubles intervening, horns at last appear on the lambs, and one young ram in particular grows a large horn, and to this one the others congregate. They are attacked again; but the Lord comes to the aid of the lambs and gives them the victory.

---

* *Op. cit.*, pp. 399 ff. † Schürer, *op. cit.*, p. 67.
‡ See chaps. 38. 4, 5; 46. 7, 8, etc. § Schürer, *Ibid.*

Here the narrative ends. Who, then, is the ram with the horns? Is it Judas Maccabeus or John Hyrcanus? The detailed comparison of the vision with the history of the time would suggest on the whole the latter.*

Certain portions of the book have been called Noachian, as relating to Noah's time, and claiming his authorship. But they contain no indications that would justify us in an attempt to determine their date.

VALUE.

The interest of the book in connexion with doctrine has already been partially indicated. The ministry of angels, future rewards and punishments, the resurrection of the dead (ch. 22), the powers of Satan and his legions (chaps. 40, 65) are forcibly exhibited. "In doctrine the Book of Enoch exhibits a great advance of thought within the limits of revelation in each of the great divisions of knowledge. The teaching on nature is a curious attempt to reduce the scattered images of the Old Testament to a physical system. The view of society and of man, of the temporary triumph and final discomfiture of the oppressors of God's people, carries out into elaborate detail the pregnant images of Daniel. The figure of the Messiah is invested with majestic dignity as 'the Son of God' (ch. 105. 2 only), 'Whose Name was named before the sun was made' (ch. 48. 3), and Who existed 'aforetime in the presence of God' (ch. 62. 6 : comp. Laurence, *Prel. Diss.* li. f.). And at the same time His attributes as 'the son of man,' 'the son of woman' (ch. 62. 5 only), 'the elect one,' 'the righteous one,' 'the anointed,' are brought into conspicuous notice."†

---

* So Schürer, *op. cit.*, p. 66. But Thomson (*op. cit.*, p. 405) points out, that if, as he strongly holds, the writer was an Essene, he would not speak in such favourable terms of Hyrcanus, with his Sadducean leanings.

† Smith's *Dict. of Bible* (2nd ed.), Article, "Enoch, Book of" (Bp. Westcott), p. 943.

LANGUAGE.

The Ethiopic version is a translation from a Greek text (not now extant), which evidently agreed substantially with the quotations found in the Greek Fathers. But it is probable that Hebrew or Aramaic was the original language, although, if so, it is strange that the book was not more used by Rabbinical writers. The Hebraic style would not of course be conclusive either way. But the names of the angels all suggest Hebrew etymology, and as a book of this kind would probably be written in Palestine, the fact constitutes a further argument in the same direction.

The Book of Jubilees.

Like the Book of Enoch, this work also, after disappearing for centuries, was found in 1844 by a German missionary, Krapf, in Ethiopia, and so brought into notice in Europe. Unlike the former case, however, an old Latin version has also been discovered.*

Another name for the work is *The Little Genesis*,† which describes faithfully enough its subject, but must not be taken to imply that it is shorter than the opening book of the Old Testament. It was very possibly written with a close regard to the impression to be produced upon cultured members of the Hellenic world. Accordingly, it deals with the patriarchal history from the apologetic side, smoothing over or omitting the points which the author judges likely to prove to such readers either distasteful or more or less incredible. Thus there is no mention of the expulsion from Eden, the curse upon Cain, or the cruelty practised upon Joseph by his brethren. On the other hand, the commentary is of an eminently *bizarre* character.

---

* By Ceriani, Librarian of the Ambrosian Library, Milan, in 1861.
† λεπτογένεσις, more strictly, Genesis *spun out fine*.

and we may observe in every thing relating to genealogy and chronology an amplitude of detail far exceeding that of the book on which it professes to be a Midrashic commentary. It gives us the names of the patriarchs' wives and many other particulars of a like nature. It also arranges events in accordance with the Jubilee periods of forty-nine years. Each of those periods is subdivided into seven year-days of seven years; and the book, in fixing the date of an occurrence, gives minute particulars of time in accordance with this method. Hence is derived its name. The author also set much store by the ceremonial law, annual feasts, new moons, Sabbaths, etc., bringing down his history to the institution of the Passover (Exod. 12). It should be added that he makes the Law as given on Sinai to be only a reproduction or copy for the use of earth of that which from time immemorial had been written on heavenly tablets and observed by the angels above.*

Authorship and Date.

The emphasis laid upon the observance of the Sabbath, as well as other indications, have suggested that the book is the work of an Essene. Against this it is urged (*a*) that there is no suggestion that the author disapproved of animal sacrifices, as did the Essenes; (*b*) that there is no mention of those washings or purifications which held so prominent a place among Essene observances. The latter argument, however, has the weakness which belongs to one which is only negative; and possibly this might be said to some extent of the former one also. At any rate, if the writer was an Essene, he seems to have been one with strong Pharisaic leanings.

The date, too, is difficult to decide. We have here no world history to afford us a clue.† The book indicates a strong dislike to Edom, which may either mean the Herodian

---
* Comp. Heb. 9. 23.   † See p. 214 f., *supra*.

dynasty, or be a disguise (as it is in many Hebrew post-Biblical compositions) for Rome. The author makes large use of the Book of Enoch,* and is himself quoted in the Testaments of the Twelve Patriarchs, a work which is probably to be placed in the 1st century A.D. As a piece of literature which very possibly at any rate falls within the limits of the present work, we have given the Book of Jubilees a place in our list of this class of writings.

Its original language was Semitic † (whether Hebrew or Aramaic we cannot determine), and doubtless, therefore, it was written in Palestine.

The Apocalypse of Baruch.

As the last-named work was framed upon the lines of the first of the *historical* books of the Old Testament, and as the Psalms of Solomon took as their basis the Canonical *Psalter*, so here we have an apocalypse claiming by its name a companionship, and so challenging a comparison, with the old *prophetic* teaching.

The book represents Baruch as bidden by the word of the Lord to proclaim the impending fate of Jerusalem at the hands of the Chaldeans. Details concerning supernatural events on the occasion of the siege, forecasts of coming judgment on the nations which successively oppress Israel, the setting up of the Messianic kingdom, the future blessedness of the righteous, a further vision and its interpretation—these constitute the main features of the book.

DATE.

The only passage which throws any light on this point, shews at the same time that, to say the least, it is far from

---

* *See* Schürer, *l.c.*, p. 70.
† This appears from St. Jerome's references to it, *Epist.* 78 (*ad Fabiolam*), *Mansio* 18, and *Mansio* 24.

certain that the book has any right to be reckoned as a part of the literature of the period we are considering in this volume.

In ch. 32. 2–4 it is declared that Jerusalem, after the overthrow by the Chaldeans, shall be rebuilt, *but shall later be again destroyed*, and long lie waste before the time comes when it shall be restored for ever. It seems plain that that second destruction can only refer to the one which took place at the hands of Titus (70 A.D.), and this makes the book a product of Christian times. The only ground for mentioning the work here is that the above inference has been denied. Thomson* considers that the prophecy is satisfied by the horror caused through the forcible entrance of Pompey into the Holy of Holies (63 B.C.).

The book is at any rate older than the time of Papias,† who borrows from ch. 29. 5.‡ It exists in the Peshitto in a Milan manuscript; § but apart from this no ancient version is found.

Second [Fourth] Esdras.

Unlike the other books called by the name of the famous post-captivity scribe, this work does not claim to be a history, but a prophecy in the apocalyptic shape.

Properly speaking it may be said, as we shall presently see, with even greater certainty than that last dealt with, to fall outside our period. ‖ But we have decided to include it here, inasmuch as by so doing we complete our notices of the variety of works which form the deutero-canonical books attached to the Old Testament.

---

* *Op. cit.*, p. 261.   † Fl. circ. 130 A.D.
‡ *See* him quoted in Iren. v. 33. 3. (Migne, *Patrol. Gr.* viii. 1213.)
§ Edited by Ceriani, in the original Syriac, in *Monumenta Sacra et profana*, vol. v., fasc. 2. (Milan, 1871), pp. 113-180, and in a Latin translation by the same editor, *ibid.* i. 2 (Milan, 1866), pp. 73-98.
‖ Although Hilgenfeld makes it pre-Christian (30 B.C.: *Zeitschift*, 1867, p. 285).

APOCALYPTIC LITERATURE. 229

We may at once dismiss the first two and last two chapters
of the book, as it stands in our English versions, and in the
Latin text from which they are taken. While the body of the
work is of Jewish authorship, these are obviously additions by
a Christian hand.* They indicate knowledge of the New
Testament.† Moreover, Israel is there rebuked for rebellion.
They reject offers of mercy, and the Gentiles are summoned to
receive the favour which the Jews have forfeited (chaps. 1, 2).
The latter of these two sections was perhaps composed
260–270 A.D., as the passage 5. 28 ff. has been thought to
refer to wars of that period. Chaps. 1, 2, may have been
written either at the same time or somewhat earlier.

OUTLINE OF CHAPTERS 3—14.

When dealing with the Book of Enoch, we noted the contrast between its tone of joyful anticipation and the melan-
choly which is a conspicuous feature of this apocalypse. We
are here carried back to the 30th year of the Captivity, and
presented with the sorrowful thoughts which may have been
supposed to fill Ezra's mind as he mused in the outskirts of
Babylon over the fortunes of his people, and the prolongation
of the Exile.‡ He cannot account for the calamities (3. 1–36)
of the righteous, and the prosperity of their oppressors. The
archangel Uriel is sent to reprove him (4. 1–21) and solve his
doubts as to the ways of Providence. He does so by means of

---

* In the best Latin MSS. they are separated from the rest, and they are not
contained in the Oriental Versions. See below. We may note that in 7. 28 "*filius
meus Jesus*" (my son Jesus), which is not found in the Oriental Versions, is
doubtless a Christian interpolation existing as early as Ambrose (*ob.* circ. 397 A.D.),
who quotes it (*Comm. on Luke* 1. 66). (Migne, *Patrol.* xv. 1503).

† Comp. 1. 30, 33 and Matt. 23. 37, 38; 1. 37 and John 20. 29; 2. 13 and Matt. 25. 34;
2. 26 and John 17. 12; 2. 42 ff. and Rev. 7. 9; 15. 8 and Rev. 6. 10; 19. 2; 15. 35 and
Matt. 24. 30; 16. 54 and Luke 16. 15.

‡ He is thus placed about ninety years before his real time, but chronology was
not a strong point with Jewish writers in the days with which we are dealing.

seven visions. These are intended to teach him that wickedness has its appointed time. In spite of appearances, God does not cast away his people. He is still ready to shew Himself cognisant of their needs, and faithful to His promises. The greater part of the trouble is already past. When the signs (enumerated in the visions) shall present themselves, then the Son of God, the Anointed One, shall appear and reign for four hundred years. Thereupon He and all in whom is the breath of life shall die, and for seven days there shall be no living thing on the earth. This week of dread silence shall be followed by the Resurrection and the Judgment (**7.** 26-35). The majority shall go into perdition, but a few shall be saved (**7.** 70). For as "silver is more abundant than gold, and brass than silver, and iron than brass, lead than iron, and clay than lead (**7.** [56])"; so the wicked outnumber the righteous. Each receives according to his deserts, and although the righteous have often interceded effectually on behalf of the ungodly as regards this life, such intercession shall be of no avail for the world to come (**7.** [102-105]). Men's ruin is brought about through their own sinfulness, and it is therefore unfair to lay all the charge upon their inheritance of Adam's guilt (**7.** 46-61).

There follows an allegorical representation of the establishment of the Temple and its services, and the overthrow of Jerusalem (**9.** 26--**10.** 59), the vision of the eagle (**11.** 1—**12.** 51), which we shall examine immediately, as determining the date of the composition, and a further vision representing redemption, restoration (including the return of the ten tribes), and peace (**13.** 1-58). Finally, Ezra is warned by a voice from a bush to prepare for his departure from the world, and is bidden to record, with the assistance of five writers, that which he shall be inspired to dictate (**14.** 1-48).

Date and Authorship.

The vision above referred to is briefly as follows :—An eagle rises from the sea. It has twelve wings, from which grow eight subordinate wings : it has also three heads. All these are rulers of some sort. The twelve large wings rule successively. It is noticed that the second of them rules more than twice as long as any of the others. Of the eight subordinate wings all but two disappear after ruling or attempting to do so. Of the three heads also the middle one rules over the whole earth and dies. The second devours the third, and reigns alone. A lion (the Messiah) announces to the eagle its approaching destruction. The third head disappears. The two remaining wings now rule, but feebly. Finally, the eagle is wholly consumed by fire. The angel gives Ezra hints for the interpretation of the vision.

Explanations which would involve the history of Rome before the later part of the post-captivity period (when that power began to have an interest for the Jews), or which would make the wings refer to Greek, but the heads to Roman rulers, are inadequate. If, on the other hand, we take the twelve chief wings to represent Julius Cæsar, as followed by the eight succeeding Roman emperors * (of whom Augustus, in accordance with the vision, did in fact reign more than twice the span of any other, viz., reckoning from his first consulate 43 B.C., fifty-six years), and lastly by three usurpers,† we may assign the subordinate wings to other and less well-known persons who claimed supreme power.

The three heads remain. By the above arrangement we have reserved for them the three last of the twelve Cæsars, viz., the Flavian Emperors, Vespasian, Titus, and Domitian. Of

---

* Augustus, Tiberius, Caligula, Claudius, Nero, Galba, Otho, Vitellius.
† Vindex, Nymphidius, Piso.

these the second was not in point of fact slain by the third; but there was a current belief at the time to this effect, encouraged by Domitian's demeanour.*

As the Messiah (the lion) appears during the reign of the third head (Domitian), it follows that this is the time when for the writer history changes to prophecy. We therefore place the book in Domitian's reign (81–96 A.D.).†

CHARACTER.

"The doctrine of the book offers curious approximations to that of St. Paul, as the imagery does to that of the Apocalypse (*e.g.* 2 Esd. **13.** 43, *sq.*; **5.** 4). The relation of 'the first Adam' to his sinful posterity, and the operation of the Law (**3.** 20 *sq.*; **7.** 48; **9.** 36); the transitoriness of the world (**4.** 26); the eternal counsels of God (**6.** *sq.*); His Providence (**7.** 11) and long-suffering (**7.** 64); His sanctification of His people 'from the beginning' (**9.** 8), and their peculiar and lasting privileges (**6.** 59), are plainly stated; and, on the other hand, the efficacy of good works (**8.** 33) in conjunction with faith (**9.** 7) is no less clearly affirmed."‡

LANGUAGE.

Unlike the two works which we have discussed, this book has been continuously known to the Christian Church from early times. It was handed down in a Latin version of a Greek original,§ preserved only in one or two fragments. There are several Oriental versions differing in value. Of these the Syriac

---

* *See* Schürer, *op. cit.*, p. 106, for references.

† We need not do more than mention Gutschmied's view that the three heads are Septimius Severus (193–211 A.D.) and his sons Caracalla and Geta, and that the date of the book is 218 A.D.; inasmuch as it is quoted by Clement of Alexandria (chap. v. 35, in *Strom.* iii. 16), the period of whose literary activity was circ. 190–203 A.D.

‡ Smith's *Dict. of Bible*, Article, "Esdras, Second Book of" (Bp. Westcott).

§ There is no reason for supposing that a Hebrew or Aramaic text stands behind the Greek.

is the most important. It is found only in the famous Syro-Hexaplaric manuscript belonging to the Ambrosian Library at Milan, which has been edited in facsimile by Dr. Ceriani.* There are also two Arabic versions, as well as an Aethiopic and an Armenian version. Of these the last-named differs most widely from the Greek.

DISCOVERY OF A LOST PORTION.

It had long been perceived that in the Latin the transition in chap. 7 from *v.* 35 to *v.* 36 was abrupt.† On a close examination of the principal Latin MS.‡ it was seen that a leaf had been removed. The late Mr. R. L. Bensly, sometime the Lord Almoner's Professor of Arabic at Cambridge, was induced by a description of a ninth century MS. at Amiens to examine it. He says:—" I read on with growing interest till I approached the place of the long-familiar chasm; then, as my eyes glided on to the words *et apparebit locus tormenti* [*and the pit of torment shall appear*, the commencement of the newly-discovered Latin section], I knew that the oldest and best translation of this passage was at last recovered; that another fragment of the old Latin was gathered up; and that now at last—an event which can scarcely happen again in these latter days—a new chapter would be added to the Apocrypha of our Bible."§

It should be added that the Rev. John Palmer, Professor of Arabic at Cambridge from 1804 to 1819, found the passage in a Latin eighth century MS. in Spain in 1826; but his transcript only appeared (long after his death) in 1877.

---

* Also edited by him in *Monumenta sacra et profana*, vol. v. fasc. 1 (1868), p. 45, ff.

† The Oriental versions have a connecting passage.

‡ Known as Codex Sangermanensis (*i.e.* from *St. Germain des Prés*, a Benedictine monastery).

§ *The Missing Fragment, etc.*, Cambridge, 1875, p. 7.

Use of the Book.

Several passages in the Epistle of Barnabas may contain a reference to the book, but in each of them the evidence falls short of being conclusive. The first certain quotation is that to which we have already referred, by Clement of Alexandria.* Ambrose is the patristic writer who quotes the book most fully and clearly.

The Council of Trent excluded it from the Canon, but it stands in copies of the Vulgate printed before the Council's decree, and even now occurs in that Version, but after the New Testament. Passages taken from it are still found in the Roman services. Although standing among the Apocryphal Books which the 6th Article of the Church of England enumerates, it is not now represented in the Lectionary.† In the pre-Reformation Church of England (as still in the Roman Missal), chap. 2. 36, 37 stood as an Introit for Whit Tuesday.

---

* See p. 234 supra.
† It may be noted that the well-known words of St. Jerome, quoted in that Article, do not in strictness refer to either of the Apocryphal Books of Esdras, being used expressly of others, viz., Tobit, Judith, Wisdom, Ecclesiasticus, and Maccabees. Of Second [Fourth] Esdras he speaks contemptuously, *Adv. Vigil.* vi. ("A book which under the name of Esdras is read by you and those like you . . . a book which I have never myself read. For what need is there to occupy oneself with what the Church has not received?") Migne, *Patrol.* xxiii. 344.

CHAPTER XVII.

THE SEPTUAGINT.

WE can only attempt here to give in the merest outline a small portion of a wide subject, and to notice the most striking features of this the first translation of the Old Testament—and we may venture safely to add the first considerable translation of any kind from Hebrew into Greek—viewed as a part of the literature of the period which we have under consideration.

Its Origin.

As we have already frequently had occasion to remark, the "Dispersion," that is, the Jews who lived beyond the limits of Palestine, formed a large proportion of the nation. Of these the dwellers in Alexandria constituted, if not the most numerous, at all events the most cultivated and influential division. From an early date there had been Jews resident in Egypt. In 650 B.C. Psammetichus I. is said to have employed as mercenaries troops of that nation in his war against Ethiopia.* In later times the number appears to have been inconsiderable,† till Ptolemy I. (Lagi) introduced from Palestine captives and many others as settlers.‡

But Egypt also contained a strong Greek element. According to Herodotus there were 30,000 Ionian and Carian mercenaries, who lived in a fertile district on the Pelusiac branch of the Nile.§ After Alexander's conquests, and under the rule of

---

* *See* Schürer, *op. cit.*, II. ii. 227, for authorities.
† Jeremiah (42. 17 ff.) prophecies "sword, famine, and pestilence" for those who fled to Egypt upon the overthrow of Jerusalem.
‡ *See* Schürer as above cited ; also Jos. *Ant.* 12. 1. 1.
§ *Herod.* ii. 163. Jeremiah (46. 21) likens them to "calves of the stall."

the Ptolemies, the Greek tongue and Greek influence and culture became thoroughly established in Egypt.

At the time of the foundation of Alexandria the rights of citizenship were bestowed upon Jewish settlers. They were located in the immediate neighbourhood of the river, and took a prominent part in the commercial activities of the place.

Under these circumstances there was nothing, apart from the influence of their inherited religion and patriotic or literary motives, to prevent Greek from completely supplanting for all purposes their traditional language. It is probable that in the third century B.C. the Sacred Books in their original garb would have been almost or quite unintelligible to the great majority of Jews resident in Egypt.

It was thus clear that, if the Greek-speaking Jews were to retain any general acquaintance with the Scriptures, they must be presented to them in the language which had become their mother-tongue. Moreover it was an age of enquiry and cultivation. Antiochus I. (Soter, 281-262 B.C.) had begun the fashion of causing the literature of other nations to be translated into the tongue of the cultured world. " Berosus, the Chaldean, published the mythology and history of Babylon from the cuneiform records by order of the king. . . . . It was doubtless at his suggestion that Manetho translated a similar work from the hieroglyphics on the history of Egypt for Philadelphus." *

The above remarks will serve to indicate two distinct views which have been held as to the immediate cause of the translation of the Old Testament, or more strictly speaking, of the Pentateuch, into Greek. Those views are as follows :—

(i.) The impetus was given from outside, viz., by Ptolemy II. (Philadelphus, 283-247 B.C.). According to the traditional

---

* Mahaffy, *Alex. Emp.*, p. 137.

account, contained in the forged letter which was ascribed to Aristeas,* a court official of Ptolemy, that king was induced by his librarian, Demetrius Phalereus, to apply to the Jewish high-priest Eleazar, who in response sent seventy † elders to Egypt. Graphic details are given of the circumstances under which the translation was made, all tending to the general aim of the glorification of the Jewish nation and their Law. It was doubtless from the number of the translators as given in the traditional account that the name of the Version is drawn.

Apart from the embellishments of the story, it is of course quite possible that one so ready to encourage letters as Philadelphus took measures to procure for his library a translation of the first part of the Jewish Scriptures.

A certain Aristobulus ‡ supports this view, while he also states that portions of such a work existed much earlier. But a doubt is thrown upon the trustworthy character even of this more prosaic narrative, by the probability that Demetrius had been banished from Alexandria before Philadelphus's accession.

(ii.) Thus the alternative view is more probable, viz., that, as we have already suggested, the translation was made to supply the needs of the Jews themselves, who, living at a distance from Palestine, had partially or altogether lost their hold upon the language of their fathers. In Palestine, after the Return, although the Law was read in Hebrew, it had to be interpreted to the congregation in Aramaic, which for everyday life had supplanted the older tongue. Similarly we may conclude that to Alexandrian Jews

---

* This celebrated letter may be seen in Hody, *De Bibl. Textibus orig.*, Oxford 1705, pp. i.-xxxvi. Its substance is given by Josephus (xii. 2. 1 ff.).

† Or, according to another form of the story, seventy-two, six from each tribe.

‡ In a fragment preserved by Clement of Alexandria (*Strom.* i. 22, Migne *Patrol. Gr.* viii. 894), comp. Eusebius (*Praep. Evang.* xiii. 12).

the Sacred Books were expounded in Greek. Translations of portions of the Scriptures may also have been made for private use.* And thus the way would be paved towards a version on a larger scale and possessed of authoritative sanction.

Important as was the part played by the Septuagint under God's Providence in bringing about the conversion of the Gentile world, we cannot suppose that a desire to satisfy the curiosity of the surrounding heathen population can have been more than a very subordinate motive for the production of this version. It is true that various historical works of which fragments survive in late writers were composed for the purpose of placing Jewish sacred history in a favourable light.† But the Septuagint, as supplying a want necessarily felt by the Jews themselves, evidently stands in a different position.

The Septuagint the work of various Authors and Times.

The Law was first translated, as being the part of the Old Testament Scriptures held in highest veneration, and earliest adopted for public reading.‡ Afterwards, as in Palestine (but probably at a much later time in Egypt), the "Prophets" also began to be used in the synagogue worship of Alexandrian Jews. Thus gradually the whole of the Old Testament came to be rendered into Greek, for public or private use, while the

---

* This circumstance easily lent itself to corruption of the text. A student would not hesitate to make marginal annotations on his private copy, and these might easily be introduced by the next copyist into the body of the work.

† e.g. by Demetrius, a Jewish Hellenist in the time of Ptolemy IV. (222-205 B.C.), who wrote a Greek history of the Judean kings; by Eupolemus (in all probability to be identified with the leader of a Jewish embassy sent by Judas Maccabeus to Rome; 1 Macc. 8. 17; 2 Macc. 4. 11), and others; among the rest by Jason of Cyrene, of whose book, as we saw (p. 152), 2 Maccabees is an abridgment. For any details that are known as to such works see Schürer, op. cit., pp. 200 ff.

‡ We have noticed above that the comments on the Old Testament in Wisdom are confined to the Mosaic history. Even a writer as late as Philo makes comparatively few quotations from other parts.

volume was also permitted, as we have seen, to include other works unknown to the Palestinian Canon.

The fact that the version is thus due to different hands and periods is illustrated by the varying degrees of merit with which different books or even portions of the same book * are rendered. While the "Books of Moses" are in the main a faithful and scholarly reproduction of the original, there is a large amount of inaccuracy and blundering in some prophetical parts, *e.g.* in Isaiah and the Minor Prophets. On the whole it may be said that the poetical are inferior to the historical. Moreover, in the case of a translation made by different persons and at such different times, it was clearly impossible, even had the idea suggested itself to the scholarship of the day, to have a comprehensive revision of the parts in order to secure something like uniformity of phraseology. Thus names as well as other words vary in their rendering in different books. †

From the Prologue to Ecclesiasticus, however, which we have had already such frequent occasion to notice, we gather that not only the Law, but the Prophets and the "rest of the books," had been translated by the time of its writer. We may therefore conclude that the LXX. as we now have it was nearly, if not quite, complete by the middle of the second century B.C. ‡

Linguistic Features.

(i.) The translation, as we might expect, is strongly Hebraic in character. When the mother tongue is yielding place to an adopted language, the idioms of the former sometimes

---

* For an example of the latter kind, we may compare the LXX. version of Exodus 35—40 with its rendering of the rest of that book, or indeed of the Pentateuch as a whole.

† Examples are found in the renderings of the Hebrew for Urim and Thummim, Passover, Philistines.

‡ The earliest certain extant quotation of the Pentateuch in this version is by Demetrius, a Jewish Hellenist (*see* note on p. 238), who seems to have lived in the time of Ptolemy IV. (222–205 B.C.). *See* Schürer, *op. cit.*, II. iii., pp. 200 f.

shew a greater degree of tenacity than its vocabulary. Hence, even though it is probable that the translators thought in Greek, not Hebrew, yet their work bears plain traces, in idiom, as well as in vocabulary, of the influence of the latter language, as well as of the cognate Aramaic.*

(ii.) When they fail to understand a word, they either transliterate it, or guess at the meaning with more or less success, or avoid it altogether.

(iii.) We find cases where a word or expression in the original is dealt with twice over. Such cases are technically called *conflate* renderings, or *conflations*. Although some of them are combinations of distinct renderings, and therefore do not mean that the *original translator* rendered the same Hebrew word twice over, yet all cannot be explained thus. Moreover, in some cases we have a transliteration and a translation combined.†

(iv.) Many errors arose from wrong vocalisation of the Hebrew words, ‡ from wrongly dividing words, from the mistaking of one letter or Hebrew root for another, etc.

(v.) In some passages the treatment is rather of the nature of a commentary (Midrash) than a translation.

(vi.) Some inaccuracies seem to have arisen not from a failure to understand the original, but from national or local feeling, from deference to Egyptian susceptibilities, from the desire to avoid bringing discredit upon their own nation, or the applying of harsh language towards them, and such like considerations.

---

* Many Greek words which correspond to one meaning of a Hebrew word are without further ceremony made equivalent to the whole extent of the meanings comprised in the Hebrew word, and thus significations are forced upon words which they do not at all possess in Greek (*e.g.* the words δόξα, εἰρήνη, and many others).

† *See* Driver's *Samuel*, Oxford, 1890, p. lxi. Examples of this characteristic and of those that follow will be found in that work, in Smith's *Dict. of Bible*, Article, "Septuagint" and in the present writer's *Double Text of Jeremiah*, pp. 19 ff.

‡ Vowel points did not come into use in Hebrew till some centuries later.

(vii.) Liturgical reasons had their influence on the rendering. In Lev. 24. 7, it is directed that frankincense be placed on the shew-bread. The LXX. adds to the word frankincense "*and salt*," so as to make the passage accord with the actual use of their time. Other examples of the same influence at work may be found in Jer. 3. 16 ; 5. 15.

(viii.) The fear of doing what might savour of impiety caused modifications of phraseology. The most conspicuous instance is the constant substitution of the word Lord* for the name which we pronounce as Jehovah, but for which there had been already substituted in reading another word (Adonai). So in Exod. 24. 10, for the words "saw the God of Israel" they from similar motives of reverence render "saw the place where the God of Israel had stood."

IMPORTANCE OF THE SEPTUAGINT.

(i.) *Influence on the Jews of the "Dispersion."*—On this point we need not further dwell. Suffice it to say, that it was one of the most important safeguards in preventing Jews external to Palestine, and Greek-speaking Jews in Palestine, from losing hold, together with their national language, upon their nation's faith. While learning of necessity the ways of the heathen around them, and attracted by their culture and philosophy, they were enabled, through the possession of their Sacred Records in an intelligible form, to continue to adhere to the religion, and in large measure to the usages, which differentiated them from all other nationalities.

(ii.) *Influence on other nations.*—The Greek Bible has been well described as "the first Apostle that went out from Judaism to the Gentile world." To it "we may ascribe in great measure that general persuasion which prevailed over the

---

* Κύριος.

whole East . . . of the near approach of the Redeemer, and led the magi to recognise the star which proclaimed the birth of the king of the Jews." *

(iii.) *Influence on the New Testament.*—To the writers of the New Testament the LXX. stood in the relation of the "Authorised Version." It supplied them with vocabulary, it coloured their phraseology, and to a large extent was cited by them in their quotations even where it was by no means an exact rendering of the Hebrew. Thus it forms the connecting link between the Hebrew of the Old, and the Greek of the New, Revelation.

(iv.) *An independent witness to the substantial accuracy of the Hebrew text of the Old Testament in its present form.*—By means of the LXX. as dating some hundreds of years behind the period when the present (Massoretic) text was fixed, and also behind the oldest of the other versions, we have a witness of high value in point of antiquity. From time to time we are able by the evidence which it affords to restore the original reading, which had been corrupted in the long interval between the epoch when this translation was made, and the date of the witness standing next in chronological sequence.† Its very mistakes are often of value, as shewing with more or less certainty what the Hebrew text lying before the translator presented as the reading which alone made his error possible or likely. Even when, as noticed above, the LXX. translators failed to understand the expression and so transliterated it, they unconsciously rendered us a valuable service in the same direction.

(v.) The variations of reading in the LXX., as illustrated in New Testament quotations, throw light upon the amount of tolerance shewn in those times to a certain laxity as regards

---
* Smith's *Dict. of Bible*, article " Septuagint," p. 1203.
† *See* the example (1 Sam. 20. 19, 41) given by Rob. Smith, *op. cit.*, pp. 80 f.

the reproduction of an original text in a version.* " To the older Jewish tradition its variations appeared, not in the light of deviations from an acknowledged standard, but as features fairly within the limits of a faithful transmission or interpretation of the text." †

(vi.) The method employed in the composition of some of the Old Testament Books has light thrown upon it by the existence of this version. From the sub-titles found in the course of the Book of Proverbs in the Hebrew itself ‡ we see that the book is formed by the combination of collections originally separate, and a certain difference of arrangement in the LXX. helps to indicate that original separation of what is now combined. For instance, the Hebrew section **30.** 1–14 stands in the Greek after **24.** 22.

The most conspicuous example of this kind is afforded by the Book of Jeremiah. There we have a collection of prophecies against foreign nations. In the Hebrew they stand as chaps. **46–51.** In the LXX. they follow immediately upon **25.** 13. The sequence of these various prophecies among themselves is also quite different in the Hebrew and Greek texts.

It is not necessary to suppose (and the same remark will apply to other cases) that the LXX. altered the arrangement which they found existing, either as regards the position of the prophecies as a whole, or their grouping among themselves. In the case of Jeremiah, *e.g.*, it may simply have arisen through the existence of his prophecies in Egypt in a more or less detached form. They may consequently have been put together by

---

* Even an orthodox Pharisee like Josephus, as we have seen in commenting on 1st Esdras, does not hesitate to make use of the LXX. where it differs from the Hebrew text.

† Rob. Smith, *op. cit.* p. 88.

‡ "The Proverbs of Solomon" (1. 1), "These also are Proverbs of Solomon which, etc." (25. 1), "The words of Agur" (30. 1), "The words of King Lemuel" (31. 1).

those who are responsible for their arrangement in the Greek without conscious reference to their grouping in Hebrew copies.

(vii.) *Indications of the influence of Greek philosophy in Alexandria at this period.*—The LXX., as Prof. Drummond remarks, is "the earliest work of undeniably Alexandrian origin."* It is not to be expected that a translation, even a very loose translation—and there is a considerable amount of the LXX. which cannot be charged with this fault—should introduce many traces of the philosophical opinions of its day. And in point of fact there is but little phraseology to which we can point with any confidence in this connexion. The modification of expressions which seemed to them wanting in reverence, as ascribing to the Divine Being a human body or human imperfections, would scarcely come under this head. † Such modifications are found in later Jewish writings also,‡ and indicate a general tendency to adopt more elevated views of the nature and attributes of the Godhead.

Drummond, however, accepts one instance at least where we detect the influence of the Platonic doctrine, that earthly things are fashioned upon the model of a heavenly type. In Isa. 45. 18, ὁ καταδείξας stands for the Hebrew root *yatsar*, "to form" or "frame," and thus seems to indicate the bringing of the invisible image of the universe into visible existence. The same Greek verb is used in Isa. 40. 26 to represent the Hebrew *bara*, "to create."

Thus, although the LXX. is far from indicating that the developed form of Greek philosophy which may be found in

---

* *Philo Judæus, etc.*, London and Edinburgh, 1888, I. p. 156.
† *e.g.* Enoch and Noah pleased God (for "walked with God"), Gen. 5. 22; 6. 9; God took it to heart (for "repented"), Gen. 6. 6; the Lord is one who crushes wars (for "a man of war") Exod. 15. 3; *the power* (for "the hand") of the Lord, Josh. 4. 24; *the glory* of the Lord (for "his train"), Isa. 6. 1.
‡ *e.g.* the Targums.

Philo had already any conspicuous hold upon Alexandrian Jews, it nevertheless brings us to a point where we "have come within the range of Greek society, and caught at least the popular echoes of its philosophical terms and ideas. At the same time we have witnessed a movement towards higher metaphysical conceptions of the Divine Being." *

---

* Drummond, *op. cit.*, p. 163.

CHAPTER XVIII.

CONCLUSION.

WE proceed to sum up very briefly the main purposes and results of our enquiry.

We have sought, after giving an outline of the history of this period, to estimate the new position in which the Jews found themselves from and after the captivity, as supplying the clue to the general characteristics of the literature which formed our main subject. Owing to the "Dispersion" they were no longer one people in a strictly political sense, but in patriotism, and still more in their religious belief, they began to realise more vividly than ever the strength of the bond which united even the most distant of them to the conutry and faith of their fathers.

At the same time there becomes apparent the greater width of view imposed upon them by their new circumstances, although the extent of its influence finds expression in very various degrees in different kinds of literature.

We have considered in detail the general characteristics discernible in the writings of this period. Idolatry is abhorred and monotheism emphasized, while there is also an obvious shrinking from any expressions which might be conceived as inconsistent with the most exalted conceptions of the Divine nature. Jewish national pride leads to occasional misstatements in the way of numbers, and to exaggerations of view as to the importance which the world of that time would impute to Jewish matters. There is perceptible now and then an artificiality and lack of freshness, as compared with the style of the Canonical Books. Sapiential writings now meet us, both in a strictly Jewish direction, and combined with a decidedly Hellenic colouring. We also perceive a development in doctrine. There come gradually into view the conceptions of a Judgment, of a future life with rewards and punishments, of angels, and even of angelic mediation. Messianic hope, on the other hand—at any rate the expectation of a personal Messiah—is vague, and on the whole contrasts unfavourably with the teaching in some of the Canonical Books. We see that the religious romance was a method employed in order to enforce duty, whether that duty took the form of domestic piety or heroic self-sacrifice. Then, as well as later, an extravagant value was attached in many quarters to ritual subtleties and ceremonial developments of the Law. It was, however, also a time in which much store was set by the fear of God and uprightness of life.

Dealing more directly with the claims of the Apocryphal Books as deutero-canonical, we have considered the attitude adopted towards them by Palestinian and by Alexandrian Judaism, as well as afterwards by the Greek and Latin Churches, and we have noted the cause of the confusion of thought found in the Western Church on this subject. We have concluded that the acceptance or rejection of these Books did not turn upon questions of the language in which they were written,* nor upon decisions of the "Great Synagogue," but came about through the Divinely guided instinct of the Jews of Maccabean and pre-Maccabean times. There was an obvious difference in strength of claim between, *e.g.*, Proverbs and Ecclesiasticus, Chronicles and Maccabees. Testimony external (*e.g.* the Jewish Church, and the absence of

---

* Although, in point of fact, no Greek original was ever accepted.

quotations by New Testament writers) and internal (lack of simplicity and of vigour, apparent consciousness on the writer's part of inferiority, absence of historical verisimilitude, distortion of Old Testament narratives)* alike support their exclusion from the Old Testament Canon. Nevertheless the value and interest of the books cannot easily be exaggerated, and they well repay study. They form a link between the Old and New Testaments. They shew the preparation of Graeco-Jewish thought and language as an instrument to be used in Apostolic and other hands for the spread of the Christian faith. They testify by their quotations from the LXX. to the completion of the Canon as well as to that of the earliest version of the Old Testament Scriptures. Finally, we should not forget that they clear up many allusions in other literature, which would otherwise fail to receive recognition.

The books thus dealt with *in globo* have next been considered with reference to their individual peculiarities and value—historical or quasi-historical and prophetic, poetic, gnomic and philosophical, and apocalyptic.

Lastly, we have noted the main characteristics, as well as the wide-reaching influence and value, of the Septuagint, a version which "performed a still greater work than that of extending a knowledge of Judaism to the heathen world : it wedded Greek language to Hebrew thought, the most exact form of expression with the most spiritual mode of conception." †

---
* These are, of course, only adduced as occasional features, and are by no means all of them to be ascribed to each apocryphal book.
† Bp. Westcott, *Introduction to the Study of the Gospels*, London, 1888 (7th ed.), p. 78.

APPENDIX A.

THE ASSIDEANS AND THEIR RELATION TO THE PHARISEES.

WE read in the Book of Numbers * the regulations prescribed for those who bound themselves by the vow of a Nazirite. According to the report of Samson's mother to her husband concerning the words of the man of God, the child was to be "a Nazirite unto God from the womb to the day of his death." †

With these Nazirites, taking their vows temporarily or for life, and lasting on through subsequent Jewish history, the Assideans seem to have been closely connected. The word Assidean, or "pions," is in this sense of frequent occurrence in the Old Testament,‡ and generally denotes those who were strict in the rigid observance of the Law, as opposed to "the impious," "the lawless," "the transgressors" (1 Macc. 1. 11; 3. 6, 8, etc.). They formed the synagogue of the Assideans according to 1 Macc. 2. 42. §

They acquired consistency and sharpness of outline as a party or sect through the circumstances of the time. The relations between the Jews and the Hellenic influences which to a large extent surrounded and even penetrated Palestine,

---

* 6. 1-21.   † Judg. 13. 7.
‡ Specially in the Psalms (e.g. 29. 5; 31. 24; 37. 28). Ps. 149. 1 ("and his praise in the assembly of the saints") has been taken to refer to the Assideans.
§ A less probable reading is that of the Codex Sinaiticus (א), 'Ιουδαίων. The language used of them in 1 Macc. 2. 42, "everyone that offered himself willingly for the law," seems to imply that they bound themselves by some kind of vow.

gradually divided the nation into two camps, consisting of those who yielded more or less fully to the attractions of new manners and new modes of thought, and on the other hand of the steadfast opponents of all change in matters social or religious. The Assideans were the emphatic upholders of tradition.

As early as the days of Simon II. (in other words, at the beginning of the 2nd century B.C.) they had become a firmly established party, making an earnest protest against concessions to the Hellenism which was becoming fashionable in certain Jewish circles. The excesses of the Greeks and of their admirers in Judea were met by a more rigid asceticism on the part of "the pious," just as the Puritans of our own history protested similarly against the riotous conduct of many of their political opponents. No doubt for a while the mass of the Jewish people took up a neutral position between the two parties, but, as the contest went forward, more and more were forced to declare themselves on one side or the other.

When the country began to suffer acutely from its Seleucid oppressors, the influence of the Assideans was intensified by the circumstances of the struggle, and on the outbreak of the rebellion they warmly supported the Maccabean leaders, as fighting for the cause dearest to them, viz. that of the Law, the sacred trust of the nation. Nevertheless they caused those leaders considerable trouble owing to the rigidity of their views as to Sabbath observance (1 Macc. 2. 32–38).

Two prominent men among them were Jose the son of Joezer of the town of Zereda and Jose the son of Jochanan of Jerusalem. These two constituted one of the pairs which according to Jewish tradition were links in the chain connecting later times with the "prophetic men" of the days of inspiration. "They both founded schools. The one laid more value upon the theoretical study of the Law, the other upon the practical results of its teaching.* Jose of Zereda taught his disciples, 'Let thy house be a place of assembly for the wise; powder thyself with the dust of their feet; drink in their words with thirst.' Jose of Jerusalem taught on the other hand, 'Let thy house be opened wide; let the poor be thy household, and prolong not converse with women.'" †

Simon II., though an earnest upholder of the Law, never fully sympathized with the extreme views of the Assideans. Onias III. (who succeeded his father Simon circ. 198–195 B.C.) on the contrary was a leader among them, and we have accordingly noticed earlier in this volume the enmity with which he was regarded by the chief supporters of Hellenism, the Tobiades and their adherents.

On the triumph of the patriotic cause and the consequent relaxation of the contest, Assidean support to the Hasmonean princes ceased.‡ The latter were not content to have gained the day in fighting for religion. They desired as the result of their efforts to establish their nation in a more influential position from a strictly political point of view. And here it was they and the Assideans parted company. The latter were willing to accept Alcimus as High Priest. They desired to preserve the ancient ritual in all its integrity, but, except so far as this was affected, cared but little under what government they lived.

Thus after the death of Judas Maccabeus (circ. 160 B.C.) we may see three distinct parties, the Hellenists (to whom belonged the bulk of the priests), the Assideans, and the upholders of the Hasmonean family. The two last were both animated

---

* Graetz, *History of the Jews* (Eng. trans.), London, 1891, i., p. 451.
† *Pirḳe Aboth*, i. 4, 5.
‡ Even before the death of Judas the suspicions entertained by the Assideans with regard to his aims induced them to desert him at the battle of Eleasa, in consequence apparently of a treaty which he had made with the Romans.

with strong feelings of patriotism, but while that of the Assideans was purely of a religious character, and aimed in no sense at political aggrandisement, the supporters of the ruling family on the other hand "differed from them in their wider perception, in their greater knowledge of outward circumstances, in their manly energy, which could not be deterred from its purpose." *

They seem gradually to have merged into the party of the Pharisees, of which they were the forerunners. The general position of both towards the Law and its requirements is virtually identical. The names also are cognate in their signification, "the saints," the "separate." We may compare the change in our own historic nomenclature of religious bodies from Puritan to Nonconformist. The Pharisees, however, unlike their predecessors, did not refuse, as we have seen in the historical sketch, to take a side in the political questions of their times, and after remaining in the shade for a while, while the Sadducees with their leanings towards Hellenism were in the ascendant, to assume under Alexandra an influential position in the state.

The tendency to exclusiveness was reproduced in a much more intense shape in the Essenes of later time, " but whether these [the Essenes] were historically connected with the Chasidim as divergent offshoots of the original sect, or whether they represent independent developments of the same principle, we are without the proper data for deciding."†

---

* Graetz, *op. cit.*, i., p. 506.
† Lightfoot, *Colossians*, London, 1876 (2nd ed.), p. 355.

APPENDIX B.

TRADITIONAL ACCOUNT OF THE SUCCESSION OF LEADING JEWISH TEACHERS DURING THE PERIOD FROM EZRA TILL THE DESTRUCTION OF THE TEMPLE BY THE ROMANS.

EZRA'S promulgation of the Law and directions for public worship had produced a permanent impression upon the mind of his nation. But as the Rabbinic schools of later centuries looked back to the period which followed the Return from Babylon, they perceived that records of Jewish history were almost *nil* from Ezra till the commencement of the Greek epoch. And although there were among them those who believed that the interval referred to did not exceed thirty or forty years, yet, whatever its length, there was the need of giving some reply to the question that naturally suggested itself, viz., what was during that space the form of religious government? The kind of answer they gave may well have arisen from the visible existence of the religious body called the Sanhedrim at the time when the above-mentioned problem sought a solution. "The Great Synagogue," whatever varieties of detail are found in the traditionary accounts, would appear to have been a general expression for those learned in the Law during the interval whose history was thus strangely lacking. We may, however, observe that there is no early Jewish testimony connecting the men of the Great Synagogue with the completion of the Canon of the Jewish Scriptures.

The existence of any such body as "the Great Synagogue," is, to say the least of it, far from being established by uncontrovertible testimony. For a full statement and criticism of the evidence the reader may be referred to Dr. Ryle's *Canon*, etc., already mentioned.* An interesting article on the other side will be found in the *Jewish Quarterly Review*,† by Dr. Samuel Krauss. The last member of "the Great Synagogue" is said to have been Simon the Just. As we have seen in the body of this work‡ some placed him in the early Greek period: others, with more truth, at the end of the third century B.C. While the Old Testament, the Apocrypha, Josephus, and Philo, are silent as to the existence of the Great Synagogue, the Jewish treatise *Pirḳe Aboth* (a part of the Mishnah which goes to constitute the oldest part of the Talmud) is the earliest testimony in their favour. Then the succession from Moses to Simon is thus given :—" Moses received the Law from Sinai and delivered it to Joshua, and Joshua to the elders, and the elders to the prophets, and the prophets to the men of the Great Synagogue. . . . . Simon the Just was of the remnants of the Great Synagogue."§ Thereupon comes the succession of individuals or pairs who carried on the traditions from Simon's death. It is impossible to determine the chronology of all these with precision. We here give (*a*) the direct succession, which preserved a species of ecclesiastical continuity from Simon as far as Gamaliel I., and (*b*) a supplementary list of leading teachers flourishing within (approximately) the same limits, in the case of most of whom there are preserved sayings in early Jewish writings.‖

---

* P. 103. † Vol. x. pp. 347-377.
‡ See p. 179, *supra*. § i. 1. 2.
‖ For notices of many of them I may refer to Wolf, *Bibliotheca Rabbinica*, four vols.. Hamburg, 1721, also to Dr. C. Taylor's *Sayings of the Jewish Fathers*, Cambridge, 1897 (2nd ed.), and to the *Translation of the Treatise Chagigah*, Cambridge, 1891, by the present writer.

APPENDIX B.

(a) *The Direct Succession.*

	B.C.
Antigonus* of Sokho	190
Jose (or Joseph) ben Joezer ⎫ Jose (or Joseph) ben Jochanan ⎭	170
Joshua ben Prachya ⎫ Mattai (Nittai) the Arbelite ⎭	140–110
Jehudah ben Tabbai	·100
Simeon ben Shatach	90
Shemaiah and Abtalion	65–35
Judah ben Bethera and his brothers Joshua and Simeon, who seem to have yielded the presidency to Hillel on his coming from Babylon	35–30
Hillel	30

Shammai, his great rival, who was for a time his pupil.

Simeon ben Hillel, president either with or next after his father. Hillel is supposed to have died about 13 A.D.

Gamaliel I.† (called also Gamaliel the elder, or simply Gamaliel) *ob.* 52 A.D.

(b) *Other Leading Teachers of the same Period.*

Zadok and Baithus (or Boethus), said to have been pupils of Antigonus of Sokho, but their existence is doubtful.

Admon, a judge along with Chanen ben Abishalom, and a contemporary of Abtalion.

Choni ha-Maagal (*the charioteer*), fl. 63 B.C.

---

* It is significant that he is at once the first who bears a Greek name, and also a connecting link between Simon the Just, a strict upholder of the Law, and Zadok (if indeed there was such a person), said by tradition to be the founder of the Sadducees.

† Acts 5. 34–40; 22. 3.

Akbia ben Mahalalel, a contemporary of Hillel.

(Jochanan) ben Bag Bag,* a contemporary of Hillel and Shammai.

Samuel ha-katan (Samuel *the Little*), a pupil of Gamaliel. It has been sought to identify him with St. Paul, the suggestion being supported by the similarity of meaning between ha-katan and Paulus (little), and by the fact that both were pupils of Gamaliel I. But there is no further evidence, unless it be that while St. Paul before his conversion persecuted the Christians, so this Samuel is credited with the authorship of eighteen curses directed against the Minim (the Rabbinic expression for heretics, Christians).

Chanina ben Dosa, a contemporary of Gamaliel. He saw the destruction of the second Temple.

Chananyah ben Hezekiah ben Goren. He lived before the destruction of the Temple, and defended from alleged inconsistencies with the Law certain passages in the Book of Ezekiel. Had it not been for his exposition of the case, that book (says the tradition) would have been withdrawn from the Canon.

Jochanan ben Ha-Chorani lived before the destruction of the Temple, and is said to have put an end to strife between the schools of Hillel and Shammai.

Baba ben Bota, a pupil of Shammai.

Jochanan ben Zakkai. He is said to have been a pupil of both Hillel and Shammai, and to have lived for five years after the destruction of the Temple.

Nechunyah ben ha-Kanah, a pupil of Jochanan ben Zakkai; fl. before 70 A.D.

(Abba Chelkiah, a grandson of Choni ha-Maagal. It is not however certain that he falls within this period.)

---

* Also called Ben He He, a name considered identical with the above on the Jewish principle of permitting the substitution of letters, so long as their several numerical values shall leave the value of the whole unaffected.

APPENDIX C.

THE DATE OF THE BOOK OF DANIEL.

THE Book of Daniel, if we accept its traditional date, stands apart from the literature treated of in the body of this work.

That date has been challenged by (*a*) unbelievers, (*b*) certain Christian writers.

Two views are taken :

(i.) The book is simply the product of the times of the Maccabees (circ. 167–164 B.C.), the writer making more or less use of traditional stories (Haggadoth). His purpose was to warn against apostacy to Hellenism, and to encourage under Seleucid persecution.

(ii.) The book in its present shape has suffered more or less from interpolations (*e.g.* chap. 11) and other alterations. These apart, the date to be assigned to its original form may well be the traditional one, viz., soon after the Persian Empire had established itself.

The former is the view now generally taken by the assailants of the traditional date. But much of what appears below will apply to either alternative. Hereupon follow—

(A) Arguments in defence of the traditional date, accompanied in most cases by the rejoinder of its assailants.

(B) Objections, other than those thus dealt with in A, to the traditional view.

(A.)

I. Universally accepted by a catena of Christian writers. (*See* Fuller, *Speaker's Comm.*, vi. 222, for details.)

Ans. This does not preclude re-investigation, aided by modern scientific methods.

II. Josephus (*c. Apion.* i. 8) says that the Canon was closed in the days of "Artaxerxes" (the Ahasuerus of Esther. *See* Ryle, *Canon, etc.*, p. 172).

Ans. Josephus may have been mistaken.

III. External evidence—
(*a*) Ezek. 14. 20 ; 28. 3.
(*b*) Zech. 1. 18-21 (Fuller in *Speaker's Comm.* vi. p. 213*a* adds Zech. 6).
(*c*) 1 Macc. 2. 59, 60 refers to Dan. 3. 27, 6. 23 ; 1 Macc. 1. 54 = Dan. 9. 27. Also there are references to Daniel in 3 Macc. 6 and 4 Macc. 16. 21 ; 18. 12.
(*d*) The existence of the book is indicated by Story of Susanna (= Judgment of Daniel), Song of the Three Children, Bel and the Dragon.
(*e*) Sibylline verses, iii. 388 ff. refer to LXX. Version of Dan. 7. 7, 8, 11, 20, and *l*. 613 to verses 23, 24. Alexandrian and Palestinian Jews of second century B.C. very ignorant of each other's literature or institutions. Improbable therefore that a Palestinian work *of the time of Epiphanes* would make any impression on, or even be known to, the presumably Egyptian Jew, who was author of Sibylline passages. J. E. H. Thomson (*Thinker*, iii. 493) argues that these Sibylline references to Daniel are not later than B.C. 170.
(*f*) Book of Enoch, in a section (Book of Similitudes) not later than B.C. 210 (for argument *see* J. E. H. Thomson,

Thinker, iii. 495), chaps. 84–90, gives a description of the Last Judgment, admittedly drawn from Daniel.

(*g*) Testimony of Josephus. He speaks of Daniel as a prophet (*Ant.* x. 11. 7), and says (*ib.* xi. 8. 5) that Jaddua the high-priest shewed the book to Alexander on his visit to Jerusalem. Josephus also embodies in his narrative a considerable amount of the historical portion (with additions), and relates the vision of the ram and the he-goat. Further, it is remarkable that "when he speaks of the miracles of the Book of Daniel, his remarks are unrestrained by that hesitation which is usually visible in his treatment of the supernatural events of the Bible." (*Speaker's Comm.* vi. 220*a*.)

(*h*) In Baruch **2, 3**, the prayer is modelled on the words of Dan. **9**.

(*i*) New Testament references : Matt. **24**. 15 (Mark **13**. 14); (?) **21**. 44; **26**. 64; 1 Cor. **6**. 2; 2 Thess. **2**; Heb. **11**. 33, 34; Apocalypse.

Criticisms on the above.

(*a*) Ezekiel's references do not suggest a contemporary, but an older Daniel, otherwise unknown. But see *Thinker*, iii. 216.

(*b*) Too vague to build upon.

(*c*) Mattathias's speech enlarged and embellished after the manner of historians of those times.

(*d*) These are alleged to be all accretions of post-Maccabean date.

(*e*) The date of the passage is placed by others B.C. 140. So Schürer, *The Jewish People in the Time of Jesus Christ*, II. iii. 281.

(*f*) The book is chaotic in arrangement and authorship. But B.C. 110 is the date which we must on the whole accept. See discussion in R.A. Lipsius in *Dict. of Chr. Biog.* ii. 126 f.

(g) Josephus's testimony that Alexander visited Jerusalem is not corroborated by others. See further in Farrar, *Daniel* (the Expositor's Bible), pp. 105 f., and Bevan's *Daniel*, p. 4 note.

(h) Baruch not earlier than B.C. 160; very possibly as late as, or later than, Vespasian. Smith's *Dict. of Bible* (ed. 2), "Baruch, Book of," p. 361.

(i) "Spoken of by Daniel the Prophet" (Matt. 24. 15) may be the comment of the Evangelist, or even "an ecclesiastical note," which latter is the explanation given by Alford (*ad loc.*) of "let him that readeth understand," in the same verse. In the parallel passage of St. Mark Daniel is not mentioned; in Luke (21. 20) not even necessarily alluded to. But on this point (as well as many others referred to in this Appendix), see Dr. Kennedy's *The Book of Daniel from the Christian standpoint* (in the same series with the present work), pp. 5 ff.

IV. Historical accuracy, such as would not have been forthcoming at the time of the Maccabees.
(a) Women at feasts (v. 2).
(b) Burning alive as a punishment (iii.).
(c) Consultation of diviners (ii.).
(d) Nebuchadnessar's colossal image (iii.).

N.B. *See* Fuller in *Expositor*, 3rd ser. vol. i. (1885), pp. 217 ff. for possible connexion with colossus of Rameses II. as seen by Nebuchadnezzar on occasion of an invasion of Egypt.

(e) The name Belshazzar (Bil-sarra-utsur) has been found in the cuneiform texts. In the absence of his father, he would be the *de facto* king in Babylon. He was apparently the "son of the king" referred to in the "Annalistic Tablet of Cyrus" (so Sayce, *Higher Criticism and the Monuments*, p. 525), which further mentions that "the *son* of the king died."* Comp. Dan. 5. 30.

---

* Such is the rendering in Smith's *Dict. of Bible*, Article "Belshazzar" (Pinches).

(*f*) Further, Daniel is acquainted with the various classes of wise men existing at Babylon (*see* 5. 7, אָשְׁפַיָּא גָּזְרַיָּא 1. 20, 2. 2 הַרְטֻמִּים), with the sacredness of the Babylonian number *seven* (3. 19 ; 4. 16, etc.), with the details of Babylonian dress (3. 21).

Criticisms on the above.

(*a*) The Book of Esther shews the same knowledge.

(*b*) But see Jer. **29.** 22. N.B. The context in Daniel shews familiarity with this chapter of Jeremiah.

(*c*) But comp. the story of Joseph in Egypt.

(*e*) It is true that Belshazzar was son of Nabonidus (Nabu-nahid), the last king of Babylon, and he may well have held command for his father in Babylon, while the latter took the field against Cyrus ; but it is difficult to think that this could entitle him to be spoken of *by a contemporary* as king. (See Driver, *Introd. to Lit. of O.T.*, 6th ed. p. 499.) Further, Nabonidus was a usurper, not related to Nebuchadnezzar, whereas Nebuchadnezzar is spoken of throughout ch. **5** (*vv.* 2, 11, 13, 18, 22) as his father (*ibid*).* Lastly Sayce (p. 502) renders " the *wife* of the king died."

V. The phenomena belonging to the Greek versions are a strong argument for the antiquity of the book. For (*a*) we must allow a long period for the interpolations and other additions and corruptions found in the LXX. to grow up ; (*b*) a comparison of the Chigi MS. (representing the LXX.) with the version of Theodotion, with a view of ascertaining the form of the original (Heb. and Aram.) Daniel, lying behind the texts on which the Greek versions were made, shews that we must allow a considerable interval of time between those versions and that original. See this worked out by J. E. H. Thomson, *Thinker*, iii. 116 ff.

---

* *See*, however, on this last point Anderson, *Daniel in the Critics' Den*, p. 29, note, and Kennedy, *op. cit.*, 180.

Ans. We cannot argue with any certainty that those changes might not easily accrue in a generation or two.

VI. Argument from the character of the language.

(*a*) The Aramaic parts much resemble in their phraseology and style the Aramaic of Ezra, and are of a much earlier type than the Aramaic of the Targums.

(*b*) A romance of the Maccabean period would have been written in Aramaic throughout, Hebrew having by that time long ceased to be the vernacular. Moreover, Daniel's Hebrew is much what we should expect for one living in Babylon, whose language therefore might well have somewhat deteriorated from that of earlier models.

(*c*) The many Persian words (fifteen in number) which occur are natural to one writing under Daniel's circumstances.

Criticisms on the above.

(*a*) On either hypothesis as to the date of the book there was time for the changes in style which the Targums exhibit to take effect, inasmuch as probably they did not reach their present form till the third or fourth century A.D. (*See* Driver, 503 f. for further details, and, for Prof. Cheyne's cautious words on this point, *see* Kennedy, pp. 149 f.)

(*b*) The recent discoveries of large portions of the original of Ecclesiasticus shew that a Hebrew book, written in the second century A.D., was at least not impossible, although as yet it stands alone. Nevertheless it should be noted that there are not lacking in Ecclesiasticus grammatical forms more clearly indicative of a late date than anything of the same character in Daniel.

Delitzsch's account of Daniel's Hebrew (later editions of Herzog's *Real-Encyclopädie*, iii. 470, Art. "Daniel,") is that "it attaches itself here and there to Ezekiel and also to Habakkuk; in general character it resembles the Hebrew of the Chronicler

APPENDIX C. 263

[see Bevan, *Daniel*, p. 29 f. for examples] who wrote shortly before the beginning of the Greek period 332 B.C., and as compared either with the ancient Hebrew, or with the Hebrew of the Mishnah, is full of singularities and harshness of style." See Driver, *l.c.* pp. 504 ff., and Behrmann, *Das Buch D.* iii., for fuller treatment.

(c) *Some* of the Persian words used, *e.g.*, *path-bag* (Dan. 1. 5, 8, 13, 15, 16 ; 11. 26), are very unlikely to have been in use among the Babylonians so early as the beginning of the Persian dominion. *See* Driver, p. 501.

VII. The age of the Assideans is not one in which the Canon could be easily tampered with.

Ans. If "Daniel" were himself "a faithful Chasid in the days of the Seleucid tyrant" (Farrar, p. 118),* his work might well find currency.

VIII. The following arguments are also advanced in support of the traditional date. (*See* Thomson, *Thinker*, ii. 209 ff.)

(*a*) If the book was written in a time of strong religious emotion, such as was the time of the Maccabean persecutions, then for a history (religious or otherwise) to be accepted under such circumstances, either there must be a unity of purpose (which Daniel lacks), or it must be a record of facts. There is no real unity in Daniel. It changes from history to apocalyptic visions, none of which are ever placed in the time of Nebuchadnezzar, the prominent figure of the earlier part of the book. Further, Nebuchadnezzar is not really like Epiphanes. The contrast between them is even strengthened, if we assume that ch. 11 is an insertion of Maccabean date, giving thus the impression made by Epiphanes on the Jews of his time.

---
* Of which, however, it need scarcely be said we have nothing in the shape of direct historical evidence.

(b) Why should a romance writer choose Daniel as his mouth-piece. His "wisdom" (Ezek. 28. 3) would naturally suggest gnomic utterances, as the Books of Wisdom or Ecclesiasticus.

(c) If the purpose was to encourage against Epiphanes, we ought to have a tale of Nebuchadnezzar's *armies* overthrown by Jews.

(d) No successful work of fiction was ever composed in two languages.

(B.)

(Objections, other than those which have been already dealt with in A, to the traditional date).

I. Alleged historical inaccuracies.

(a) Nebuchadnezzar's expedition against Palestine and Egypt, which (Jer. 25. 1 ; 36. 1 ; 45. 1 ; 46. 2) took place in the fourth year of Jehoiakim, is referred (Dan. 1. 1) to his *third* year.

Ans. This was the Assyrian mode of reckoning. The year broken by a new reign was assigned to the king with whom it began. *See* Douglas in *Thinker*, vii. 24 ff.[*]

(b) Discrepancy between the three years of 1. 5, 18, and the "second year" of 2. 1.

See Ans. to (a).

(c) There are no deportations in Jehoiakim's reign.

Ans. 2 Chron. 36. 6 mentions a deportation, and Berosus implies it. See Anderson, pp. 15 ff. On the other hand see Bevan, p. 17, on the question whether Berosus is trustworthy in this passage.

---

[*] He refers to Geo. Smith's *Assyrian Canon*, p. 21, in confirmation of his statement. But this says that the reign was reckoned from the New Year's Day *either before or after* the accession—generally indeed after; "but there are cases of the year of accession being reckoned as the first year." The writer goes on to give examples of the latter kind, Nebuchadnezzar being one of them. *See also* Prof. Oppert in *Proceedings of the Society of Biblical Archæology*, Vol. xx. Part I. (Jan. 1898), pp. 24–47.

(*d*) There was no *king* Belshazzar, and B. was not son of, or related to, Nebuchadnezzar.

See IV. (*e*) under A above.

(*e*) "Darius the Mede" (5. 31) is unknown to secular history, and there is no room for him. He is a reflection into the past of Darius, son of Hystaspes (Sayce, p. 528).

Ans. He may well be identified with Gobryas, or some other person appointed to restore order after the overthrow of Nabonidus.* So Anderson, pp. 39 ff. But see also Fuller in *Expositor*, 3rd ser. 436.

(*f*) Babylon supposed to be captured by assault. This is " a reflection into the past of the actual sieges undergone by the city in the reigns of Darius, son of Hystaspes, and Xerxes." Farrar, p. 56.

Ans. Daniel does not assert that it was so captured.

(*g*) There were not only two Babylonian kings within the period, as Daniel implies, but five.

Ans. The death of Belshazzar has really nothing to do with the end of the Babylonian Empire.

(*h*) There were not only four Persian kings, but twelve.

Ans. The number is to be regarded, not as historical, but cyclical. But see Anderson (p. 14) for another explanation.

(*i*) Nebuchadnezzar's lycanthropy is unknown.

Ans. The secular history of the time is by no means complete, and if it were in other respects much fuller than it is, this is a fact that might very well be omitted or disguised.

II. Other improbabilities.

(*a*) Daniel is said to have been made "chief ruler," and to have been placed over all the wise men. They would not

---

* But the language of Daniel 6. 1. is hard to reconcile with the idea of a mere viceroy or deputy of any kind.

have tolerated this, nor would the monotheistic Daniel have accepted such a position.

(*b*) We have no evidence to support the view that death or apostacy was ever the alternative offered by the Babylonian power to members of subjugated states.

(*c*) How is it that no mention is made of Daniel in ch. **3**?

(*d*) Aramaic ("the Syrian language," **2.** 4) would not have been used by the "Chaldeans" in addressing the monarch and his courtiers, but the native Babylonian tongue spoken by them as late as the time of the Parthian king. "Assyrian and Babylonian differed from Aramaic as much as French differs from Portuguese" (Sayce, 537).

(*e*) How was it that (5. 8) the "Chaldeans" could not read plain Aramaic, a language which must have been so familiarly spoken in the market?

Ans. It may however well have been the application, and not the meaning of the words, which constituted the puzzle.

(*f*) The names Belteshazzar and Abed-nego are impossible ones. See Farrar, p. 20, and Sayce, p. 532.

Ans. Granting that the latter is a corruption of Abed-nabu, servant of Nebo, Balatsu-utsur, "Save his life" may be an abbreviated form of the prayer, Bel-balatsu-utsur.

(*g*) Ch. **1.** 21 is inconsistent with **10.** 1.

Ans. The earlier passage only means that Daniel continued beyond the Babylonian *régime*.

(*h*) Daniel accepted adoration from Nebuchadnezzar (2. 46).

St. Jerome replies "*Non tam Danielem quam in Daniele adorat Deum.*" *

(*i*) In Daniel the word "Chaldean" has partly † lost its national and territorial significance (comp. *gypsy*) and has

---
* Migne, *Patrol.* xxv. 504.   † Not altogether; for *see* 1. 4.

become the equivalent of "sorcerer," "magician." This changed sense has come to the word through a *Greek* channel. See Sayce, 535.

See however the national application of the word surviving in 1 Esdras 6. 15.

(*j*) Daniel would not have spelt the word Nebuchadrezzar incorrectly (*n* instead of *r*).*

(*k*) Three Greek words occur among the names of musical instruments in 3. 5, 7, 10, 15, viz. κίθαρις, ψαλτήριον, συμφωνία. The first may have been borrowed by the Babylonians from Greece. But ψαλτήριον does not occur in Greek before Aristotle (*ob.* 322 B.C.) and συμφωνία not before Plato (*ob.* 347 B.C.). In the sense of concerted music (or, possibly, of a definite musical instrument), συμφ. is first used by Polybius in his account of the festivities in which Antiochus Epiphanes indulged (Pol. xxvi. 1; xxxi. 4).† See Driver, p. 502.

It is evident that these objections will have very varying force with different minds. It is also clear that certain of them, *e.g.* (*d*) (*e*) (*i*) (*j*), may deal with difficulties which have their origin in editing rather than in the original narrative. See Anderson, pp. 47 f. As regards the introduction of Greek words and names into Hebrew long before the Alexandrine age, see Flinders Petrie, *Ten Years' Digging in Egypt*, p. 39.

III. Direct arguments which have been adduced in favour of the Maccabean date.

(*a*) The post-exilic prophets and Ezra are silent about Daniel. He is absent from the list of heroes in Ecclus. 44 ff.

---

* But we cannot say that Daniel's spelling (so in Kings and other O. T. Books) may not indicate the contemporaneous way of pronouncing the name in Hebrew or Aramaic. In the Heb. and Aram., for *two*, these letters are interchanged. Comp. *London* with *Londres, Londra*.

† E. S. Shuckburgh's Ed., London, 1889.

His prophecies are not quoted in Maccabees.* We are called upon to observe the *cumulative* evidence of these omissions.

Ans. The argument from omission is always a somewhat perilous one. Ecclesiasticus also omits Ezra, Job, Esther, and Mordecai. Moreover, for a certain amount of capriciousness to be observed in the notices of " famous men," *see* p. 178.

(*b*) Each vision leads up to Antiochus as climax.

Ans. This is no real objection, even if true.

(*c*) The prophecy of the 70 weeks (**9.** 24-27) brings us to the climax of Seleucid profanation, immediately after which come the days of the Messiah.

Ans. This is not so, according to the traditional school of interpreters. True, they differ much from one another in details. But this does not of itself shew that their opponents are right. These too are much divided.

(*d*) The elaborate detail given in ch. **11** is wholly contrary to the analogy of prophecy.

Ans. It may be an interpolation. But in any case we cannot set bounds to the character which prophecy may assume. It is not to be tied down by unvarying rules. Further, if the prophecy is a *vaticinium ex eventu*, it is strange that parts of it should be so obscure.

IV. The Jews placed the book among *K'thubim*, and not among the Prophets. This shews that they are dissatisfied with, or suspicious of, the traditional date.

Ans. It is in a natural historical order between Esther and Ezra-Nehemiah. See further in Smith's *Dict. of Bible*, Article " Daniel, the Book of " (Bp. Westcott), i. 708*b* (2nd Ed.), and in Thomson's Article, " Daniel : In relation to the Canon," *Thinker*, iv. 13 ff.

---

* Although mentioned in 1 Macc. ii. 60. *See* A. III. c. above, with subsequent criticism.

V. Neither our Lord nor His Apostles point to the evidence of the prophecy of the 70 weeks (**9. 24–27**)—a proof so definite and so chronological.

For *Ans.* see Anderson (p. 64), who argues that such proof would have been discredited by the erroneous chronology which, as Josephus indicates, was prevalent in their day.

It has been thought well that an attempt should be made, as above, to set forth with as much fairness as possible the main arguments on both sides of this difficult question.

In a case like this, where, as in so many literary enquiries, we cannot hope in the present state of our knowledge to attain to positive proof, we must anticipate a divergence of opinion. On the other hand, considering how remarkable are the discoveries of one literary treasure after another, which characterize the present day, we may well expect with considerable confidence that further light will be thrown on some, or even many, of the points indicated above as involved in the discussion. In the mean while different minds will return different answers to the question, How far have the impugners of the traditional date acquitted themselves successfully of the task that they have undertaken, viz. to disprove the view which at any rate has been held with practical universality by the Church till very recent times ?*

---

* For a very full, clear, and elaborate defence of the traditional view, see J. Fabre d'Envieu, *Le Livre du Prophète Daniel*, Paris, 1888 (4 vols.).

INDEX.

Aaron	178
Abtalion	84, 255
Achiacharus	136
Adasa	45
Admon	255
Ahab (the false prophet)	163
Ahasuerus	104, 161
Akbia b. Mahalaleel	256
Alcimus	44 f., 47, 130, 251
Alexander the Great	4, 6, 146
Alexander Zabinas	56
Alexander, son of Aristobulus	78, 80
Alexandra	65, 71 f., 75, 129, 206
Alexandria	89, 126, 235
Almsgiving	16, 95, 135 ff., 140
Ambrose	234
Anahita (Anaitis)	3
Ananias	66
Andromachus	6
Angels, doctrine of	48, 93, 136 f., 208, 216 f., 224
Anna	135, 139
Anthropomorphisms avoided	92, 244
Antigonus, brother of Aristobulus	65
—— son of Aristobulus	80, 82, 86 f., 88
—— Doson	25
Antioch	88
Antiochus I. (Soter)	236
—— III. (the Great)	11, 12, 25 ff.
—— IV. (Epiphanes)	24, 27, 29 ff., 131, 220
Antiochus IV., massacre of Jews in Jerusalem	32, 125, 147, 205
—— erects altar to Zeus in Jerusalem	34
—— death	43
—— V. (Eupator)	43, 48
—— VI.	50
—— VII. (Sidetes)	52 f., 54 f.
—— VIII. (Gryphus)	56, 66
—— IX. (Cyzicenus)	56 f., 66
—— XII. (Dionysus)	69
—— Theos (father of Seleucus II.)	10
Antipater (governor of Idumea)	75
—— his son A.	75, 80 ff., 85
Antony	81, 86 f., 221
Apocalyptic writings, style of 213 f.	
Apocrypha, compared with Canonical Books	91 f.
—— attitude of Palestinian Jews, of Alexandrian Jews, of Greek and Latin Churches towards	99 ff.
—— restriction in public reading of	102
—— why excluded from Jewish Canon	103
—— not quoted in New Testament	107
—— value of	109 ff.
—— forms a key to literary allusions	110
—— testifies to completion of Canon and to age of LXX.	111

INDEX.

	PAGE
Apollonia	24
Apollonius	28, 33
Apollos	192
Apostolic constitutions	169
Arbela	4
Aretas	69, 77
Aristeas	125, 237
Aristobulus	
64 f., 71 ff., 76 ff., 80, 87, 206 f.	
—— (story of LXX.)	237
—— (teacher of Ptol. Philom.) 192	
Aristomenes	26
Arphaxad	128
Arses	4
Artaxerxes I.	2, 123
—— II.	3
—— III. (Ochus)	4, 203
Article VI. of Church of England	234
Asmodeus (Ashmedai)	137
Asmoneans. See Hasmoneans.	
Asophon	66
Assideans (Chasidim)	
29, 34, 36 ff., 44, 46, 58, 180, 249 ff.	
Assur-bani-pal	128
Athanasius	98
Athenion	11
Attalus of Pergamum	48
Augustine	98
Baba b. Bota	255
Babylon	128
—— overthrow of	164
Bacchides	44, 47
Bagoas (Bagoses)	4
Baithus (Boethus)	255
Balas	48 f., 56, 146
Baltasar (Belshazzar)	168
Barnabas, Epistle of	100, 222
Baruch, Apocalypse of	
169, 217 f., 227 f.	
—— Book of 101, 167 ff., 210, 212	
Barzaphanes	86

	PAGE
Bascama	50
Belmerodach	164
Benedictus, etc.	209
Bensly, Prof.	233
Berenice	10
Berosus	236
Beth-horon	40
Beth-zur	42 f., 50
Bruce, the traveller	222
Bubastis	125 f.
Cæsar	30 ff., 85
Caligula	157, 192
Cambyses	2, 10, 123
Canon, foundation of O.T.	103 f.
—— closed long before N.T. times	107
Caphar-salama	45
Carthage, council of	101
—— destruction of	220
Cassius	80, 85
Chakamim	178
Chananya b. Hezekiah b. Goren	255
Chanen b. Abishalom	255
Chanina b. Dosa	255
Chasidim. See Assideans.	
Choni ha-Maagal	255
Chronicles, Books of	
105 f., 108, 113 ff.	
Circumcision	39
Clemens, Alex.	97, 100, 220, 232
—— Rom.	100, 129, 220
Cleomenes	225
Cleopatra, mother of Ptol. Lathyrus	66
—— wife of Ptol. Philom.	125, 160
—— VI.	221
Codomannus	4
Colonies, Greek	9, 23
Corinth, destruction of	220
Crassus	80
Cyprian	100

INDEX.

Cyril of Jerusalem . . . 98
Cyrus . . . . 1, 123 f.

Daniel . 5, 16, 18, 30, 168, 216
—— *précis* of arguments as to
   date of . . . 257–269
—— additions to . 93, 109, 161 ff.
Darius I. . . 2, 113, 123 f.
—— II. 4
David, son of 208
Dedication, feast of the 43, 152, 200
Demetrius I. (Soter) 30, 44, 42
—— II. . . 49, 52, 56, 129
—— III. (Eucærus) . . 69
—— Phalereus . . . 237
—— a Jewish Hellenist . 238 f.

Dositheus 160
Dualism 18

Ecbatana 128
Ecclesiastes . 15, 107, 176, 187
Ecclesiasticus
   95, 100 f., 103, 105 f., 137 f., 143,
   176 ff., 208 ff., 239.
—— portions of original dis-
   covered . . . 184 f.
Egypt, Greek element in . 255 f.
—— Jewish element in . . 236
—— throws off Persian yoke . 3
—— value of, as a province . 7
—— attractive to Jews . . 8
Elasa 45
Eleazar 34, 144
—— Maccabeus . . . 39
Elijah, expectation of
   21, 42, 52, 150, 183
Emmaus (*Amwas*) . . . 41
Enemessar 133
Enoch, Book of
   93, 137, 150, 210, 216 ff., 221 ff.
Esarhaddon 133
Esdras 1st [3rd] Book of
   95, 102, 112 ff., 126 f., 143

Esdras 2nd [4th] Book of
   93 f., 97, 102, 112, 169, 218,
   228 ff.
Essenes . . . 59, 226, 252
Esther, Book of . 17, 150, 157
—— additions to . . 158 ff.
Euergetes. *See* Ptolemy.
Euphemisms 73
Eupolemus 238
Evil spirits . . 137, 183, 224
Exaggeration, tendency to . 91
Exile, changes in religious life
   during the 15
Ezekiel, canonicity of . . 105
Ezra 2, 107, 112 ff., 229 ff., 253

Fasting . . . 95, 134 f., 140
Future life . 195, 217, 224, 235

Gabinius . . . 78 f., 80, 82
Gadara 67
Gamaliel I. . . . . 254 f.
Gaza . . . . . 4, 66 f.
Gazara 50, 55
Genesis 108
——, the Little . . 225 ff.
Gerizim 57
Gnostics 97
Gorgias . . . . 40 f.

Habakkuk 165
Haggadah . . 23, 94, 161
Halachah 23
Hanniba 25
Hasmoneans 38, 46 f., 106, 206 f.
Hebrews, Epistle to 153, 194 ff.
Heliodorus . 28 ff., 144, 152
Helkias 66
Hellenists (Hellenism)
   24, 31, 36 f., 46 f., 58, 92, 180,
   207
Hermas, Shepherd of . 100, 102

S 7551.

INDEX.

Herod . . . 84 ff., 88, 134
Hezekias 8
Hillel 255
Holophernes . . . 4, 130
Homilies 141
Hyrcania 203
Hyrcanus, John
    37, 53 ff., 61 ff., 87, 104, 129
—— son of Joseph . 12, 27, 30
—— son of Alexandra
    71 f., 76 ff., 81 f., 84 f., 206 f.

Idolatry, abhorrence of . . 91
Idumeans 56
Ipsus 9
Irenæus 100
Issus 4
Itureans 64

Jaddua 4, 52
Jakim. *See* Alcimus.
James (St.) 187
Jannæus (Jannes) . 65 ff., 129, 163
Jason . . . 29 ff., 180
—— of Cyrene . 152 ff., 238
Jehoiachin . . . 119, 163
Jehudah b. Tablai . 73, 75, 255
Jeremiah . . . 243 f.
Jerome
    98, 101 f., 112 f., 131 f., 151, 159, 166, 184, 234.
Jerusalem sacked by Antiochus
    32, 125, 147, 205
—— Pompey's siege of . 77 f.
Joachim 127
Joakim (in Judith) . . . 129
—— (husband of Susanna) . 163
Job 140, 175
Jochanan (John) Maccabeus
    39, 47 ff., 53, 128
—— b. Bag Bag . . . 256
—— ha-Chorani . . . 256
—— Zakkai 256

Jonathan Maccabeus 39, 47 ff., 145
Joppa . . . 50 f., 55, 82
Jose, son of Jochanan 250 f., 255
—— son of Joezer . 250 f., 255
Joseph 10, 27
Josephus as to cessation of prophecy . . . . 103 f.
—— relation to 1st [3rd] Esdras . . . 123 ff.
Joshua b. Bethera . . . 255
—— b. Prachya . . . 255
Josiah 126
Jubilees, Book of
    210, 218, 221, 225 ff.
Judah b. Bethera . . . 255
Judas Maccabeus
    39 ff., 129, 145, 224
Judas, son of Simom Maccabeus 53
Judea 6
—— divided into provinces . 78
"Judeans" 16
Judges 107, 132
Judith
    94 f., 101 f., 108, 127 ff., 133 f.
Justin Martyr 99

K'thubim . . . 108, 204
Koheleth. *See* Ecclesiastes.
Krapf 225

Lactantius 220
Laodicea, council of . . 101
Laomedon 8
Legalism 19, 21 f., 35, 94 f., 130, 134
Leontopolis, temple at . 155, 160
Lepidus 221
Lewis, Mrs. 185
Libya 220
Litany 141
Luther 141
Lysias . . . . 40 ff.

INDEX. 275

Lysimachus 9
—— son of Ptol. Philom. . 160

Maccabean age, features characteristic of religious literature 89 ff.
—— influenced by earlier writings 90
Maccabees, enumeration of family 39
—— derivation of name . . 39
—— revolt of . . . 38 ff.
—— Temple cleansed by . 42
(*See also* Mattathias, Judas, etc.)
—— 1st Book of 95, 101, 103, 105 f., 129, 143 ff.
—— 2nd —— 94 f., 101, 108, 152 ff., 170, 208
—— 3rd —— . 143 f., 156 f.
—— 4th —— . 94, 143 f., 158
—— 5th —— . 143 f., 158
Malachi quoted . . 15, 21
—— time of 20
Malichus 85
Manasses, Prayer of . 102, 171
—— Talmudic references to . 171
Manetho 236
Mariamne 187
Marriage Service . . . 141
Mattai (Nittai) the Arbelite . 255
Mattathias . . . 38 ff.
—— tomb of . . . 38, 148
—— son of Simon Macc. . 53
Megabyzus 3
Melito 99
Menelaus 31 f., 42, 44, 125, 180
Messiah, expectation of 93, 150, 183, 196, 208 f., 215, 219, 221, 224, 230.
Mishnah, the . . . 35 f.
Mithridates . . . 77, 206

Mizpah 41
Mnemon 3
Modiim (Modin) 38, 45, 53, 62, 70
Monotheism 91
Mordecai 159
Moses 178

Nabateans 57
Name, avoidance of the Divine 19, 147, 150
Naphthar (nephi) . . . 17
Nazirites 249
Nebuchadnezzar 128, 130, 134, 136, 168
Nehemiah . 2, 17, 107, 112 ff.
Nicanor . . 40 f., 45, 152 ff.
Nineveh 128, 133
Nittai. *See* Mattai.

Obedas 68
Octavian 86, 221
Offertory sentences . . 135, 141
Onias I. 6
—— II. 10
—— III. . . . 29 ff., 251
—— son or grandson of O. III. 125 f.
Origen . 98 f., 131, 151, 166
Originality, lack of, in Apocrypha 92, 108
Orophernes 4
Orthodox (Jewish) party . 24

Palmer, John 233
Panium (Panion) . . 12, 26
Papias 228
Parthians . . . 86 f.
(St.) Paul & (St.) Peter, anticipation of teaching of . . 194
Perdiccas 7
Perseus 32
Persian worship, influences on Jews of 17

Pharisees
  58 ff., 67, 71, 73, 84, 207, 209, 252
Phasael . . . . 84 ff.
Philadelphia 10
Philip v. 25
Philippi 85
Philo . . . 188, 192, 238
—— attitude towards O.T. . 99
—— Apocrypha . . . 100
Philosophy, distinctive features of Jewish and Greek . 172 f.
—— books illustrating these features 173
Philoteria 10
Plato 190, 215
Polybius, epoch for commencing his history 23
Polycarp 133
Pompey
  77 ff., 81, 85, 149, 205 f. 225
Popilius Lænas . . 33, 45
Prayer . . 95, 135, 137, 139 f.
—— for the dead . . . 156
Prodicus 97
Proverbs, Book of
  105 f., 175, 181, 187, 243
Psalms, are there Maccabean or post-exilic . . 105 f., 199 ff.
—— of Solomon. See Solomon.
Psammetichus I. . . . 235
Pseudo-Aristeas. See Aristeas.
Pseudo-Smerdis . . . 2
Ptolemais 10
Ptolemy I. (Soter, son of Lagus)
  7 f., 235
—— II. (Philadelphus)
  9 f., 125, 236 f.
—— III. (Euergetes I.)
  10, 25, 178 f.
—— IV. (Philopator)
  11, 25, 157, 193
—— V. (Epiphanes) . . 12

Ptolemy VII. (Philometor)
  48 f., 125, 160, 220
—— IX. (Euergetes II., Physcon) . 157, 178 f., 193, 220
—— son of Abubus . 53 f.
—— Auletes 80
—— Lathyrus . . . 66
—— general of Antiochus Epiphanes . . . 40 f.
Punishment, future
  194, 217, 224, 230
Purim . . . . 159 f.
Raguel 139
Raphael 136
Raphia 11
Resurrection 183, 193, 208, 224, 230
Returning exiles, character of . 1
Righteousness, peculiar use of word 16
Romans
  25, 30, 45, 48, 50 f., 77 ff., 80 ff., 85 ff., 146, 231 f.
Ruth, Book of . . 132
Sabbath 38, 226
Sadducees . . 58 ff., 207
—— Greek influence on - . 61
—— their relations with Hyrcanus . . . . 61 ff.
—— their rule as to perjury 73, 163
—— their hostility to Antipater 83 f.
Salome. See Alexandra.
Samaria 6
—— demolished . . . 57
—— rebuilt and freed from Jewish oppression . . 79
Samaritans . . 113, 121, 124
Samuel ha-katan . . . 256
Sanhedrin . 129, 133, 136, 253
Sarbeth Sabanaiel . . . 151
Sarchedonus 133
Scaurus 77

	PAGE
Schechter	. 184
Schools	. 23, 74
Scopas	. 12
Scribes	35 f., 94 f.
Scythopolis	. 79
Seleucus	. 7
—— II. (Callinicus)	10 f.
—— IV. (Philopator)	28, 44, 152
Sennacherib	. 128, 133, 136
Septuagint, story of	. 237
—— linguistic features of	239 ff., 244
—— importance of	. 241 ff.
—— indications of Greek Philosophy in	. 244 f.
Shalmaneser	. 133
Shammai	. 255
Shechem	. 57
Shekels. *See* Simon Maccabees.	
Shemaiah	. 255
Sibylline Books	122, 124, 209, 211 ff.
Simeon b. Bethera	. 255
—— b. Hillel	. 255
Simon I.	. 179
—— II.	. 29, 179, 250 f.
Simon the Just	. 6, 10, 22, 179
Simon b. Shatach	65, 67, 72 f., 75, 130, 163, 255
—— Maccabeus 39, 50 ff., 130, 145	
—— his shekels	. 52
Sira(ch), meaning of	. 177
Solomon, Odes of	. 214
—— Psalms of 95, 150, 168, 204 ff.	
—— Song of	. 107
Song of the Three Children 93, 162	
Sosius	. 88
Soul, immortality of	. 94
Stoics	. 190
Suffering, problem of	140, 156, 174 ff., 182 f., 194
Susanna, History of	93, 98, 108, 162 f., 166

	PAGE
Synagogue, the Great 23, 103, 253 f.	
Synagogues, establishment of	. 16
Symmachus	. 122
Syrian Kingdom, Jews abounded in various parts of	. 26
Talmud on Manasseh	. 171
Tarquinius Superbus	. 218
Temple-tax	. 73
Tertullian	. 100
Testaments of the Twelve Patriarchs	. 227
Theodore of Mopsuestia	. 203
Tiamat	. 164
Tigranes	. 71 f.
Titus	. 136, 205, 228
Tobiades, the	. 13
Tobiah	. 10
Tobias	. 139
Tobit	18, 93, 95, 100 ff., 108, 132 ff., 216
—— miracles in	. 140 f.
Trajan	. 129
Trent, Council of	. 102, 113, 234
Trypho	. 50, 53, 220
Tyre	. 4
Uriel	. 229
Ventidius	. 87
Vespasian	. 158
Wisdom, Book of	91, 94 f., 100, 176, 187 ff., 238
Zabinas. *See* Alexander Zabinas.	
Zadok	. 98, 255
Zechariah	. 214
Zedekiah	. 119, 128, 167
—— the false prophet	. 163
Zerubbabel	. 2, 14, 124, 127, 134
Zoroaster	. 97

www.ingramcontent.com/pod-product-compliance
Lightning Source LLC
Chambersburg PA
CBHW032102230426
43672CB00009B/1609